Ambassadors for Christ

BOOKS BY EDWARD WAGENKNECHT
Published by Oxford University Press

NATHANIEL HAWTHORNE: *Man and Writer (1961)*

WASHINGTON IRVING: *Moderation Displayed (1962)*

EDGAR ALLAN POE: *The Man Behind the Legend (1963)*

HARRIET BEECHER STOWE: *The Known and the Unknown (1965)*

HENRY WADSWORTH LONGFELLOW: *Portrait of an American Humanist (1966)*

JOHN GREENLEAF WHITTIER: *A Portrait in Paradox (1967)*

WILLIAM DEAN HOWELLS: *The Friendly Eye (1969)*

JAMES RUSSELL LOWELL: *Portrait of a Many-Sided Man (1971)*

AMBASSADORS FOR CHRIST: *Seven American Preachers (1972)*

CHAUCER: *Modern Essays in Criticism (1959)*
Edited by Edward Wagenknecht

AMBASSADORS FOR CHRIST

Seven American Preachers

EDWARD WAGENKNECHT

Let us not be afraid to surprise
the human heart naked ... even
in the saints ~ SAINTE-BEUVE

NEW YORK
OXFORD UNIVERSITY PRESS
1972

Library of Congress Catalogue Card Number: 76–179361
Printed in the United States of America

In memory of
CHESTER CARWARDINE,
whom I first heard preach
Christ's Gospel with power, and of
WILLIAM E. BARTON,
my Pastor in Oak Park days.

CONTENTS

1 LYMAN BEECHER:
Great by His Religion 1

2 WILLIAM ELLERY CHANNING:
Messages from the Spirit 40

3 HENRY WARD BEECHER:
God Was in Christ 68

4 PHILLIPS BROOKS:
The Lord Our God Is a Sun 118

5 D. L. MOODY:
Whosoever Will May Come 148

6 WASHINGTON GLADDEN:
Where Does the Sky Begin? 183

7 LYMAN ABBOTT:
The Life of God in the Soul of Man 214

APPENDIX: *A Postscript on the Beecher-Tilton Scandal* 249

BIBLIOGRAPHIES AND NOTES 255

INDEX 303

The illustrations appear in a group following p. 150

Ambassadors for Christ

1

LYMAN BEECHER

Great by His Religion

I

Frances Alda divided her operatic contemporaries into men, women, and tenors, and Leonard Bacon thought his country inhabited by saints, sinners, and Beechers. It has been said of Lyman Beecher that he was the father of more brains than any other man in America; seven of his children are in the *Dictionary of American Biography*. To be sure, he had his failures. He guided (or shanghaied) all seven of his sons into the ministry, but James, who was both a preacher and a soldier, committed suicide, probably while of unsound mind, and George may have done the same, though in this case the coroner ruled his death accidental, which is what the Beechers themselves believed. It is not always easy to tell just where eccentricity turns into irresponsibility. Lyman[1] himself had his share of eccentricity; even his most famous children, Henry Ward Beecher and Harriet Beecher Stowe, were not wholly free of it; and I, for one, cannot quite believe in the sanity of Isabella Beecher Hooker, who expected, like her "adorable brother Jesus," to "grow into the hearts of men and women and children by the power of God our common Father" and ultimately to be "called to the presidency of a matriarchal government, which would spread from the United States across the whole world and . . . be merged with the kingdom of Christ in a great millennial period." [2] But Edward Beecher, pastor, college president, and highly individual theologian, was certainly an impressive and respect-worthy figure, and so was Thomas K. Beecher, pioneer of the institutional church, who was Olivia Langdon's pastor in Elmira, New York, before she became Olivia Clemens and the wife of Mark Twain. Catharine Beecher was a pioneer exponent of higher education for American women; she has never had quite the recognition she deserves.[3]

Lyman Beecher is an incomparably vivid and exhilarating subject with whom to open a volume of character studies of great preachers; from this point of view indeed, the only disadvantage is that none of his successors could possibly be expected to match him, not even D. L. Moody hot on the trail of sinners nor his own son Henry Ward under accusation. If, as many biographers seem to believe, enlivening anecdote is the prime desideratum in vivid biographical writing, who could fill the bill better than this man, who always carried a watch that was never running and borrowed pencils indiscriminately from everyone, depositing them in his own pockets after he had finished with them, but who seems to have kept himself supplied with any number of pairs of glasses, so that whenever he needed to read a passage in one of his sermons, he could pull out a pair and pop them on his nose? When he came to the end of the passage, the spectacles would be swept up over his forehead, and since he always forgot what he had done with them, he would be obliged to bring out a fresh pair for the next quotation, sometimes creating a glass shield over his head, so that it was said, "The doctor has got his spectacles on behind and before; he means to look into the matter all round." Since his father was famous for collecting the eggs in the barn into his pocket, and then coming into the house to sit on them, Lyman may be said to have come by his absent-mindedness honestly, and there were almost no limits to his own achievements along this line. He himself said he had spent half his life looking for his hat, and he was quite capable of carefully depositing his printer's copy in one headpiece and then starting out for the printshop wearing another. Riding in the stage, he would habitually remove his false teeth, which were uncomfortable, placing them on the seat beside him, and never thinking of them again until he sat down that evening to supper. Once, while visiting, his eye fell upon a clock which he had not seen before, whereupon he demanded of his hostess, "Wife, where did you get that clock?"

None of this, however, seems to have interfered unduly with either Lyman's efficiency or his enjoyment of life. He sawed firewood for himself and for his neighbors too, for the sheer enjoyment of it, exercised on gymnastic apparatus in the back yard, and kept a load of sand in the cellar so that when it was too stormy to go out, he could limber up his muscles by shoveling sand from one side to the other. When he found a burglar stealing the clothes out of his room, he pursued him into the street, continued the chase even after the thief had dropped his booty, caught him, mastered him, disarmed him of a dangerous weapon, and took him back to his room, where he made him lie on the floor until morning, when he turned him over to the authorities. Once reckless drivers crowded his conveyance off the road and down a sharp declivity. When he yelled for help, they leaned over the edge, crying, "How shall we get down there?" and Lyman replied sharply, "Easy enough; come as I did."

One Sunday morning, on his way to church, he saw a particularly desirable fish under the bridge he was crossing. He stopped long enough to catch the fish, slipped it into the back pocket of his ministerial coat, and never thought of it again until his wife came to brush the coat for him to wear on the following Sunday. After the Sunday night service, he always had to "run down" by playing with his children.

Often [writes Harriet] his old faithful friend the violin was called into requisition, and he would play a few antiquated contra dances and Scotch airs out of a venerable yellow music-book, which had

> come down the vale of years with him. . . . Auld Lang Syne, Bonnie Doon and Mary's Dream were the inevitables; and a contra dance which bore the unclerical title of "Go to the devil and shake yourself" was a great favorite with the youngsters.

Sometimes Lyman himself would dance, in his stocking feet, but this could be done only when his wife (it was the second wife, Harriet Porter, by this time) was off guard. Mrs. Beecher did not object to her husband's dancing, but she did object to his wearing out his socks.

It will be granted, I think, that few clerical (or lay) figures can match this record. But let no one suppose that these matters are recorded here merely for their entertainment value. We shall see the same temperament which is revealed here manifesting itself again in all Lyman's activities, even the most serious. And I think we must admit that if he has a great advantage over some of his companions in this book on the score of "human interest," there are other aspects in which he performs under a handicap. It would distress him to know that these are not "human" but religious aspects. To preach on "The Bible as a Code of Laws" is not to make the most rewarding possible approach to religion for the needs of modern readers, and now that nobody cares particularly what John Calvin taught, those who wade through the story of Beecher's trial for heresy will be less interested in whether or not he successfully defended his orthodoxy than in whether what he had to say made sense in itself. Even here, however, Lyman succeeds wonderfully well in escaping from some of his handicaps. His son Henry Ward went to the heart of the matter when he remarked that though his father "thought he was great by his theology, everybody else knew he was great by his religion."

II

The Beecher family came to New England in 1638, and Lyman was born at New Haven, Connecticut, on October 12, 1775, the seven-months child of David Beecher, "the learned blacksmith," and his third, tubercular wife, Esther Lyman, who died two days later. Because the baby was so frail that he hardly seemed "worth raising," the midwife wrapped him in a blanket and laid him aside while she tended his mother. When she got back to him, she was surprised to find that he still breathed, which she thought a pity.

Lyman was brought up by his uncle Lot Benton and his aunt on their farm at Guilford, from which, having manifested no great aptitude for farm work, he was sent to Yale College in 1793. During his junior year he was converted, and after his graduation in 1797, he studied theology under President Timothy Dwight, whom he loved and greatly admired. Completely inept in mathematics, he was rated good in Latin, yet when, in one of his ecclesiastical disputes, one of his opponents corrected his Latin, he was only amused. "Well, all this proves that they understand Latin better than I do. Everybody knew that before; they need not crow over it so." Lyman read Jonathan Edwards and Butler's *Analogy* and other works and authors, but he was hardly a bookman even in the theological field. The impressive list of church fathers and other authorities cited in his defence before the presbytery was indebted to his scholarly son-in-law, Calvin E. Stowe, but Lyman was too impatient to continue gathering his material in Stowe's fashion and ended by taking much of it "out of Scott's reply to Tomlin." [4] Stowe quotes Lyman as lamenting that Dwight did not put him to the study of the Greek New Testament—"it would have been worth more to me than all the theologians I have ever read." He also lamented that he had not read more history, but this was for a rather belligerent, unscholarly reason: "it furnishes a public speaker with illustrations and matter-of-fact argument, which is the most knocking-down argument in the world."

Lyman was licensed to preach in 1798, and in 1799 he both married his first wife, Roxana Foote, and became pastor of the Presbyterian church at East Hampton, Long Island, where he remained until 1810. Thereafter until 1826 he was pastor of the Congregational church at Litchfield, Connecticut, where, in 1816, Roxana died. The next year he married Harriet Porter, and in 1826 he was called to the Hanover Street Church in Boston, where he girded himself to take on two enemies—Unitarianism and the Pope. Stowe says that he laid out "extensive plans of aggression beyond the limits of his own congregation," attended councils, made speeches at public meetings, wrote essays and reviews, watched over theological discussion, and took care of "all the young men he could drum up for the ministry." The church edifice burned in 1830. Part of its basement had been rented out to a merchant who, without the knowledge of the temperance reformer who was the pastor, had stored liquor there. This did nothing to quench the flames, but it gave the irreverent a chance to say that "Beecher's jug was busted," a description all the more appropriate because the square tower of the church had been split by the heat.

In 1832 Beecher became president of Lane Theological Seminary in Cincinnati and pastor of the Second Presbyterian Church there. Since he was by this time almost obsessed with the idea of winning the West for Christ and for the Protestant religion, and since he believed that the future of the American nation would be decided there, this was regarded as a heaven-sent opportunity. Arguments over slavery very nearly wrecked the project. Lyman took up a "moderate" position against the "extreme" abolitionists, but whatever may be thought of his views, there is no questioning his faith and courage. It was to him alone that the seminary was indebted for its continued existence; even Calvin Stowe, who had accompanied him as a professor, was ready to give up. Oberlin College was an offshoot of the controversy at Lane.

The stay in the West was further embittered by Lyman's trial for heresy before the Cincinnati Presbytery on charges brought by the Reverend Joshua L. Wilson. The decision was in Beecher's favor, though he was asked not to "philosophize" so much on the questions under dispute but to content himself with "exhibiting in simplicity and plainness these doctrines as taught in the Scriptures." Wilson appealed to the General Assembly, but nothing significant came of this.

Harriet Porter Beecher died at the time of the trial, and in 1836 Lyman took his third wife, Mrs. Lydia Jackson. In 1846 he made his only trip abroad, to attend a temperance convention in London. "My dear madam," said one English clergyman to Lydia, "go home and take care of that blessed man, for his like is not to be found." He resigned from the Second Presbyterian Church in 1843 and from Lane Seminary in 1850. After his return to the East he continued to preach as long as he was able, having one very successful series of meetings at Andover. He lived first in Boston but moved in 1856 to Brooklyn, where he died on January 10, 1863.

His most important publications were *A Plea for the West* (1832), *Views in Theology* (1836), and three volumes of collected *Works* (1852–53). A larger collection had been contemplated, but Lyman was no longer fit for the editorial task. Nor was he able to carry out his original plan of publishing his *Autobiography* as a work of his own composition. Instead, he reminisced at length to his children, especially Harriet; Charles Beecher took notes, collected letters and papers, admitted contributions from brothers and sisters, and in 1864 published the work which is our principal source of information concerning Lyman Beecher and the home life of his children.

III

Lyman Beecher seems to have planned to be a preacher even before he was converted; if this was not a "calling," it was at least a strong, almost irresistible inclination. He could preach either extemporaneously or from manuscript, and once at least he was so eager that he forgot what Protestant ministers have sometimes been guilty of thinking of as the "preliminaries" and rushed into his sermon as soon as he entered the pulpit. According to Harriet, his sermon

> consisted invariably of two parts: first, careful statement and argument addressed purely to the understanding, and, second, a passionate and direct appeal, designed to urge his audience to some immediate practical result. The first part was often as dry, condensed, and clear as a series of mathematical axioms. If preaching upon a doctrine, he commenced by the most clear and carefully-worded statement of what it was not and what it was, before attempting to prove or disprove. It very often happened that these simple statements disarmed prejudice and removed antipathy, and, to a people somewhat predisposed to return to the faith of their fathers if they could see their way, rendered the succeeding argument almost needless.

Harriet may seem to be suggesting more than she says when she writes that "Father is to perform tonight in the Chatham Theater, 'positively for the last time this season.' " I have no doubt Lyman could be very dramatic when he so chose. One listener found in him "a mighty uplifting of passionate emotion, . . . a tender but grand upheaval and on-moving power which was like the rolling of a tidal wave on the beach of the sea," and another calls him a thunderbolt. "You never knew where it would strike, but you never saw him rise to speak without feeling that so much electricity must strike." The same writer adds, significantly, "I have never yet met the man in whose presence, whenever I met him, I always felt so small as in his." [5] Lyman advised his Lane students to fill themselves full of their subject, "then pull out the bung and let nature caper." But though he himself says that in his early days he "tore a passion to tatters," he does not seem to have been a noisy preacher. Certainly it could never be said of him as of Donne that he "preached from a cloud." In the pulpit, in his classes, and in the inquiry room, he watched his listeners intently and responded to their every mood, using "careful instruction," metaphysical speculation, or "the highest action and strongest arguments" as they might be needed to secure conviction, always trying to avoid "the spirit of rebuke" and ironical or sarcastic expressions or seeming to suggest that there was a great gulf fixed between his hearers and himself. He spoke of his "clinical theology," and he employed terms like experimental phenomena, exhausted sensibility, melancholy temperament, and morbid sensibility, which were not in the vocabulary of many preachers of his time.

The church [he said] is not a place where none but the perfect associate, but a conservatory association (a "spiritual hospital") in which the first movements of holiness are cherished and strengthened, up to the confirmed and perfect health of heaven.

His preparation for preaching was as erratic as everything else about him. " 'Squire Langdon used to say," he himself wrote of one period during his early ministry, "that when he saw me digging potatoes on Saturday night, he expected a good sermon Sunday morning," and he once told Lowell Mason, ten minutes before a service in Boston, that he could not give him the numbers of the hymns to be sung because he had not yet made up his mind what he was going to preach about.

The time that he spent in actual preparation for a public effort [writes Harriet] was generally not long. If he was to preach in the evening he was to be seen all day talking with whoever would talk, accessible to all, full of every body's affairs, business, and burdens, till an hour or two before the time, when he would rush up into his study (which he always preferred should be the topmost room of the house), and, throwing off his coat, after a swing or two with the dumbbells to settle the balance of his muscles, he would sit down and dash ahead, making quantities of hieroglyphic notes on small, stubbed bits of paper, about as big as the palm of his hand. The bells would begin to ring, and still he would write. They would toll loud and long, and his wife would say "he will certainly be late," and then would be running up and down stairs of messengers to see that he was finished, till, just as the last stroke of the bell was dying away, he would emerge from the study with his coat very much awry, come down the stairs like a hurricane, stand impatiently protesting while female hands that ever lay in wait adjusted his cravat and settled his coat collar, calling loudly the while for a pin to fasten together the stubbed little bits of paper aforesaid, which being duly dropped into the crown of his hat, and hooking wife or daughter like a satchel on his arm, away he would start on such a race through the streets as left neither brain nor breath till the church was gained. Then came the process of getting in through crowded aisles, wedged up with heads, the bustle, and stir, and hush to look at him, as, with a matter-of-fact, business-like push, he elbowed his way through them and up the pulpit stairs.

Think of the nerve strain such methods must have involved for a man who preached as much as Lyman did,[6] and then read Henry Ward's amusing account of how his father prepared himself for the Cincinnati trial.[7] But Lyman knew exactly what he was doing: he was about as innocent as Little Eva, played by a raddled *Uncle Tom's Cabin* veteran of sixty-five. "I took all my books and sat down on the second stair of the pulpit," he afterwards wrote. "It was in my church. I looked so quiet and meek my students were almost afraid I shouldn't come up to the mark." They need not have worried. Nobody needed to worry except Dr. Wilson. It was he who never had a chance.[8]

IV

Lyman Beecher was about five feet, seven inches tall, and weighed 140 to 150 pounds. He had a large head and he combed his hair straight back from his forehead, which was one of the reasons he had a kind of bustling, bristly appearance. Physically he was a very strong man. The day he was eighty-one he wished to attend one of Calvin Stowe's lectures at the seminary in Andover. True to form, he was not ready when the time came to leave, and Calvin started off "in the usual path" without him. "Presently he came skipping across lots, laid his hand on the top of the five-barred fence, which he cleared at a bound, and was in the lecture-room before me."

But, like his father, Lyman was racked with dyspepsia, and when an attack came on, he would collapse into an intense and all-embracing melancholy.

> Depression is an inevitable symptom of the disorder, and mine at times exceeds any thing I ever experienced. It is *flesh and heart failing.* It is desolation like a flood, and extinguishes at times all hope that I shall recover my health and usefulness.

It would take a better doctor than I am to figure out how much of this was physical and how much (as we should now say) psychosomatic, and Lyman learned enough from his experiences to be able to distinguish pretty shrewdly between physical and spiritual ailments in his penitents, some of whom may have been shocked when he asked them whether their bowels moved, when they expected him to inquire about their souls. But it is always easier to be wise for others than for oneself. Lyman had an illness of about a year very early in his ministry, and his near collapse when he arrived in Boston to slay the Unitarian giant seems to have been motivated by a well-founded fear that this countryman who never got over talking about "natur" and "creeturs" even in the pulpit was not really going to be accepted at the American Athens. Between the melancholia induced by his recurrent illnesses and his inborn tendency to dramatize whatever situation he found himself involved in, he never played down any indisposition but instead found himself afflicted with tuberculosis or "cancer internal," with fine impartiality.[9]

The active life Lyman led probably helped to keep him in condition. In his early days he was a mighty hunter of squirrels, quail, partridges, muskrats, minks, etc.; he might have gone after wolves and deer if they had not by his time pretty well disappeared from the region. Once he tried to climb a tree twenty feet high because he had shot a squirrel which ran into a hole in the tree and he was determined to get it, and once in the dark he threw a book at what he supposed to be a rabbit but which turned out to be a skunk. Even in the thirties he kept a gun loaded in his study, so that when migratory pigeons came over in clouds, he could rush out and have a shot at them. But it was fishing which was, as he says, his "passion"; he could fish all day and feel sorry when night came. Sometimes he even caught fish with his hands. Sometimes he was in the water with the fishes, and once at least he was nearly drowned. When he visited St. Paul's Cathedral in London, he alone of the party mounted to the very top of the dome and crawled into the ball on its summit.

Like some trees, like Jonathan Swift, and like his daughter Harriet after him, Lyman died from the head down, and from the early fifties until his death in 1863, he was increasingly withdrawn not only from his usual activities but finally almost from all communication. Even so, as Calvin Stowe says, the failure was

> not so much of mind as of the power of expressing himself. . . . Very gradually the intellect withdrew itself from the outward world; but the heart was still alive to all human and all divine affections. He forgot the living for the most part, but the dead were ever fresh in his recollection.

It was a great sorrow to him that he could no longer preach; if he had only been given ten years more, he thought he might have been able to do much better. Sometimes, during the early years of his retirement, he did speak extemporaneously in prayer meeting, and on one such occasion he confessed pathetically, "If God should tell me that I *might* choose—that is, if God said that it was *his* will that I *should* choose whether to die and go to heaven, or to begin my life over again and work once more, *I would enlist again in a minute!*" When he attended Plymouth Church, he worshipped God and his son together. "Thought I could preach," he said, "until I heard Henry." One day, Harriet was combing his hair as he lay on a couch before her. "Do you know," she asked lovingly, "that you are a very handsome old gentleman?" and Lyman impishly replied, "Tell me something new," which does not sound much like a failing mind.

Lyman's cultural and aesthetic equipment was no less mixed—nor less interesting—than the physical. "When I used to be out hoeing corn and saw two thunderclouds rising," he tells us, "my nerves braced up, and as it grew darker the excitement increased till finally when the thunder burst it was like the effect of a strong glass of wine!" He thought "meanly" of the world only when it was "considered as our god"; "as a place of probation" it showed "the mercies of God" clustering round us, "new every morning and fresh every moment. It should neither, therefore, be put upon the throne nor trampled in the mire, for one is idolatry and the other ingratitude." As for himself, he loved the earth and hated to leave it even for heaven, and he dreaded the experience of physical death. Once, when his son congratulated him on nearing the end of his pilgrimage, the old man snapped, "I don't thank my children for sending me to heaven till God does."

He did not grow up in a bookish environment; he was not a great reader in childhood, and, as has already been noted, he never became one, even in the professional field. He once said that for years he had recommended hardly any book but the Bible. Yet he was capable of intense response to literature (Satan's plight in *Paradise Lost* reduced him to tears), and he was not hostile to the other arts either. For him, as for so many in his time, it took Scott to break down the prejudice against "trashy" novels. One summer the children read *Ivanhoe* through seven times (Harriet, as a novelist, was never to get over it), and when the father and his children worked together making apple sauce, they made the time pass by telling stories out of the Waverley novels. But Lyman's great "crush" was Byron—"Oh, I'm so sorry that Byron is dead. I did hope he would live to do something for Christ"—and he believed that if only he and his friend Dr. Nathaniel Taylor had had a chance to talk to the poet, they might have saved his soul.

As to the performing arts, Lyman opposed theater-going because of the profligacy connected with the theater, but amateur theatricals were not wholly unknown to the Beechers, nor did he condemn all those who attended public performances. Music was in another class altogether. His own interpretations of "Go to the Devil and Shake Yourself" and kindred masterpieces had no great musical significance, though he himself once lamented that he had never heard Paganini and then added that if he could "only play what I hear inside of me," he could beat him! It was a great day when the Beecher family obtained a "fine-toned," second-hand, upright piano, after which the children, with their voices and their instruments, were drawn into "domestic concerts," to which their father contributed with his violin. When Lyman was a pastor in Boston, the great Lowell Mason was his choirmaster, which means that his church was in the forefront of the development of American church music.[10]

V

Lyman Beecher's relations with others were about what might have been expected from what has already been said. He knew that humility is a Christian virtue, and there is no reason to doubt his sincerity when he speaks of himself as an unprofitable servant. Nevertheless he was a masterful man, and it is hard to see how such a human dynamo, with his strong convictions and great personal efficiency, could have been expected to be anything else. Sometimes in preaching he was astonished by his own "wisdom and eloquence," and once when Stowe congratulated him on an address, he said, "I do believe it was about as good a thing as ever I did." Stowe suspected he often did not listen to sermons delivered by others but that after the text had been announced, he went off constructing a sermon of his own in his mind. Stowe admits too that his father-in-law was vain, but insists that he had no envy and that the vanity was "harmless and amusing as a child's."

He had a strong sense of his own individuality, and when, in his old age, he looked back upon his youth for the purpose of dictating his reminiscences, he never doubted his own identification with the youngster whom he described. Even at sixty he responded to life with the eagerness of a boy; when it was first suggested that he should head up Lane Seminary, he rushed home to tell the news but was so excited that at first he could not bring out a word. He may, as he claims, have avoided personal attacks whenever possible—certainly he showed real forbearance toward Dr. Wilson, who had called him not only a heretic but a hypocrite—but he still knew the joy of conflict, for he speaks of hewing down his antagonists, wringing their necks off, and hanging them on their own gallows. "I hope the man is not dead," he wrote of one enemy, "for I have some terrible things in reserve that I should not like to hurl at a dead man," and of one synod meeting he writes, "When my turn came, I rose and knocked away their arguments, and made them ludicrous. Never made an argument so short, strong, and pointed in my life. I shall never forget it." Sometimes, too, he disarmed an adversary by seeming to agree with him and thus making him feel ashamed.

Though Lyman was deeply devoted to such men as Timothy Dwight and Nathaniel Taylor, I do not get the impression that he had many close friendships. With love the situation was different, but it may well be that Lyman's large family so absorbed his social and amative proclivities that there was not much left over for the outside.

The Puritans were legalists, not ascetics, where sex was concerned, and, as everybody knows, Lyman married three times and fathered many children. Surely nobody ever prized domestic happiness more highly. Once indeed he goes so far as to call happiness "the important thing in the universe of God. . . . It is the thing which God commands *us* to seek, both for ourselves and for others. To be happy as we can be, and to communicate as much happiness as we are able, is the *chief end of man.*" There is not much suggestion here that the world is the vale of soul making, though there may be an echo of the *Westminster Catechism*:

Q: What is the whole duty of man?
A: Man's chief end is to glorify God and to enjoy Him forever.

But surely the *Catechism* has the more comprehensive statement of the two and the more deeply Christian.

One aspect of domestic life which seems very important to the average couple does not seem to have interested Lyman very much. Money was the snakes-in-Ireland element in the Beecher story; the family never had enough to worry about it. Whatever he did, Lyman's salary was fixed in terms which to us seem fantastically small—for in these inflationary days even the indigent spend in terms which would have seemed wildly extravagant to him—and, to make things worse, the whole amount pledged was seldom paid. He was allowed to leave both East Hampton and Litchfield for lack of a few hundred dollars to pay him a living wage. Lyman could think about money very clearly when the occasion arose,[12] but he could be as cavalier in handling it as he was in every other aspect of his life. One day he came rushing into the house, demanding that his wife give him five dollars immediately to cover the vital, urgent needs of one of the Lane students. Since this was all the money they had, she demurred, but he merely assured her that the Lord would provide. And here, as so often in the Moody story, He did, this time in the shape of a fifty-dollar wedding fee.

Of the three wives, the first was the only one who really counted. Roxana was one of the brilliant Foote girls, born into a Tory, Episcopal family, and brought up, after their father's death, in the home of their legislator grandfather, General Andrew Ward. Lyman had made up his mind never to marry a weak woman, for he wanted "sense" and "strength to lean upon," while she had been waiting until she found a man like Sir Charles Grandison. "I presume she thought she had," said Lyman dryly —which remark has sometimes been quoted as an example of his egotism—but he had too much humor to intend that such a statement should be taken literally.

Roxana was a very shy, intensely domestic woman, much given to blushing, and unable to participate in any of the public functions often assigned to ministers' wives. But she loved beauty in every aspect—in nature, in literature, and in the arts—and she could both read and speak French fluently. At one time she ran a girls' boarding school in the parsonage. She sang, playing her own accompaniment on the guitar, used both pencil and brush, and was a gifted needlewoman. She decorated her furniture and household appliances with her handiwork, and at East Hampton, where everybody else had sanded floors, she made a beautiful rug from scratch, even to spinning the cotton, then sized it and covered it with painted flowers; after it was laid, Lyman's parishioners were afraid to come in for fear of stepping on it, and one of his deacons asked him if he thought he could have all this and heaven too. Nor were her extra-domestic interests purely aesthetic in character. How startling it is to come upon this in a letter to her sister-in-law, otherwise crammed with domestic news:

As for reading I average perhaps one page a week. . . . I expect to be obliged to be contented (if I can) with the stock of knowledge I already possess except what I glean from the conversation of others. . . . Mary has, I suppose, told you of the discovery that the fixed alkalies are metallic oxyds. . . . I think this is all the knowledge I have obtained in the circle of the arts and sciences of late; if you have been more fortunate pray let me reap the benefit.

When Roxana and Lyman became engaged, he worried over their religious differences, and worried her about them too until her family feared for her reason. In good old Calvinistic style, he tortured himself trying to decide whether he would be willing, should God require it, to resign his "dear Roxana," which, since God did not require it, would appear to have been an unrewarding subject for anxiety. In the long run, however, she seems to have had more influence on him than he upon her, for when he put to her the stock Hopkinsian question about whether she would be willing to be damned for the glory of God, she replied that if being damned meant anything, it must mean being terribly wicked. She did not wish to be terribly wicked; neither could she conceive of her wickedness as redounding in any way to God's glory. "Oh, Roxana," cried Lyman, "what a fool I have been!" and headed straight for the day when, hearing a Christian worker put this same question to a poor soul in the inquiry room, he broke in to advise the interrogator to be damned himself if he thought he would like it.[13]

Lyman once told a female friend that his wife was less obedient to him than the friend was to her husband and that he was content to have it so, though he gave a rather odd reason for his satisfaction: "I could never know the sweets of power if she never rebelled a little, just to try my strength, and manifest the predominance of her conscience over her will." He told Harriet that the closest he and Roxana ever came to a quarrel was one day when he was beating some hogs that had annoyed him. Roxana came to the door and cried, "Lyman, don't, don't!" "I said something sharply, and she turned to go in. But oh, I had not time enough to get to the door and say, 'I am ashamed, I am sorry,' when one of the sweetest smiles shone out on her face, and that smile has never died and never will."

If Roxana had a fault, it was that there was something almost inhuman about her control; Lyman says he "scarcely ever saw her agitated, so perfect was her faith and resignation." The one infant the Beechers lost, the first Harriet, died while, at Lyman's command, Roxana slept the sleep of exhaustion from tending her, but when she woke she showed no emotion. "She was so resigned that she seemed almost happy."

> After the child was laid out, she looked so very beautiful that [Roxana] took her pencil and sketched her likeness as she lay. That likeness, a faint and faded little thing, drawn on ivory, is still preserved as a precious relic.

When the time came for her own passing, she was equally calm. "I do not think I shall be with you long," she told her husband one winter night, as they were driving home from a visit to a parishioner, and when the startled man inquired how she knew, she replied, "I have had a vision of heaven and its blessedness." Shocking as this was it must have been twice as chilling to hear of her "*more* than willingness to leave him and her children," all eight of them, the eldest sixteen and the youngest a baby. It worked out so exactly as she had said that if we did not know she died of tuberculosis, we might be tempted to believe that she had willed herself to death.

From the modern point of view, Lyman had worn her out with childbearing, but that was what women were for at the beginning of the nineteenth century; Lyman's father, David, used up five of them. Yet there can be no question that Lyman loved Roxana according to his lights. For a whole year after her death the world was an empty place for him, with "not motive enough" in it anywhere to move him. He wrote many sermons, but none of them were good for anything, and he never used any of them in later years. "Amid the smiles and prattle of children, and the kindness of sympathizing friends, I am alone; *Roxana is not here*." Many years later he endorsed one of her old letters in his by then shaky handwriting: "Roxana, beloved still, this Dec. 5, 1854."

Lyman's last marriage, to a Boston widow with several children, seems to have ended in catastrophe. We do not know much about it in its earlier stages, but when Lyman was an old man, Lydia dunned both Harriet and Henry Ward for money, and in 1862 the old man's doctor decreed that he must be "entirely separated from his wife for an indefinite period. . . . He ought not to see her nor know that he has a wife." And so it was done.

The problem is the second wife, Harriet Porter, stylish daughter of a Portland physician. The second Mrs. Beecher was a virtuous and pious woman who came into her husband's family determined to do all that could be done for his motherless children, and at first it seemed to go well enough. "I think our father's marriage with our present mother is as blessed an event as ever happened to our family," wrote William to Edward. "She is a dear woman. I can but love her, she is so kind and so careful, and appears to take as much care of the children as if they were her own." In one respect at least, Roxana would surely have approved of her: when Lyman tried to read Jonathan Edwards' hair-raising sermon on "Sinners in the Hands of an Angry God" to her (one would think he might have learned better than that from having been married to Roxana), she swept from the room declaring she would not listen to such libels on the character of her Heavenly Father. As time went on, however, there seems to have been less satisfaction on either side, and after the Beecher removal to Cincinnati, which she hated, Mrs. Beecher gradually lapsed into melancholia. Henry Ward thought her cold and unapproachable, and the best Edward could say for her after her death was that he wished he could have done more to make her happy. All in all, one can hardly avoid feeling that the rambunctious Beecher household and its highly developed individualists were rather more than Harriet Porter could cope with.[14]

Lyman was the same Beecher with his children as with his wives. His theology made it impossible for him to entertain a Wordsworthian reverence for them, for though he disbelieved in infant damnation, he thought their conduct proved children to be unregenerate before conversion. But he romped with his offspring and played with them and worked with them on household chores and took them with him on hunting and fishing expeditions, and a wonderful time was had by all. In this aspect, as in others, he sometimes suggests Theodore Roosevelt, but Roosevelt could never have behaved as Lyman did when, for example, he doused Catharine's head, without warning, in a wash-tub to see how she would take it or swung her by her hands out the window to see if she would be afraid (she wasn't). The baby of the family, Harriet tells us, always had the job of getting him out of bed in the morning, and this involved taking him by the nose and kissing him many times.

Oftentimes he would lie in bed after his little monitor had called him [writes Harriet], professing fears that there was a lion under the bed that would catch his foot if he put it out, and requiring repeated and earnest assurances from the curly head that he should be defended from being eaten up if he rose; and often and earnestly the breakfast-bell would ring before he could be induced to launch forth. Great would be the pride of the little monitor, who led him at last gravely into the breakfast-room, and related in baby phrase the labors of getting him up.

Charming as this is, one is not quite sure whether Lyman is entertaining the baby or merely indulging himself. Certainly his ways did not make for an orderly household. "Mother," writes Catharine, "was of that easy and gentle temperament that could not very strictly enforce any rules, while father . . . was never celebrated for his habits of system and order." But she also says that he had one or two or three sessions with each child in early youth "in which he taught them that obedience must be exact, prompt, and cheerful, and by a discipline so severe that it was thoroughly remembered and feared." There are also indications that Lyman sometimes failed to distinguish properly between teasing and torture. He could play his violin *against* the children as well as with them, as when he would deliberately destroy the rhythm when they wanted to dance, or produce a hideous tone or play the same monotonous series of notes over and over again, and we hear of Roxana coming to him at such times and, without a word, taking the fiddle out of his hands and carrying it off, as she might have done with a child.

To his own way of thinking, Lyman was always a devoted father.

William, why do you not write to your father? [he once inquired]. Are you not my first-born son? Did I not carry you over bogs a-fishing, a-straddle of my neck, on my shoulders, and, besides clothing and feeding, whip you often to make a man of you as you are, and would not have been without? and have I not always loved you, and borne you on my heart, as the claims and trials of a first-born demand? Don't you remember studying theology with your father while sawing and splitting wood in that wood-house in Green Street, Boston, near by where you found your wife?

Once he prevented Tom from going away by telling him how much he loved him—"Tom, I love you; you mustn't go 'way and leave me. They're all gone—Jim's at college. I want one chicken under my wing"—but opinions will differ as to whether this was prompted by affection for Tom or consideration of his own needs. As for his confidence in his own opinions, it could hardly be better illustrated than by reference to his letter to Edward when he heard he was flirting with the Baptists:

> I have no doubt of what is true on the subject, and do not expect that you will have any when you shall have had time calmly to examine it. But to me it seems as if you had better come home and be with me, and supply my exchanges, and attend the inquiry meeting, and a few such things, and be ordained when you are ready, especially if your way is veering to the Baptist side of the question. I should be sorry to have it acquire any considerable momentum that way till I see you.

Maintaining your individuality and making your own decisions in the presence of a father like that would have its problems; as James said of his own consideration of the ministry, "Father will pray me into it." Yet we ought in fairness to remember that though Lyman got all his sons into the ministry, none of them accepted his theology, nor his daughters either, yet he remained on good terms with them all. What could be more delightful than his comment upon Edward's attempt to account for original sin on the hypothesis of pre-existence? Lyman admitted that Edward had "destroyed the Calvinistic barns" (what in the world would Dr. Wilson and the Cincinnati Presbytery have said to that?), but told him he must not delude himself into thinking that the animals were now going to come into his "little theological hencoop"!

The only harsh word I have ever heard about Lyman as a father comes from Henry Ward, who says that he was "too busy to be loved." Edward speaks of the energizing effect he always had upon his children, so that all their mental vigor was activated by his presence, and Catharine says that "his society seems always to give a new impulse to the affection of the heart, and to every intellectual power," while Harriet, who wrote more about him than did any of the others,[15] speaks of "my blessed father, for many years so true an image of the Heavenly Father."

VI

Conversion was very important in Beecher's religious thinking. Though he was not prepared to say that the change *must* occur instantaneously, he did believe that, whether they realized it at the time or not, all Christians must at some time cease loving the world better than God and begin to regard Him "with an interest and affection wholly new in kind and superior in degree to their love for any other object" [*sic*]. As we have seen, he himself was converted during his college years, but he went through a long period of mental and spiritual anguish,[16] and even though Roxana had been conscious of no comparable experience, it sometimes appears that he was determined nobody else should escape what he had gone through. Listen to the stern words with which he took leave of his unconverted parishioners at East Hampton:

> And what shall I say to you, my dear hearers, of decent lives and impenitent hearts, to whom, through the whole period of my ministry, God has called by me in vain? God is my witness that I have greatly desired and earnestly sought the salvation of your souls, and I had hoped before the close of my ministry to be able to present you as dear children to God. But I shall not. My ministry is ended, and you are not saved. But I take you to record this day that I am pure from your blood, for I have not shunned to declare, to you especially, the counsel of God.

The *Autobiography* contains many examples of his dealings with individuals who had been touched by the Spirit.

> Before evening service, one Sabbath, news came to me that two of Deacon Shirrell's sons were under conviction. Oh, how I went down there! Whether walking, or flying, or on tiptoe, I don't know. When I got into the deacon's seat, oh how I preached!

In his book nobody became a Christian without an effort. "May you not be deceived in what you now feel?" he asked one parishioner, who had the courage to reply, "No, I can not!" But this was nothing compared to the struggles he undertook to bring his own children into the fold.

> But while I am as successful as most ministers in bringing the sons and daughters of others to Christ, my heart sinks within me at the thought that every one of my own dear children are [*sic*] without God in the world, and without Christ, and without hope. . . . A family so numerous as ours is a broad mark for the arrow of Death. I feel afraid that one or more of you may die suddenly, and I be called to mourn over you without hope.

"*You must not continue stupid*," he cries elsewhere. "Oh, my dear son, *agonize* to enter in. You *must* go to heaven; you *must not* go to hell!" But even here it was his will that must prevail, and never mind for the moment that it might be assumed to be God's will too.

As a theologian, Lyman is most notable for his struggles with the Calvinistic doctrine of election or foreordination. To be sure, such struggles were not peculiar to him. There were Old School Calvinists and New School Calvinists, Edwardians and Hopkinsians. John Elmer Frazee says of Lyman that he "tried to render the Edwardian doctrine of free agency consistent with the Calvinistic doctrine of divine sovereignty, and to make them both harmonize with the *Westminster Confession of Faith*." His conclusion "astonished both the 'Old School' and the 'New School' factions, and exposed him to the assaults of both."

These relationships cannot be studied in detail here, for our subject is Lyman Beecher himself and not his theology nor his place in American church history. But what he believed—and what he refused to believe—shows much about the man he was. And even to those who find his theology meaningless in itself, his own feelings and convictions in relation to it are significant for the understanding of his character.

Lyman's grandson, Charles Edward Stowe, was to describe Calvinism as "a mighty giant on the pathway of history who walked on two legs: the agency of God and the agency of man. He was always going lame in one leg or the other, and flopping over into fatalism on the one side or Arminianism on the other." Lyman could never reconcile himself to having either leg disabled. "My people know that I am not always banging their ears with the doctrine of natural ability. I alternate the two edges of the sword, and smite as to me seems good." This was conviction but surely it was temperament also. We shall see that Lyman facing the slavery problem was the same man who confronted the Calvinist dilemma. "I am not afraid of the ground of controversy between the Colonizationists and the Abolitionists. I am myself both without perceiving in myself any inconsistency." As a matter of fact, he was no expert in such perceptions.

He gives us an unmistakably clear statement of what he did *not* believe:

> We know that Calvinism is often represented as teaching that infants deserve damnation, and that hell is paved with their bones; that all men are, by nature and necessarily, as depraved and wicked as they can be; that an atonement has been made only for the sins of the elect, —a very small part of mankind; that the elect will be saved, though they should conduct ever so wickedly; and that the non-elect cannot be saved, though they should conduct ever so religiously; and that men to whom pardon is offered, without special grace to enable them to repent, are in the condition of captives in a dungeon,—insulted with the offer of liberty, and threatened with punishment if they do not embrace it, when their hands are bound, and their feet put in fetters.

What God actually has decreed is something very different:

The decrees of God are His determination to create a universe of free agents, to exist forever under the perfect laws of his moral government, perfectly administered; for gratification and manifestation of his benevolence, for the perfect enjoyment of all his obedient subjects; with all that is implied therein, and all the consequences foreseen.

Lyman distinguished sharply between physical and moral omnipotence. God controls the material universe by "simple power," but "he must act in the government of the mind by laws, and motives, and moral influence, with reference to the formation and continuance of free agency, and accountability, and character."

"Total depravity" means not the destruction of all good qualities in human beings but simply the perversion of their nature so that in them the love of God was not supreme. Lesser goods had usurped the place of the Supreme Good. "No, the fall did not destroy free agency or accountability. It did create a powerful bias, so that there was an inevitable certainty that man would go wrong. But it did not destroy his capacity for going right." Lyman would not grant that the devil himself had reached a state of "natural inability."

I have no doubt the devil would be glad to think so. It would relieve his deep and unsupportable anguish, if he could believe that he had never sinned but once, and that ever since that he has been a poor, helpless creature. No! he has sinned since his fall, and will sin again.

This is the Edwardian distinction between natural inability and moral inability, and it is here, of course, that many believe Lyman chose to have his cake and eat it too. "Original sin" exists "anterior to actual sin or any knowledge of law." But Adam was no sinner until he chose to sin, nor was he holy in the absence of having chosen to do right. We are not accountable for Adam's sin; it is not "imputed" to us; and we are not condemned for having inherited his corrupted nature. But that corrupted nature does create an "obstinate perversion" in us, and the "guilt" with which the Confession charges us indicates a "liability to evil." This is why we need Christ's atonement, and this too is why the renewing and redeeming agency of the Holy Spirit is necessary for us. By the Spirit, God can "make to the mind of man such an application of the truth as shall unfailingly convince him of sin, render him willing to obey the Gospel, and actually and joyfully obedient."

Christ made a complete atonement for all sinners, and God desires the salvation of all. There is no malignancy in God; when the Scriptures assign such human passions as anger to Him, they are to be taken analogically. Always He is "disposed to defer the infliction of the penalty and continue the means of reformation in behalf of the transgressor." His decrees, therefore, do not compel the sinner to sin; neither will God shut him out of heaven. His departure from God is voluntary; so is his refusal to return to Him through Christ. God

> will leave to walk in their own way none who do not deserve to be left; and punish none for walking in it who did not walk therein knowingly, deliberately, and with wilful obstinacy. He will give up to death none who did not choose death, and choose it with as entire freedom as he himself chooses holiness; and who did not deserve eternal punishment as truly as he himself deserves eternal praise. He will send to hell none who are not opposed to him, and to holiness and to heaven; none who are not, by voluntary sin and rebellion, unfitted for heaven and fitted for destruction as eminently as saints are prepared for glory.

How many would thus be lost Lyman did not attempt to say, but it is clear that he hoped there would be few. He emphatically rejected the notion that the numbers of the damned would equal or surpass those of the redeemed.

Who ever heard of a prison that occupied one-half of the territories of a kingdom? and who can believe that the universe, which was called into being, and is upheld and governed to express the goodness of God, will contain as much misery as happiness? How could the government of God be celebrated with such raptures in heaven, if it filled with dismay and ruin half the universe?

There was one special topic connected with the doctrine of election about which Lyman's feelings were especially strong—the alleged damnation of infants—and there is nothing else he had to say which shows more clearly his own kindness of heart. In his eyes, infants were "innocent" though not "holy," and since damnation was conceivable only as a sequel to deliberate, positive, responsible sin, they could not be damned if they died before achieving the age of responsibility.

I am aware that Calvinists are represented as believing and teaching the monstrous doctrine that infants are damned. . . . But, having passed the age of fifty, and been conversant, for thirty years, with the most approved Calvinistic writers, and with distinguished Calvinistic divines in New England, and in the Middle and Southern and Western States, I must say that I have never seen or heard of any book which contained such a statement, nor a man, minister or layman, who believed or taught it.

The last part of this was certainly an overstatement, and Lyman elsewhere admits the existence of Calvinists who believed in the damnation of non-elect infants, but he insists that a creed must not be judged by the eccentricities of ill-balanced persons who may hold it. In his opinion, the Calvinistic rejection of baptismal regeneration supported his view; so did the Edwardians in repudiating the doctrine of imputation. The Bible nowhere states that infants will be damned nor that anyone not guilty of actual sin can finally suffer reprobation.[17]

Lyman Beecher was not the first Calvinist to raise questions about infant damnation, but he brought the question into the open more successfully than did his predecessors. It would hardly be an exaggeration to say that he delivered the world's dead babies from the hell which they had hitherto inhabited in many clouded minds. "All infants are saved by the grace of Christ through the wonderful efficacy of the Spirit." Lyman Beecher must share very importantly in the credit accruing from the fact that this finally became the official Presbyterian doctrine.[18]

VII

The attentive reader will not need to be told that there were weaknesses and inconsistencies in Lyman Beecher's theological thinking. Even in his affectionate memorial article, Calvin Stowe thought it necessary to attack his father-in-law's distinction between natural and moral inability. "He checked the theologically more adventurous spirit of [Nathaniel Taylor] and by his love prevailed on his friend still to draw as much as possible in the old harness of Edwards. The result was not happy." With this I believe the modern editor of the *Autobiography*, Barbara M. Cross, would agree; Lyman, she writes, was "rather feckless about theological subtleties." He himself never claimed that he had seen the whole problem of election clearly. He could not go beyond Romans 5 on the subject of original sin. "All is confusion and darkness beyond this. I have no light and pretend to no knowledge. And surely there is no heresy in ignorance." Even in his old age the pitfalls and subtleties of the doctrine of election seem to have plagued him. He was never really at ease in Zion. He hoped for, but he had no positive, settled assurance of, salvation. This shows, if you like, that he never really recovered from the Calvinist nightmare, but it also shows a very attractive humility.

It would not be difficult to find utterances of Lyman's which would seem to contradict what I have quoted here. But the whole force of his nature, his faith, and his hope stand arrayed against these statements. On this point as elsewhere, Harriet is a safe interpreter. Her father "firmly believed in total depravity," she says, "yet practically he never seemed to realize that people were unbelievers for any other reason than for want of light, and that clear and able arguments would not at once put an end to skepticism."

This, of course, is why he became such a powerful revival preacher. Temperamentally he was less interested in speculating about God's part in human redemption than he was in persuading, driving, or dragooning men to do theirs, so as to make the mercy of God operative in their behalf. His primary interest was not God in His heaven, which is a subject for religious philosophy, but God in this world, or God moving in the hearts of men, which is religion. That is why Frazee says that "the principle of free agency with all its implications was the life-giving spirit with which Beecher endeavored to resuscitate a 'dead orthodoxy.' "

Serious objections might be raised also to other aspects of Lyman's religious thinking. He seems virtually to have regarded Bible and revelation as synonyms ("no doctrine, and no institution which cannot be found in the Bible without the aid of ecclesiastical history, can be recognized as of divine appointment"). Yet he never defines what he means by inspiration. He argues the harmony of the Old and New Testaments, but to maintain this he is driven to such desperate expedients as seeing Christ as "the acting Divinity of the Jews," indicated wherever the Angel of the Lord is mentioned. His treatment of miracles cannot, I think, mean much to modern readers, for he is credulous in accepting Biblical miracles and peremptory in rejecting all others, for example, "the private miracles of Mahomet, or the modern Catholic miracles." [19]

Lyman is even more unsatisfactory on the Trinity and the Atonement. His Trinitarianism seems at least to have approximated tritheism, for his Trinity comprised three real, divine Persons, "sustained and developed by the eternal essence," and their functions were clearly differentiated. The Father is "the guardian of the law." The Son assumes "a sphere subordinate to the Father; so that he is said to be sent by the Father, and God is said to have made the worlds by him," while the Spirit is "subordinate to the Son" and "the divine agent to whom is committed the work of commencing and perfecting holiness in the hearts of men," all of which sounds more like Milton than it does like Christian orthodoxy. In his *Autobiography* Lyman advises praying "to Christ as God, for he is God as truly as the Father, as is also the Holy Spirit," and Harriet says that he himself prayed to all three Persons.

Though his God is benevolent, he has little to say about divine grace or love, and his Atonement remains largely a legalistic conception, basically Grotian in character. Christ came "to vindicate and establish" God's law, "to redeem mankind from the curse, and to bring them back to the obedience of the same law from which they have revolted." His action was necessary because the repentance and faith of the sinner were in themselves not sufficient to secure his salvation. He must have a Mediator to intercede for him with God. Through the Atonement, "God can maintain the influence of his law and forgive sin, upon condition of repentance toward God, with an assurance of pardon and eternal life if [sinners] comply." But as Frazee says, "what it is that Christ suffered; how it is that the death of Christ justifies the sinner; or how the sinner is saved in consequence of what Christ did—all these vital inquiries" Lyman leaves unanswered.

VIII

A man who could describe the Bible as a "statute-book" for moral government might not seem well qualified to become a champion of religious toleration. It is even more difficult to perceive tendencies in this direction in such a statement as:

Popery is a system where science and ignorance, refinement and barbarism, wisdom and stupidity, taste and animalism, mistaken zeal and malignant enmity may sanctimoniously pour out their virulence against the Gospel, and cry Hosanna, while they go forth to shed the blood and to wear out the patience of the saints.[20]

Nevertheless the tendencies were there.

Lyman believed that scepticism was an evil, caused by fallen man's alienation from God, but he would not have it repressed by "authority" or "the odium of hard names." As he saw it, it was not heaven's intention "that truths which lie within the sphere of evidence should be obtained without mental effort," and this meant that those who miss the mark must not be treated as outlaws. Instead he relied wholly upon what it is now fashionable to call "dialogue" to establish truth, and he taught his children not to "find fault if their arguments were roughly handled" or "grumble and get angry at being bruised and floored in fair debate." "Dare to think for yourself," he cries; "but give to others the same liberty; and never raise the pusillanimous cry of intolerance, because others will not think your opinions to be harmless or as correct and salutary as their own." Those who rejected religious truth were not in his eyes necessarily wicked. "Ignorance, or prejudice, or simple misapprehension" might well take the place of "real enmity," and only God could judge. In all these matters, Calvinist and supernaturalist though he was, Lyman was a true child of the Enlightenment.

He did not see religious "establishments" as necessary to Christianity; often indeed it seemed to thrive more in spite of them than because of them. Denominations, with their formulated creeds and disciplines, had their place, but he regarded it as immoral for any denomination "to hinder the prosperity of other denominations, by any monopoly of governmental influence and favor," and he himself served both Congregational and Presbyterian churches. For all his loathing of Unitarian theology, he refused to read Unitarians as such out of the Christian Church: "It is my opinion that there are many among Unitarians who feel a solemn reverence for God, and his Word and worship, the active power of a tender conscience, and the pressure of an honest and earnest desire to know what is truth."

In the early days, he supported a state church in Connecticut, and when disestablishment came, he at first regarded it as a blow against the Kingdom of God itself; later he found "that I was on one side and God on the other, and God's side proved the best." Disestablishment turned out to be a blessing in disguise and the best thing that had ever happened to the church. Instead of destroying the power of the clergy, as had been feared, disestablishment increased it by placing it upon the only truly tenable, that is, a purely spiritual, basis.

As for those outside the Christian communion altogether, Lyman rejected the liberal idea that the "heathen" were "not accountable for their depravity of heart, nor criminal for their idolatry, and scarcely for their immoralities," and he could not see that "the light of nature" had "ever developed and maintained a correct and universal system of morals," for "the best men in pagan history were, with few exceptions, men, who, in Christian lands, would be regarded as stained by practices of flagrant immorality." His account of "heathen" sins is one-sided, showing no real understanding of any non-Christian civilization (he made an exception of Judaism only because he could read Christianity back into it). Nevertheless he was not willing to assert that those to whom the Gospel had not been preached could not be saved without it. It was different of course with those who wilfully rejected it.

If Lyman Beecher's toleration was not wholly to have been expected from his prepossessions, the same thing was not true of his interest in reform. The term "Social Gospel" had not been invented in his time, but he was well aware that the Kingdom of God could never come on earth without man's active cooperation. The very first lecture in his *Works* opens with a startling observation.

In all past time the earth has been owned, and knowledge and power have been monopolized, by the few, while the people, the laboring classes, the great body of mankind, have been left to grope their way in darkness and slavery, tilling the earth they did not own, on the borders of starvation, and liable by a few days' sickness to become paupers.

This condition can never be alleviated, he adds elsewhere, until the earth shall be owned by those who till it.

Lyman may not have meant by that quite what Karl Marx would have meant. He believed that "our nation has been raised up by Providence to exert an efficient instrumentality in this work of moral renovation," and it was clearly his view that some of the worst abuses had already been corrected here. Jonathan Edwards had believed that the millennium would begin in America; Lyman thought it would begin in the American West. "If we gain the West," he wrote Catharine, when pondering the removal to Cincinnati, "all is safe; if we lose it, all is lost." Let us not be too much amused by this: it shows a more continental consciousness and a greater sensitiveness to the American destiny than most New Englanders possessed in Lyman's time. And he is not far from Marx when he admits that "revolutions and convulsions" are needed to establish a decent social order.

The unsurpation of the soul will not be relinquished spontaneously, nor the chains be knocked off from the body and the mind of man by the hands which for ages have been employed to rivet them. He that sitteth upon the throne must overturn and overturn, before the rights of man will be restored.

All in all, he achieved an amazing combination of millenarianism, revolutionism, social consciousness, and an exuberant, optimistic faith in American destiny.

It is true that not all the reforms Lyman sponsored seem as important to us as they did to him. He was a strict Sabbatarian, and he found virtue in stopping the Sunday mails which we can hardly be expected to discern there. Nevertheless he was considerably more than a one-eyed man among blind reformers. He made his first bid for public recognition by speaking out emphatically against the duel when that relic of barbarism was still accepted as honorable, even obligatory, by a great many fools who ought to have known better,[21] and his "Lectures on Intemperance" make out a case for total abstinence which can still be regarded as air tight. In the early days, Lyman himself had accepted moderate drinking, and there was a time when, as college butler at Yale, he had sold alcohol to his fellow students, so that, as one of his descendants has remarked, "the future founder of the American temperance movement" developed out of "a retail liquor dealer." He changed because he was disgusted by the disabling drunkenness of the society in which he lived, where the atmosphere of the grog shop invaded even ecclesiastical gatherings and preachers themselves drank and smoked as much as anybody. He made an important beginning toward the development of the temperance sentiment, which continued to gain power in America until the passage of the Eighteenth Amendment caused it to become fashionable to break the law and we headed straight for the morass into which we now sink a little deeper every year. Lyman Beecher was not so foolish as to imagine that any great reform could be brought about by government action alone. ("O Lord," he prayed, in a prayer which certainly has lost none of its bite through the years, "grant that we may not despise our rulers; and grant, O Lord, that they may not act so we can't help it!") He did favor prohibition laws, but he knew they needed moral and spiritual sanctions behind them if they were to be successful. He sponsored lyceums and libraries to compete with the saloons as social clubs, and he advocated wide, tireless, often sacrificial participation in popular government at the grass-roots level. Finally, he was not willing to blame individual liquor dealers for intemperance nor slaveholders for slavery. "None of us are enough without sin to cast the first stone." He knew that "all language of impatient censure . . . would only serve to irritate, and arouse prejudice, and prevent investigation."

As for slavery itself, though legend will have it that Lincoln thought *Uncle Tom's Cabin* caused the Civil War, as a matter of fact all the Beechers were inclined to be moderate about slavery, and Lyman, who once had two "bound" girls in his home, was no exception. When he refused to join actively in William Lloyd Garrison's work on the ground that he had too many irons in the fire already, the editor of *The Liberator* told him to forget about the others and give all his attention to this one. But Garrison was more logical about it than any Beecher could be expected to be about anything when he argued that, slavery being a national sin, Beecher must come out for immediate emancipation or else repudiate his own doctrine of immediate repentance. "Oh, Garrison," cried Lyman, "you can't reason that way. Great economic and political questions can't be solved so simply. You must take into account what is expedient as well as what is right." At Lane Seminary the young firebrand student leader Theodore Weld agreed with Garrison, not Beecher, and this was the beginning of the end of Lyman's Western dream. "You are taking just the course to defeat your own object," Lane's president told Weld, "and prevent yourself from doing good. If you want to teach colored schools, I can fill your pockets with money, but if you will visit in colored families and walk with them in the streets you will be overwhelmed." So he was, but Lane Seminary was nearly overwhelmed with him.

Beecher hated standing armies, professional soldiers, and the War of 1812, which caused him to fear the suppression of free speech and the establishment of a military dictatorship.[22] He praised the Old Testament Jews for giving

exemption from military exposure for one year after planting a vineyard, or building a house, or marrying a wife. . . . What a considerate regard to the refined feelings of human nature lies in this peculiar law,—that when a man has set his heart on enjoying some peaceful work of national utility, some plan of provision for his children, some new and dear relation of life, he shall have peace.

At East Hampton he protected a nearby settlement of Montauk Indians from exploitation by rum-sellers, but he also defended the Pilgrims for their "tough" Indian policy. Apparently it never occurred to him to question capital punishment. In "The Remedy for Duelling" he declares that "the appointed punishment of murder is death. God, who defines the crime, has himself specified the penalty," though it is true that in the same sermon he argues that a Christian may not do evil that good may come. Such a choice is extended to us only in connection with natural evils. You may sacrifice a finger to save an arm, "but of two sinful things you may choose neither." Apparently he saw no contradiction here.

It would not be correct to describe Lyman Beecher as a rebel against Calvinism, but it might be fair to say that he undercut the Calvinistic system by holding it in his mind along with ideas that cannot really be reconciled with it. Leonard Bacon said of him that

The thing of all others . . . that affected me most was, not his intellect, or his imagination, or his glowing emotion, but the absoluteness and simplicity of his faith. The intensity and constancy of his faith made eternal things real to me, and impressed me from childhood with the visionary nature of worldly things, so that I never felt any desire to lay plans for this world.

So he must have affected many, this man who was great by his religion. "I might criticise unfavorably many of his opinions and some of his actions," wrote Calvin Stowe after his death. "But I will not. He was a good man, and I loved him; a great man, and I reverenced him."

2

WILLIAM ELLERY CHANNING

Messages from the Spirit

I

When Jean Lefebvre de Cheverus, the first Roman Catholic bishop of Boston, died in 1836 in France, where he had first been made archbishop of Bordeaux and later a cardinal, William Ellery Channing caused the bells of the Federal Street Church to be sounded in his honor, an unusual act of inter-denominational courtesy for those days. Not unmindful of the significance of what had occurred, the Catholics of Boston remembered until Channing himself died in 1842, when the bells of the cathedral were tolled for him—probably the only time they have thus honored a Unitarian minister.

He was a "short, spare man," with a "stooped frame, emaciated look, pallid complexion, and deep-set, almost sunken eyes." [1]

The deepening hollows in the cheeks made the cheekbones prominent and threw the good straight nose into more sharp relief, while the increasing pallor of the countenance gave the large sunken eyes even a more wonderful expressiveness than that of their earlier light. The sick look hovered about the mouth, qualifying its natural firmness with tremulous and sympathetic lines. Matter of fact people called this face emaciated and cadaverous; the more poetic fancied an attenuation of the bodily substance that revealed a spiritual presence with the least possible obstruction.[2]

They said of him also that he wore a boy's size coat. But his pulpit gown was made of beautiful, belted silk; from his house to the church he wore over it a thick, quilted silk coat or cape. His neck was swathed in the high clerical neckcloths which preachers favored in his time. When he had climbed the pulpit stairs he would sink into his seat as if he never intended to rise from it, and when the time came to speak, he might begin in "a monstrous little voice." Yet, though he disdained all the popular tricks of pulpit eloquence, he gained in power as he proceeded. He took on stature; his eyes seemed to see into another realm; and his voice, though not beautiful in the conventional sense, would be "flexible to tremulousness," running "up and down, even in the articulation of a single polysyllabic word, in so strange a fashion that they who heard him for the first time would not anticipate its effect,—how before it ceased, that voice would thrill them to the inmost." [3] For all this he paid a heavy price, for the effort of preaching was so great for him that he might be prostrated for hours, or even for days, after a sermon.

William Ellery Channing was born at Newport, Rhode Island, on April 7, 1780. He told Lucy Aikin that his ancestors had come "from Dorchester, or its neighborhood, near the beginning of the last century." He was the third of ten children, of whom nine grew up, and three (William Ellery, Walter, and Edward T.) became well known. The Channings were allied with Cabots, Lees, Jacksons, and Lowells, and with the Gibbs, Dana, and Allston families. The father, a lawyer, seems to have been an amiable man, yet his son was never so intimate with him as he was with his more irritable mother. He did not cherish his early years in memory as a kind of Wordsworthian paradise.

I look back to no bright dawn of life which gradually "faded into common day." The light which I now live in rose at a later period. A rigid domestic discipline, sanctioned by the times—gloomy views of religion—the selfish passions—collisions with companions perhaps worse than myself—these and other things darkened my boyhood.

Through the family connections, the child was, however, brought into contact with some of the great men of the time, and until he became president of Yale, Ezra Stiles was Channing's pastor.

The little boy was sent to dame school so young that he had to be carried. In 1798 he was graduated from Harvard, giving a commencement address on "The Present Age." From 1798 to 1800 he tutored in the Randolph family, at Roanoke, Virginia, an important broadening influence upon him. He had seen something of slavery in Rhode Island, but he saw more and was more greatly shocked in Virginia. Though he considered Virginians more "sensual" than New Englanders, he also thought them less commercially minded and found many virtues in them.

In 1800 Channing returned to Newport, where he formed a friendship with Dr. Samuel Hopkins, whose influence upon his thinking has been strongly affirmed and denied.[4] In 1801 he became a "regent" at Harvard; this post, which was a kind of proctorship and largely a sinecure, made it possible for him to begin his study of theology. On June 1, 1803, he was ordained and installed in the only charge he was ever to hold, that of the Federal Street Church in Boston. But it was not until 1814 that he married his cousin, Ruth Gibbs, and bought a house on Beacon Street, on the present site of the Athenaeum. A girl child, born in October 1816, lived less than twenty-four hours; in 1818 Mary was born, in 1819 William Francis. A second son, born in 1820, died in early childhood.

By this time the split between Trinitarians and Unitarians in New England's Congregational churches was all too evident, and, somewhat against his will, Channing was sucked into the war of pamphlets which was one of the results. Though he had very little interest in fine-spun theological distinctions, even when they were made in behalf of positions he himself had staked out, and though his famous Baltimore sermon, "Unitarian Christianity," was widely accepted as defining the tenets of the new faith, Channing still declined the presidency of the newly organized American Unitarian Association in 1824. Meanwhile, however, he had received a D.D. from Harvard, had travelled in England and upon the continent, and his labors at Federal Street had been greatly lightened by the appointment of Ezra Stiles Gannett as his colleague.

His health was such that, during his later years, he was able to do less and less at Federal Street; it is remarkable, therefore, that the outreach of his ministry should have expanded steadily until the end. Publishing books and articles and speaking hither and yon are not exciting subjects to chronicle, but they require energy, and they have their effect. The abolitionists long felt that Channing was taking a lukewarm attitude toward slavery, but in 1835 he began his notable efforts, carrying them finally to a point which barely stopped short of a complete break with the Federal Street Church. In 1838 he testified to his belief in free speech in the most effective possible manner when he signed a petition in behalf of the atheist Abner Kneeland. In 1842, on April 7, Channing gave his final sermon at Federal Street, and on August 2 he died at Bennington, Vermont.

II

His contemporaries did not consider Channing a brilliant scholar; sometimes indeed they professed themselves surprised that he had been able to accomplish so much with so little. "In our wantonness we often flout Dr. Channing," said Emerson, "and say he is getting old; but as soon as he is ill we remember he is our Bishop, and we have not done with him yet."

Latin he could not (or did not) learn in the classroom, but he did better when instructed privately by his father's clerk. Greek and Hebrew he must have been exposed to in his theological training, but his use of the New Testament is hardly that of a scholar. He read the masterpeice of French and German literature (finding more goodness in Schiller than in Goethe), and he so greatly admired Don Quixote that he could not accept the indignities to which Cervantes subjected him. Much of this must have been read in translation, however; in fact, he tells Miss Aikin that he cannot read German and that therefore he could not, as some persons suppose, have got his mysticism from German sources. He gave Shakespeare and Milton their due meed of praise (Coleridge's worship of Shakespeare was "one of his most innocent excesses," for "where else could he have found an influence so fitted to counteract his morbid tendencies and errors?"), and regarded Wordsworth as the greatest poet of his own time. Carlyle was important to him; so was Coleridge himself. He recognized Byron's gifts ("I always hoped, that, after the fever of youthful passion, this unhappy man would reflect, repent, and prove that in genius there is something congenial with religion") and regarded Shelley as "a seraph gone astray, who needed friends that he never found in this world." Though he admired Maria Edgeworth, I recall no reference to Jane Austen. Scott Channing greatly relished, though he rather labors the point that he did not rise above "the ideal of a man of the world." He is labored too on Dickens, who

> greatly erred in turning so often the degradation of humanity into matter of sport; but the tendency of his dark pictures is, to awaken sympathy with our race, to change the unfeeling indifference towards the depressed multitude into sorrowful and indignant sensibility to their wrongs and woes.

It is difficult to see how he can be right in both these statements. Some will feel that he would have appreciated Dickens more if he himself had possessed more humor, and I do not deny that this may be true. Theoretically, however, he appreciated the importance of humor for literature, even as he knew the values of tragedy;[5] Channing was always capable of surprises of this kind.

Though he knew his own style was anything but Addisonian, he calls Addison "my delight," and he finds Horace Walpole's letters extremely amusing though he "offends my moral sentiments perpetually." But perhaps the most amazing passage occurs in the essay on "Self-Culture":

> If the Sacred Writers will enter and take up their abode under my roof, if Milton will cross my threshold to sing to me of Paradise, and Shakespeare to open to me the worlds of imagination and the workings of the human heart, and Franklin to enrich me with his practical wisdom, I shall not pine for intellectual companionship, and I may become a cultivated man though excluded from what is called the best society in the place where I live.

Channing was always the serious reader, for he interleaved his books with slips of paper upon which he wrote with a pen the reflections which occurred to him; later these were assembled and classified. Such methods would seem better suited to science or philosophy than, say, fiction. As a student, Channing studied Locke, Berkeley, Thomas Reid, David Hume, Priestley, Richard Price, and others. In Price he found a valuable antidote to Locke's empiricism—"he gave me the doctrine of ideas" and "probably moulded my philosophy into the form it has always retained"—and what he learned from Hutcheson about "innate moral sense" and "disinterested benevolence" almost amounted to a conversion experience.

Science interested Channing from an early age—his very first composition dealt with electricity—and he is said to have had considerable aptitude in mathematics. From time to time he was inclined to wish that he could have carried his scientific interests further. But though he was a closer observer and describer of nature than many clergymen,[6] I always get the feeling that he valued science primarily for its spiritual suggestiveness, and he was in character when he escaped the phrenology craze which attracted so many in the nineteenth century because he had "a strong aversion to theories which subject the mind to the body."

Nature, however, had other than scientific aspects, and though Channing was no pantheist,[7] he loved nature as much as any pantheist could, and even reproached the Quakers for "neglecting the revelation made through Nature to the human reason," suffering "from the old dogma of the depravity of human nature" and failing to "reverence the spontaneity of the intellect and imagination as immediate gifts of God no less than conscience." Since these feelings did not grow stale with age—"Time wears out the wrinkles on Mother Earth's brow"—he took them as a sign that he had been "made to be an everlasting inhabitant of the universe."

Great natural wonders like Niagara Falls made nature and nature's God, who created it, more wonderful to him. "Instead of shrinking before the majesty of nature, my mind rather dilates into a proportioned elevation." But the sunshine and the roar of the waves on the Rhode Island beach where he had roamed as a boy caused him to "thank God that this beautiful island was the place of my birth." No other spot on earth had helped so much to form him. "There, in reverential sympathy with the mighty power around me, I became conscious of power within."

When he was too weak to work for long stretches of time, Channing would break away from his desk and take a turn in the garden with his dogs galloping around him.[8] When he built a new house in 1835 he feared he must be guilty of extravagance and self-indulgence and had to argue with himself about it.

> I spend nothing on luxuries, amusements, shows. My food is of the simplest, my clothes sometimes call for rebuke from affectionate friends, not for their want of neatness, but for their venerable age. But one indulgence I want,—a good house, open to the sun and air, with apartments large enough for breathing freely, and commanding something of earth and sky.[9]

So the physical was itself transmuted into the spiritual: "I almost wonder at myself, when I think of the pleasure the dawn gives me after having witnessed it so many years. This blessed light of heaven, how dear it is to me! and this earth which I have trodden so long, with what affection I took at it!"

So much for the beauty of nature; what, then, of beauty in the arts? The materials available for judging what they meant to Channing are not abundant. When he called his brother-in-law, Washington Allston, "the greatest genius of this country in his department," he was not an unprejudiced witness, but his judgment was not absurd. Though he thought he lacked ear, Channing still felt

a power in music which I want words to describe. It touches chords, reaches depths in the soul, which lie beyond all other influences,—extends my consciousness, and has sometimes given me a pleasure which I may have found in nothing else. Nothing in my experience is more mysterious, more inexplicable. An instinct has always led men to transfer it to heaven, and I suspect the Christian under its power has often attained to a singular consciousness of his immortality.

At the very end of his life he lamented that he had lost much pleasure in life through neglecting music, but he remembered that he had always been very sensitive to sound. "I have always been inclined to love people for their voices. A musical voice is one way to my heart; and when it communicates to me the grand and beautiful thoughts of a work of genius, it is particularly captivating."

As for the theater, not only was he enthusiastic about Shakespeare but he greatly enjoyed reading such dramatists as Cibber and Lillo. Though Fanny Kemble was at first repelled by his "unreal" and "mistaken" way of talking about the theater, she finally came to "love and adore" him. The author of *Fashion* recalled him affectionately at an amateur production at Lenox: "He was warm in his expressions of delight, and many times rose from his seat, and clapped his hands, and laughed with genuine enjoyment." She recited for him, and he criticized her pronunciation and elocution. Then he read her Bryant's "The Future Life": "his silvery tones were tremulous as he read, and his mild eyes beamed with a lustre almost angelic." [10] With the moral condition of the theater what it was, or what he though it was, he was inclined to prefer recitation, yet he could "conceive of a theater which would be the noblest of all amusements," and indeed he was always mindful of the value and importance of clean, uplifting amusements as a means of combating social vices.

If Channing had not been a preacher, might he have become a professional writer? As early as his college days, Judge Story thought he surpassed all his classmates in his "power of varied and sustained written composition," and there were those in his time who mentioned him along with Cooper, Irving, and other luminaries in the literary heavens, though some thought his style "enigmatic" where it should have been "lucid" and "perspicuous." Certainly his essays on Milton and Napoleon were the first American equivalents of the serious critical articles in the English reviews. Beethoven, of all people, was interested in his writings long before his reputation had reached its highest point, and he still has an honorable place in one of the most widely used college anthologies of American literature.

Channing began each day by writing down the thoughts that had come to him during wakeful periods in the night. Yet he professed himself so dissatisfied with his own expression of the ideas in which he profoundly believed that he often hesitated to send his productions to his friends, and he never did get round to his major projected work on "The Principles of Moral, Religious, and Political Science." Though he did not pretend to be entirely indifferent to literary reputation, writing interested him primarily as a means of achieving clarification. Contradictory views were placed side by side and various, far-reaching ramifications of his thought examined. Systematic, orderly formulation, achieved at last through seeing the flower in the crannied wall in relation to the totality of its environment—this was the goal.

One of the problems with which clergymen and writers alike have to grapple quite passed Channing by. His wife came of a wealthy family, so that after his marriage her husband was under no necessity of depending upon his own exertions for his livelihood.[11] When he went to Federal Street, his salary was set at $1200; it seems never to have risen above $2000, and it was progressively reduced with the decline of his health and the delegating of more and more work to his associate until, at the end, he was giving the little he was now able to do quite without remuneration. He made it his habit to spend everything he earned (very little of it upon himself):

> I make it my rule to spend my *whole income*, to lay up *nothing*. At the same time, I hold myself bound not to exceed my income, and it is possible that in my case, as in others, the self-denial and economy necessary to keep within this bound may pass with some for meanness.

Yet his charity could, upon occasion, be impulsive, as when, greatly moved, he gave away the whole contents of his wallet, being obliged to borrow afterwards in order to be able to feed his horse.

Though Channing found the sight of pretty girls "one of my pleasures as I walk in the streets," women do not seem to have troubled him much more than money. We have his own word for it that his college life was chaste, though, says Chadwick,

> there are various passages in his letters and journals which do not read as if the passions which assailed him were a painted flame, and it may be that, like many another stern ascetic, his preoccupation with temptation made it more real for him than if he had led a life less tense and strained.

As a mature man, he made friends with women of brains and character like Dorothea Dix and Elizabeth Peabody, and, as one of the Sedgwicks put it, "the man was never lost in the saint nor the friend in the prophet and seer." He believed in a married woman's right to hold property and encouraged Elizabeth Peabody to go into business on her own.[12] The notion that women were made for men seemed to him "suited to an age of female degradation," and though he strongly felt the charm of Mrs. Jameson's *Characteristics of Women*, he thought the author at fault because she had suggested that her sex could find fulfilment only in love. He himself, clearly, admired brains in a woman's head as well as in a man's, and he corresponded at length, and on a high level, with such British ladies as Lucy Aikin, Harriet Martineau, Joanna Baillie, and Felicia Hemans. It is interesting too that he considered Mary Wollstonecraft the greatest woman of her time. "*Can* you call her a prostitute? She indeed formed a guilty connection. But even then she acted upon principle."

We know very little about Channing's relations with his wife, but there is nothing to indicate that they were not quite contented with each other. In later years she suffered from a rheumatic affliction in her hands and eyes but always did her best to keep knowledge of her condition from her valetudinarian husband, that she might save him worry and look after his needs more effectively. His relations with his children were happy, as they ought to have been, for he allowed them a surprising amount of freedom for his time; indeed, children in general seem to have been drawn to the solemn, delicate man and to have enjoyed being with him. He even had doubts about some aspects of Bronson Alcott's teaching methods, fearing that the child's mind might be "turned inward" too much.

The free development of the spiritual nature may be impeded by too much analysis of it. The soul is jealous of being watched, and it is no small part of wisdom to know when to leave it to its impulses and when to restrain it. The strong passion of the young for the outward is an indication of Nature to be respected; spirituality may be too exclusive for its own good.

But whatever advantages Channing may have possessed in other connections was more than made up for by the limitations of his health, which must have cut down his activities by at least fifty per cent. In 1831 he wrote Lucy Aikin that two or three hours was for him a good day's work ("What I have done is so little compared with what I have hoped and proposed, and I see myself outdone by so many in various particulars"). Though Elizabeth Peabody speaks of him as a dyspeptic child, his natural health seems to have been good enough. His mother made him practice swimming without water, on the kitchen table, but he had his share of pranks and "blowouts," climbing the mastheads of brigs and schooners in the harbor, and even fighting on occasion, though he also liked taking long walks on the beach, flying his kite, or pitching pebbles into Narragansett Bay. Washington Allston calls him an accomplished wrestler and says that his laugh "could not have been heartier without being obstreperous," and Elizabeth Peabody herself speaks of Channing's horseback riding, riding in a rough wagon, and walking into the ocean with his young friends, their hands clasped, in a row. The ruination of his health is supposed to have derived from the ascetic excesses to which, for the only time in his life, he gave himself up in his student days—studying all night, wearing insufficient clothing, sleeping on a cold floor, and eating only abstemiously from foods that he did not like. This was supposed, among other things, to curb his animal passions; instead, it inflamed them; if this had not happened, he might well have continued his course of insane self-deprivation until it killed him. Unfortunately it was too late for a complete recovery. "A good night's sleep was something calling for special thankfulness. The sermon that was a delight in the preaching set the pulse flying and put brain and stomach out of gear." [13] He was deaf in one ear also, and on this account he tended to shun public lectures and other functions which depend for their full enjoyment upon normal hearing powers.

In his maturity Channing gave people a definite impression of well-being. There was a nervous vitality about him, and he advocated the physical culture cause in America long before many others had awakened to its importance. Yet I wonder whether the fantacism of his youth was ever completely outgrown. When he lived with his mother at the parsonage on Berry Street, he "took for his study the smallest room in the house, while a much better one was crying to be used, and for his sleeping-room the attic, which was ill-furnished, cheerless, cold, and every way ill suited to the condition of his health."[14] Very late in his life, Channing was fascinated by the alleged power of Fénelon and others to "transmute pain" through the power of a "devout mind." "I take pleasure in reading their triumphs of mind over body, their manifestations of spiritual energy, though I must confess they are too often deformed by some excess." He himself had sometimes thought that "by analyzing a pain, I have been able to find an element of pleasure in it. . . . Distinct perception instead of aggravating, decreases evil." By 1841 all this seemed to concern him less. "I see pain and death everywhere. All animated nature suffers and dies. Life begins and ends in pain. Then pain has a great work to do." But Channing had too much sense to carry such reasoning beyond a certain point, or, perhaps one might say, to its logical conclusion. "Mere suffering will not do us good.—Mere tears will not wash a living sin. The very severity of suffering leaves us harder,—a solemn thought. We may grow insensible." For this reason, among others, the idea of "infinite, endless punishment" did not much appeal to him. It "would make hell the most interesting spot in the universe. All the sympathies of Heaven would be turned towards it."

III

It is time to turn to what Channing preached and how. Since he considered both medicine and the law, he can hardly be regarded as a preacher predestined, but, as he himself said, it was upon his looking into the evidences for Christianity in the face of the agnostic challenge of his college days that "*I found for what I was made.*" Yet Channing was never in the least like Phillips Brooks, who poured out his sermons as the sun shines. Instead he tore them out of his vitals; there is no record of his having preached more than twenty-seven times at Federal Street during any one year, and from 1832 on he averaged only five or six sermons a year.[15]

In the ordinary sense of the term, Channing disdained pulpit eloquence altogether.

> Good preaching never enraptures an audience by beauties of style, elocution, or gesture. An easy, unbalanced, unlabored style should be the common mode of expression. . . . Let clearness, dignity, unstrained vigor, elevation without turgidness, purity without primness, pathos without whining, characterize my style.

He made a point of saying commonplace things in a commonplace manner, and he eschewed the beauties of quotation. By preaching Christ he did not understand "making Christ perpetually the subject of discourse," but promulgating "*the religion which he taught.*" This does not mean that he was keen on propaganda. As a matter of fact, he disliked theological disputation, and some Unitarians thought him too evangelical. He tried to scatter his truth abroad as nature scatters the dandelion seed, "not forcing it on here and there a mind, not watching its progress anxiously, but trusting that it will light on a kindly soil and yield its fruit."

Matthew Arnold called conduct three-fourths of life; Stevenson questioned his percentages, finding much in life neither moral nor immoral but simply amoral. Certainly Channing's approach, in the pulpit and out of it, was both moral and intellectual. In his sermons and in his articles, he is minute, careful, and systematic, deliberately reasoning his way through a whole series of considerations, and never trying to sweep the reader away on a tide of emotion. This certainly makes for what is often called rather "dry" reading, and Channing himself tended to feel that Unitarians had developed "rational and critical power" at the expense of "imagination and poetical enthusiasm." Of himself he complains, "I have composed sermons till I can with difficulty write anything else. I exhort when I should smile." Yet he calls God Himself "Perfect Morality." The world is a valley of soul-making, and "redemption is the recovery of man from sin, as the preparation for glory." As he saw it, "man's moral nature" was his "great tie to the Divinity." Only through the "inward, everlasting law" could he know God. "All other means are vain."

Channing does not lose this emphasis even when dealing with worldly affairs. To him the worst aspect of drunkenness was not the waste and degradation involved in it but the fact that it involved "the voluntary extinction of reason." He did not oppose the War of 1812, as others did, for what it was doing to the American economy, for this was a small matter compared to "its effect on our *character*." He approached slavery the same way:

> The true ground, I think, is that slavery is a *wrong*, be the yoke lighter or heavier, and that, even where it provides sufficiently for the physical being, it destroys the intellectual and moral being, and utterly extinguishes the hope and capacity of progress.

Later he even entertained some doubts about organized labor, fearing that the strength of the organization might weaken the individuals comprising it.

Channing was sufficiently Protestant to dislike having even the adjective "Reverend" set before his name. He told his parishioners specifically that he would not accept the responsibility for their spiritual salvation; as sons and daughters of Puritans, they could delegate that to nobody.

I, indeed, offer myself to you as your spiritual friend and teacher; but I do it in the full knowledge that God has given you better aids than your minister, that I am but one out of many means of your instruction, and that, after all, the chief responsibility falls upon *yourselves*.

This does not mean that he sought to evade responsibility. "No man," he says, "is fitted to preach or promote Christianity who is not fitted to die for it." Channing was no thinking machine. To us who can only read his sermons, they seem a close record and analysis of religious experience, but those who heard him were so captivated by "that solemn fire of his eye, that profound earnestness of tone" that "the whole earth seemed good to live in while they listened to him." [16]

Channing praised Rousseau as the only French writer who knew how to appeal to the heart, and he wept over tales of woe in eighteenth-century fiction until he became convinced that emotion which cannot expend itself in efforts toward the relief of suffering is mere self-indulgence. In his early days, too, he was capable of being himself overcome by the sorrows of parishioners he was striving to comfort; later he presented a front of unbroken equability. He overcame the irritability inherited from his mother; he overcame what he regarded as his own native cowardice; his tears, he finally said, did not lie close to his eyes. When, towards the end, he was asked at what age he supposed a man to be happiest, he smiled and replied, "About sixty."

When Whittier wrote his poetic tribute, "Channing," [17] he took pains to explain in a prefatory note that he did not share, nor sympathize with, the "peculiar religious opinions" of his distinguished subject. Channing's religious "peculiarity" was of course his Unitarianism, but it is ironical that a man so little inclined to controversy should so often be thought of as if he were primarily a controversialist. If Channing ever prided himself on anything, it was upon having risen "above the region of controversial theology," and he did not mean to be arrogant when he said that he had never preached against Trinitarianism but merely ignored it.[18] Channing never believed in the Trinity, but he was not emotionally involved in his opposition to it; he did not *hate* it, as he hated the Calvinistic foreordination and election. Had it been possible, he would have been glad to avoid wearing the "Unitarian" nor any other label. "Were the name more honored I should be glad to throw it off; for I fear the shackles which a party connection imposes." [19]

Even Calvinistic notes are often sounded in Channing's earlier sermons, with their heavy stress upon man's sinfulness and his consequent need of being reconciled to God. Though he clung to "the dignity of human nature," "the greatness of the soul, its divinity," and "its likeness with God," the idea of a Fall does not seem wholly foreign to his thinking. Though he told his notebook upon at least one occasion that "the science of mind removes Satan," he was reluctant to repudiate future punishment, for fear of losing a powerful incentive toward decent behavior here. Some of his later statements, taken by themselves, sound pantheistic, as when he declares that "we see God around us, because he dwells with us," but this is misleading. To the end, his God was more transcendent than immanent, and he had no idea of having human beings swallowed up by the Oversoul.

Channing was later reported by his son to have remarked in 1841 that "I am more and more inclined to believe in the simple humanity of Jesus." Possibly he was not correctly reported; possibly he meant something quite different from what a Unitarian would mean today. Certainly there is no authenticated utterance of his in which Christ appears as a "mere man." He is not God nor yet a God-man; he is, as he was for Milton, a Divine Being created by God. He existed before his human birth in Bethlehem, and the Old Testament prophets foretold his coming.

Sometimes it even seems that Channing expected him to come again. But the important thing was the believer's relationship to him. For Channing, religion was a "temper and a spirit" rather than a doctrine, God's life in the soul of man. In a peculiar sense, Christ's character was his religion, and Atonement and redemption had no meaning except as the believer's contacts with Christ enlarged his heart, exalted his mind, and made him partaker of the divine nature. This might be either a gradual or an instantaneous process. Early in life, Channing came close to what the Evangelicals called a conversion experience, which he felt so intensely that he "longed to die; as if heaven alone could give room for the exercise of such emotion." As the result of this "change of heart," he turned away from "mere moral attainments" and "solemnly" gave himself "up to God." In later years, however, he was more likely to speak of a lifelong "process of conversion."

Like Milton, Channing based his beliefs upon the Bible. What the Bible said was true, and he had no particular interest in the gabble of commentators and church councils; the trouble with the creed-maker was that "he dares not trust me alone with Jesus" but "interposes himself between me and my Saviour." It was because he found no Trinitarianism nor (as commonly conceived) Atonement in the Bible that he discarded these beliefs from his own creed, which he had no desire to impose upon others.

My conscience is a rule to myself only.—My will has no province but my own mind. I am responsible for no others. I may desire virtue, but must not interfere with their freedom. Each is to act from his own inward law—each to be turned on his own soul.

For Channing, then, the Bible was an inspired book, but inspiration and inerrancy did not, in his view, stand or fall together. He had no difficulty with miracles. Life itself was a miracle. "Without miracles the historical Christ is gone. No such being is left us; and in losing him, how much is lost!" [20] He would have had no sympathy with the early twentieth-century slogan "Back to Christ!" for he did not believe that God had died or shut up shop or retired to the country in the first century, the thirteenth, nor the nineteenth. Like the Pilgrim pastor John Robinson he looked for more and more light to break forth from the Holy Word.

I know nothing which indicates greater ignorance of the history of the church and of the history of mankind, nothing more fitted to reduce the intellect to imbecility, and to carry back the race to barbarism, than the idea that we have nothing more to learn, that Christianity has come down to us pure and perfect, and that our only duty is implicitly to receive the lessons of our catechisms.

This meant that the Bible must be interpreted by human reason, but that did not trouble Channing at all, for he knew that, for better or worse, "the ultimate reliance of a human being is and must be on his own mind." He granted that God is "incomprehensible" in the sense that finite man cannot completely take Him in; nevertheless, as far as it goes, the human mind is as reliable here as in any other area, and God Himself could not refuse to accept its findings without repudiating His own creation. Channing himself found convincing evidence for the divine origin of Christianity in the very fact that "it contained nothing which rendered it unadapted to a *progressive* state of society; that it did not put checks upon the activity of the human mind, nor compel it to tread always blindly in a beaten path." The revelation we receive through it is in harmony with "the teachings of nature and the sure dictates of our natural and moral faculties."

IV

There seems considerable difference of opinion as to Channing's usefulness as a pastor. Elizabeth Peabody thought "he administered the Communion . . . more effectively than I ever saw any one [else] do." On the other hand, so warm an admirer as Chadwick finds him

> too cloud-wrapt in his great soaring thoughts to respond quickly to the personal appeal and reach a human hand. It is hard to believe that Channing was ever a good pastor, and he did not improve in proportion to his increasing engrossment in the large, social aspect of religion.

Yet he certainly understood the importance of pastoral work, and in the early days held many meetings for prayer and for religious instruction and conversation. He knew the dangers of pastoral visitation also—how easily it degenerates into mere gossip, and that it does not automatically take on religious value simply because a clergyman is present. "Love of the teacher is, at the best, but a tottering foundation for religious principle. Truth should be heard, not for the sake of him who utters it but in its own right." Chadwick tells the appalling story of a bewildered Channing standing in the midst of a stricken family exclaiming "What a mysterious Providence!" But this needs to be balanced by others which show him bursting into tears and rushing from the room when overcome by the griefs of his parishioners.

On the other hand, one of Channing's closest friends and admirers, Henry F. Tuckerman, startles the reader when he declares that "egotism was a striking trait in Dr. Channing." "His opinions are rather announced as truths than suggested as possibilities." Chadwick at least partially agrees with this, finding the isolating conditions of Channing's way of life and the immense deference paid to him during his later years as contributing toward this end. As Chadwick saw him, Channing was likely to go to other men only for confirmation of what he himself had taught or believed; consequently he makes Milton another Channing and condemns Napoleon because he was not a man of the Channing type. (This last point is involved in Hazlitt's criticism of the Napoleon study also.) "He had no use for men who sailed by other stars. He might praise them with his lips, but his heart was far from them."

But if this be egotism, it tars the whole Transcendentalist group, and I myself do not understand how any man who has any character at all, or who has developed any individuality or strength of personality, could be expected to behave otherwise. Channing was never satisfied with what he had achieved, but he always knew what he wished to achieve. He did not set his sights by the particular job in hand.

> I was not satisfied with knowing things superficially or by halves, but tried to get some comprehensive view of what I studied. . . . I did not think of fitting myself for this or that particular pursuit, but for any to which events might call me.

All this is not to say that Channing never failed in consideration. When Gannett was appointed as his associate, the poor man often had to go to church primed with a sermon but never knowing beforehand whether he would be permitted to deliver it or whether Channing would have a message from the Spirit which he expected to offer instead. Once, when he was asked whether he intended to preach on the morrow, Channing replied haughtily, "There will be divine service in the church." He could be severe with his assembled congregation also. He would not tolerate coughing, even if he had to stop the sermon to quell it, and one auditor says his congregation hardly dared to breathe while he preached, and that "sometimes, at the end of a great passage, you could hear the long-held breath escaping in a general sigh."

It is interesting to find Channing saying that he had had "no experience of being overwhelmed by the presence of a human being." He brought a calm, cool intelligence even to the consideration of just what was involved in the command to love our neighbors as ourselves, and told his notebook that "love is not giving ourselves away. We are too great to be given away." Certainly nobody was ever franker than he was in assessing the faults and the virtues of his friends, as when he described Elizabeth Peabody's teaching methods or told Lucy Aikin that her judgment of human nature had been "perverted" by living under an aristocracy. For all that, he does not seem to have thought of himself more highly than he ought to have thought. When he was asked what he would do in a hypothetical perilous situation, he replied that he did not know; he could only tell what he thought would be the right thing to do. I do not know of anything that shows his loving character much better than his argument that though God has placed children under the power of their parents, He has also placed the children in charge of them, through the affection which their parents feel for them. He was always delighted at any manifestation of trust or affection on the part of a child, and he saw the wisdom of God in the limitation nature places upon parental influence. "The hope of the world is that parents cannot make their children all they wish." There are many stories of generous, kindly services which Channing performed for poor people. You did not have to be "good" in order to enlist his interest, for he recognized the special responsibility of the community for and to the very persons who create its most urgent problems.

It is true, however, that Channing's introspective, soul-searching way of life did not encourage social contacts. He did not think his own exterior attractive; he also thought that he lacked charm. "My countenance would not make me many friends, I fear. What has troubled me in my different portraits is, not that they have not given me a more intellectual expression, but that so little benevolence has beamed from the features." He had been brought up by the book, loved but not coddled; his parents aimed to do their duty by him and teach him how to perform his own, but they did not overcultivate the emotional side of his nature. He was not encouraged to believe that God was greatly concerned over whether His children were happy or not; what was expected was that they should obey the laws of life that He had given them. At Harvard Channing escaped from many of the contacts other students made by living in his uncle's home. He instinctively shied from ugliness and evil. "My mind seeks the good, the perfect, the beautiful. It is a degree of torture to bring vividly to my apprehension what man is suffering from his own crimes and from the wrongs and cruelty of his brother."

Yet he saw human nature as "essentially social. It wants objects of affection, companions to whom it may communicate its thoughts and purposes, and with whom it may act and enjoy." Toward the end, he felt that he had lived too much by himself, wishing a friend "more courage, cordiality, and real union with your race. . . . I sometimes feel as if I had never known anything of human nature until lately. . . . My reserve is not to be broken down in these later years of my life, but I think the ice melts."

At least one of his biographers, Madeleine H. Rice, says bluntly that Channing "was made for the public; his cold temperament made him the most unprofitable private companion." It must be admitted that there is considerable comment which supports this view, so that even Elizabeth Peabody admits that "Dr. Channing don't know how to chat." There is considerable variety in the reports we get of him as a conversationalist. Some thought him a monologuist, others a Socratic questioner. Edward Everett thought him easy to listen to but hard to talk to. Frederic Hedge says he paid no attention to questions but simply went on talking about his own concerns. Orville Dewey says one always felt like standing erect in his presence, and Henry Ware records, "I go to Channing; I listen to him; I go away; that is all." Finally, his niece, Susan Channing, who adored him, admits that he was "a very great restraint upon her," and that conversation with him—"alone, unsupported, unprotected"—was much the same as with Margaret Fuller. Channing himself acknowledges having often wasted his powers in reveries, especially during his early life. Mighty before the multitude, he felt weak before an individual.

But this is not all. During his Harvard years, Channing belonged to Phi Beta Kappa, the Porcellian, the Speaking Club, and Hasty Pudding, which does not sound exactly like a recluse. We must remember too that he was deaf, and he must often have left questions unanswered not because he wished to be rude but because he simply had not heard them. He often allowed himself warmer expressions of affection for his friends than many of us are inclined to use nowadays, and he is never more amusing that when he remarks that

> There are some who can "forgive, but not forget." The difficulty with me is, that I cannot forgive, because I so soon forget. I have so many subjects more interesting than my opponent, that he is crowded out of mind. In all this there is no virtue, but much comfort.

He may have been right too in feeling that he was made "of poor material for a reformer," but if so, then he was right again when he perceived that he needed to engage in such work

> not, as many do, to give me excitement, for I find enough, perhaps too much, to excite me in the common experience of life, in meditation, in abstract truth; but to save me from a refined selfishness, to give me force, disinterestedness, true dignity and elevation, to link me by a new faith to God, by a deeper love to my race, and to make me a blessing to the world.

In achieving this end, Channing would honor very humble duties to humble individuals, and his mother was at one time greatly annoyed by the Negro teacher who used to visit him on Saturdays, taking up his time into the evening, thus making it necessary for him to work into the night in order to get ready for Sunday.

In politics for its own sake, I do not find that Channing was ever very greatly interested. He did not believe that politics and politicians contributed much of value to the life of a people; neither did he judge politics to exercise a wholesome effect upon the lives of those professionally engaged in it. Yet I do not believe anybody who has read his discussion of the *Creole* case in the sixth volume of his *Works* could fail to realize that he had considerable knowledge of the workings of our system of government, its opportunities and its limitations.

He never believed that a society could be better than the individuals composing it, but he did know that man was not yet "mere spirit," and that therefore circumstances and conditions could make individuals either better or worse than they would otherwise be. In his time "any one who would teach how to make bread and cook potatoes well must be a public benefactor." Channing inherited the early American mistrust of England, which he lost, as many Americans did, in the face of the Napoleonic menace; at times he even seems to have a touch of nativism about him. But he learned earlier than some of his contemporaries that we cannot solve all our problems by simply proclaiming that that government is best which governs least. Theodore Parker was speaking of theological reform when he said of Channing that he was "never in the foremost rank of the movement, nor a discoverer, but defender," but the statement applies over a larger area also. Nevertheless, "he labored for temperance, for the improvement of prisons, for the abolition of imprisonment for debt, for the general welfare of the laboring man, for freedom everywhere and under all conditions, for peace instead of war." He praised and admired Father Mathew's work for temperance among Catholics, and he himself was one of eleven petitioners who once sought to ban the sale of spirits in Boston, but generally speaking, he relied not upon prohibitory legislation but upon the correction of the social and economic conditions which encouraged drinking.[21]

It is hard for us to remember that slavery was still a controversial matter in America when Channing died; as a matter of fact, manumission had not yet been quite completed in his own state of Rhode Island. Apparently slavery did not trouble him during his boyhood; his awakening did not come until he went to Virginia and saw the field hands. For some ten years, he pleased neither the abolitionists nor their opponents; even Lydia Maria Child at one time thought him timid and even time-serving. He was never really either, but he was so constituted that he could not be hurried; he had to think his problem through and reach a conclusion which he could convince himself was fair to everybody. He crossed his own Rubicon in the fall of 1834, when Samuel J. May replied with some heat to his criticism of abolitionists, asking him point-blank why he had left a necessary protest to be made by those who lacked good taste and judgment: "Why, sir, have you not moved? Why have you not spoken before?" After an "awful silence," Channing replied, "Brother May, I acknowledge the justice of your reproof; I have been silent too long." John Quincy Adams called Channing's *Slavery*[22] "an inflammatory, if not an incendiary" publication, and after it had appeared some of the writer's aristocratic parishioners stopped seeing him socially and even cut him on the street. The cantankerous Maria Chapman gave his letter to Henry Clay[23] credit for delaying the annexation of Texas for two years, and Whittier, one of the few who could combine unquestioned devotion to the cause of abolition with perfect tolerance toward those who disagreed with him, could think of only one man who had sacrificed more for the cause than Channing.[24]

The war problem brings Channing closer to us, for no late-twentieth-century American can stand in any need of being convinced that the war against war is still far from won. Channing was not an absolute pacifist; as a boy, he was an officer of a boys' military company which welcomed Rochambeau to Newport. Like Saint Thomas Aquinas he believed in the theoretical possibility of a just war but this was largely on paper. He never supported any war in which the United States was engaged or threatened to become engaged during his lifetime. He detested all forms of violence, even the corporal punishment of children, and mistrusted a standing army and all the moral effects of army life. He preached anti-war sermons in 1812, 1814, 1816, 1835, and 1838, and the Peace Society of Massachusetts was formed in his parsonage. "The field of battle is a theater got up for the exhibition of crime on a grand scale. There the hell within the human breast blazes out fiercely and without disguise." You cannot fight another *nation;* you can only maim and mutilate *human beings*, like yourself, who happen to be living under another flag. Humanity is greater than any nation, and the nation can have no purpose or justification save "to breed a noble race of men." Channing understood earlier than most people did the fatal tendency of modern war to spread beyond the confines which used to hedge it in. Conscription for a war in which the individual could not believe must be resisted even unto death; to prohibit public discussion in a nation at war would be to destroy freedom altogether and invite "war without end." Channing did not question Elijah P. Lovejoy's "right" to arm himself against the mob which killed him, but he did feel that "an enterprise of Christian philanthropy could not be carried on by force." A reformer should appeal to the laws and the moral sentiments and sympathies of the community. Only thus could support be won and prejudice disarmed.

There are many reasons for which a clergyman may become celebrated, and more than one such reason can be legitimate, but surely the very best reason is that he brings his people into contact with God. William Ellery Channing was neither a great scholar nor a significant independent thinker. Even in theology he was a transitional figure, and today he hardly seems to belong more to the Unitarians who still claim him than he does to their more orthodox brethren.

He never in his life *tried* to shock anybody, but he never hesitated to do so when it was necessary to proclaim the truth in which he believed. "Christianity is a rational religion," he said. "Were it not so I should be ashamed to profess it," and again: "if religion be the shipwreck of understanding, we cannot keep too far from it." The particular truths which he perceived and proclaimed may not seem as inevitable to the more scientifically trained philosophers of the present day as they did to him, but the years that have passed since his death have brought us nothing that makes the beauty of his spirit seem less precious.

He preached the kingdom of heaven *upon earth* [says Chadwick]. Not to save men's souls for heaven or from hell was the conscious purpose of his ministry, once he had come into clear self consciousness, but to save men in their physical, intellectual, moral, and spiritual entirety, from foolish wasting of their powers, and for the upbuilding on the earth of a divine society.

3

HENRY WARD BEECHER

God Was in Christ

I

Abraham Lincoln considered Henry Ward Beecher one of the foremost Americans of his time. He was without question the most famous of all American preachers, and it has been said of him that his influence upon religious thinking in America was greater than that of all the theological seminaries put together. But some of his admirers were not satisfied with this, and so responsible a man as John Hay called him the greatest preacher since Saint Paul.[1]

Yet his fame has been sullied. This is not only because he has been unfortunate in some of his twentieth-century commentators and biographers. He has suffered also from the reaction against nineteenth-century (and Romantic) enthusiasm and the consequent inability of much of his posterity to distinguish between sentiment and sentimentality. Even in his own time he was criticized as "too sentimental, too loose, too ready to surrender truth." "We shall take it to heart," he replied, "and strive henceforth to be slower, drier, tighter, and more obstinate." But he also admitted that sometimes he did "slop over" a little. "I am not worthy to be related in the hundred-thousandth degree to those more happy men who never make a mistake in the pulpit. I make a great many.

I am impetuous. I am intense at times on subjects that deeply move me."

He is not the only American who has suffered from our changing emotional climate. Longfellow and the "schoolroom poets" in general have felt the change. So has Daniel Webster, whose portentous portraits now seem to many of us less the image of a great man than a caricature thereof. So, too, at a later date, did Theodore Roosevelt, who is still sometimes called "Teddy" (an appellation he hated), even in what profess to be serious books, and whose achievements modern historians, as distinct from uncritical admirers, are only now beginning fairly to evaluate. His teeth, his pince-nez with their flying cord, his bucking bronchos, his big game hunting and "Teddy bears," and his exuberant determination to discern Armageddon just around the corner in connection with every issue in which he chanced to be interested —all these things have got in the way. ("Do you realize," asked Mark Hanna, when Roosevelt was nominated for vice-president under McKinley, "that only one life stands between that damned cowboy and the Presidency?")

Roosevelt had one advantage over Beecher, however: his fame was never tarnished by scandal.[2] If he was not the cleanest man who ever lived, certainly none was ever cleaner. Henry Ward, on the other hand, was the only American clergyman of foremost eminence who was publicly accused of adultery and faced a suit on that issue, and though his guilt was never proved he lived the rest of his life under a question mark, and his posterity is still divided on the issue. Except where sexual irregularity is openly admitted, people usually believe what they wish to believe about such accusations. Those who loved and admired Henry and whose spiritual lives had been nourished by his preaching and writing were touchingly loyal to him, but his long career had made him many enemies who must have welcomed the opportunity to snap at his heels; there are always those who rejoice when a man whose work or whose professions have seemed to set him up on a level higher than they themselves occupy at last gives them an opportunity to drag him down from that eminence.

Beecher's temperament, his convictions, the generally free-wheeling quality of his personality and career, even his appearance, all made him a perfect target. He had preached the love of God almost to the exclusion of His other attributes, and he had said that God loved sinners and sought to save them not because they deserved it but because it was His nature to love. Of all the words in the English language, love has probably been the worst abused; it was much easier to believe that the full-bodied Beecher had sinned with a pretty woman than it would have been to suppose William Ellery Channing to have done it. Henry Ward was about five feet, nine inches tall; his figure was bulky, his eyes large, full, and blue, his complexion ruddy. In repose the face was dreamy, even dull, but it took on unusually vivid and varied expressiveness as he came under the influence of different moods and emotions. In the early days, many found his soft and straw hats and his refusal to wear clerical garb shocking. Mrs. Beecher herself considered him "an exceedingly homely young man" when she first laid eyes upon him. But it was the "drooping eyelids" and the "loose" mouth upon which his enemies fastened, that mouth which an English paper found "suggestive of one who has little of the ascetic in his nature and who can appreciate the sweets and comforts of existence as well as lecture against their abuses." W. N. Taylor thought that as he mounted the platform at Plymouth Church to conduct a service, "he might be mistaken for a butcher in his Sunday clothes," and even Lyman Abbott admits that "my first impression of him was disappointing."

Henry Ward Beecher was born at Litchfield, Connecticut, on June 24, 1813, during his father's pastorate there. He showed little promise in his early schooling ("I had from childhood a thickness of speech arising from a large palate, so that when a boy I used to be laughed at for talking as if I had pudding in my mouth"), but in 1834 he graduated from Amherst College, from which he proceeded to Cincinnati, where his father was president of Lane Theological Seminary; here Henry's brother-in-law-to-be, Professor Calvin E. Stowe, exercised considerable influence upon him. In 1837 he graduated from Lane, but he never accepted any honorary degree and thus never became "Dr. Beecher."

He taught in rural schools during the long winter college vacations, and preached his first sermons at Northbridge, Massachusetts, in 1831. The first lecture for which he was paid was given at Brattleboro, Vermont. He received ten dollars and walked nearly fifty miles each way in order to save the money for books. Having completed his theological course, he accepted a call from the first body that showed interest in him and went to a tiny Presbyterian church at Lawrenceburg, Indiana, where he had only twenty members, "nineteen of whom were women, and the other was nothing." His salary was $250 a year on paper and something like $150 in actuality. On August 3 of the same year of 1837, he married Eunice Bullard of West Sutton, Massachusetts; two years later he was called to Indianapolis, where he remained until the newly-organized Plymouth Congregational Church brought him east to Brooklyn in 1847. That he had not left his pioneering spirit behind him in the West was shown by his choosing this experimental post over the famous and well-established Park Street Church of Boston, which was offered to him at the same time. During his stay in Indianapolis he had published the most sensational of his books, *Lectures to Young Men* (1844), and had held his first editorial post of any significance on the *Western Farmer and Gardener.*

Fortunately for Henry, Plymouth's first inadequate building burned in January 1849, which gave him the opportunity to oversee the erection of a new building, capable of holding some 2500 to 3000 persons, and constructed according to his own ideas. After the first six months he filled it at every service (when Sunday morning visitors from Manhattan inquired the way from the ferry to Plymouth Church, they were told simply to follow the crowd), and his lectures, articles, and editorials immeasurably extended his audience. He was editor, though he did little or none of the editorial drudgery, first of *The Independent*, then of *The Christian Union*, which later became *The Outlook*. Robert Bonner, of *The New York Ledger*, paid him $30,000 for his only novel, *Norwood* (1868); this and his *Life of Jesus the Christ* (1872, 1891) were, properly speaking, the only "books" he ever wrote, since all the other volumes published over his by-line reprint his magazine pieces or contain lectures and sermons, generally as taken down by stenographic reporters. He was active in the anti-slavery and other reform movements and spoke his mind freely upon many public issues. During the Civil War he championed the Union cause in a series of public lectures in England, delivered under great handicaps before noisy, hostile, heckling audiences.

His success in his own parish and in the country at large was for many years uniform and unwavering, and until the seventies there were no important changes or developments except those which Plymouth Church shared with the nation at large.

Early in the seventies, however, charges against Beecher's moral character began to be bruited about Brooklyn, and in the summer of 1874, Theodore Tilton, a brilliant but unstable young journalist who had long been closely and affectionately associated with the Plymouth pastor, openly accused him of adultery with Mrs. Tilton. This entailed (1) an investigation of the charges by Plymouth Church itself; (2) a civil court trial occasioned by Tilton's suit against Beecher for alienation of affections; and (3) a second ecclesiastical hearing before a council of Congregational churches. Both the ecclesiastical investigations found Henry Ward innocent. The civil trial opened on January 11, 1875, and ended on July 2, after 112 days in court, with a hung jury which had found three for the plaintiff and nine for the defendant. It had been one of the most sensational and widely reported court cases of the century.[3]

It cost Henry over $100,000, much of which Plymouth Church generously covered, and once it was over, he set out on a mammoth lecture tour to help repair his broken fortunes. Between April 1875 and his death, he travelled nearly 300,000 miles under J. B. Pond's management and delivered 1261 lectures. He was growing and thinking to the end, finding new causes, not even shrinking from sensation when it served his ends. He championed woman suffrage, became one of the first prominent American clergymen openly to accept evolution, rejected the dogma of eternal punishment and a fire-and-brimstone hell. During his years of trouble he thrice gave the "Yale Lectures on Preaching" on the foundation established by Henry W. Sage in honor of Lyman Beecher.

His last sermon was delivered in Plymouth Church on Sunday evening, February 27, 1887. After the service he walked out of the building with his arms around two poor children, one of whom afterwards became a clergyman. The organist was playing "Hark, Hark, My Soul," and Henry called it a good tune to die on. During the Thursday-Friday night following he suffered an apoplectic stroke but told his wife he had only a sick headache. He stayed in bed through the next day, and when she informed him it was time to get up for prayer meeting, he replied that he did not feel like getting up and was not going to prayer meeting. The following Tuesday, March 8, he died. More than 50,000 people passed through Plymouth Church to view his body. Both Brooklyn and the State of New York took official cognizance of his passing, and memorial tributes came from all races and creeds.

II

Generally speaking, Henry Ward Beecher was a strong and vigorous man; he once told Lyman Abbott that he had more health than he knew what to do with. Until his last years, his principal difficulty was the hay fever.[4] Later he lived in fear of the apoplexy which finally killed him, though he dreaded still more such mental failure as had at last overtaken his father. "I hope God will have so much consideration for my weakness . . . as to let me drop down in my harness in the full energy of work. I have no fear whatever of dying; it is only the fear of living I have before my eyes."

His health was not so exuberant, however, that he ever made the mistake of forgetting to take care of himself. He rested in the afternoon, barred the discussion of serious subjects at the table, and, except for his speaking, avoided night work. Like Lyman Abbott, who may have learned it from him, he knew the importance of resting before one's work rather than after it, and Pond speaks of his once sleeping on an office floor, with his valise for a pillow, during a lecture tour. His attitude toward remedies was pragmatic, and he was reasonably receptive to the various -isms which attracted attention during his time.[5]

On occasion we hear of his eating heartily; there is a story about his making a feast of peanuts, for example, and another about his eating a pound of "mixed candy" on a ferry boat. He has one loving reference to oysters, and *Eyes and Ears* contains knowledgeable essays on pumpkins and apples, and especially on apple pie. In later years, when they could afford it, the Beechers set a lavish table, but Henry himself does not seem to have partaken immoderately. Coffee exhilarated him, tea depressed him; when he drank both, he thought he achieved a happy average. During most of his life he was a teetotaler ("the prudent and temperate use of liquor is to let it alone"); towards the end he made occasional use of both wine and beer, partly at least for medical purposes or what the nineteenth century regarded as such. Tobacco he never touched. "It is a filthy trick to use it at all; and it puts an end to all our affected squeamishness at the Chinese taste, in eating rats, cats, and birds' nests."

He championed "muscular sports" for their health value, and even shocked some of the brethren by advocating gymnastic grounds and good bowling-alleys, "in connection with reading rooms, in every ward of the city, under judicious management." During his boyhood he himself engaged in both sports and pranks (some of them dangerous), but he was no sportsman during his mature years; "when I knew him," says Abbott, "he neither fished nor hunted, nor took long tramps, nor rode horseback for exercise." He does take a good many illustrations from this area, especially from fishing, but I doubt that he had any great interest in animals. Horses he loved, but he drove them instead of riding them, and, like Moody, he drove them fast, even making himself believe that fast horses ought to be driven fast for the horse's own sake! The only outdoor game he ever took to was croquet, which finally became something of a passion. Pond says he never played cards in his life and did not know one card from another; his wife says she and he played backgammon together after coming to Brooklyn, and that this helped him to "run down" before going to sleep.

Henry's love for nature has never been questioned. "I was brought up in a New England village, and I knew where the sweet-flag was, where the hickory trees were, where the squirrels were, where all those things were that boys enterprise after." In *Norwood* he has an elaborate passage about watching the sun rise from the Amherst chapel tower, a sight many went through college without ever having seen. Once he says that there are only two perfect months in the year—June and October—but he certainly did not confine his appreciation to these months. As a child he used to beg to be allowed to go out into the snowstorm; as a man he saw winter relieving the year of satiety, after the mind had grown "sated with greenness." He was passionately fond of flowers—"I must have flowers; I am as set and determined to have flowers as my farmer, Mr. Turner, is to have vegetables"—and, as his paper on the dandelion[6] shows, they did not have to be rare or expensive to please him. On his thirty-six-acre farm he had over 1600 varieties of ornamental trees and shrubs; he particularly loved elms, but he thought the unnecessary destruction of any handsome tree a worse piece of vandalism than the attack of the Puritans on "painted windows." His love and knowledge of nature, and his intimate familiarity with her in all her aspects, runs all through *Eyes and Ears* and *Pleasant Talk about Fruits, Flowers and Farming*. He knew agriculture and he knew everything related to it. Many a "nature writer" has swung a whole career on less.

In itself all this had nothing to do with religion, but Henry Ward was well aware that he himself found much more religious nourishment in nature than his father had found there. "No one who has experienced the solemn exhilaration of soul which comes upon high mountains," he wrote in his life of Christ, "will wonder that Jesus loved mountains for places of devotion." And in *Norwood* Dr. Wentworth asks the clergyman Buell:

> "Dr. Buell, do you believe in the Scriptures? Do you believe that those very heavens above your head declare the glory of God; or only that they *did*, four thousand years ago? 'The earth is the Lord's and, the fulness thereof, the world and they that dwell therein!'—now, today, here in this field—yonder over that meadow, just as much as in Palestine. 'Thou crownest the year—Thou visitest the earth—Thou makest the outgoings of the morning and evening to rejoice. The Lord sitteth upon the flood; yea, the Lord sitteth king forevermore!' "

Nevertheless, nature had its limitations as revelator. One of Beecher's most amusing papers is "Unveiled Nonsense" in *Pleasant Talk*, in which he replies to a silly religious writer who saw "bugs, beetles, aphides, heat, rain, and mildew" as "the messengers of God" to the farmer and worthy of being treated as such. Henry retained his faith in miracles through his unwillingness to permit God to be imprisoned in His own creation. God worked *through* nature, but He was still above it and outside of it. Even men, though, in a sense, controlled by natural law, could still themselves achieve a measure of control over it. It would be absurd to suppose that God could do less.

III

Intellectually Henry had great gifts and striking limitations. The schools never did much for him. "School Reminiscences" in his *Star Papers* is about as bitter an indictment of the old district school as has been penned. "We abhor the thought of a school. We do not go into them if we can avoid it." Even at Boston Latin the curriculum was "repulsive and uncongenial" to him, and he did not even begin to find his way until he encountered sympathetic masters at Mount Pleasant School in Amherst. In college it was his humor and his gifts as a speaker that his fellow classmen remembered. He remembered facts but not figures, names, or dates. He had a powerful visual imagination, so that he often saw what was described to him. He seems never to have been sure of the multiplication table, but for some reason or other, the list of Latin prepositions governing the ablative stuck in his memory, and he was always prepared to rattle it off at the drop of a hat. In preparing his sermons, he habitually used the Greek New Testament, but he had left his Hebrew behind him in the seminary. "If I should conclude to study my text from the Old Testament in Hebrew, I think it would take me most of the week to ascertain what it was!" He said that when he went to Paris, he could read French newspapers as easily as the English, but, like many other Americans, he could not understand French as the Parisians spoke it.

Though the guesses that have been offered as to the number of volumes he owned have varied from six to fifteen thousand, Beecher was beyond doubt a passionate book collector. He himself recognized collecting as a passion equal to the craving for drink, and his insistence that bookbuying is a duty is all the more striking in view of his presentation of religion as not that but a privilege. The man who denies himself other things to buy books "rises at once," he says, "in our esteem." [7]

Henry Ward himself thought that under different conditions he might have become a scholar. I doubt this, though he shows considerable skill as a personal essayist in his *Star Papers*. Yet he hated to write; even as an editor he put off the composition of his editorials until the boy was crying for copy. He himself tells us that of the books he read in his childhood only *Robinson Crusoe* and *The Pilgrim's Progress* stayed with him. "The children's tales, the Jack the Giant-Killer and his compeers [were] gone forever," and even *The Arabian Nights* had lost "its wonderfulness." Bunyan always remained "like a tree planted by the rivers of water, that bringeth forth his fruit in season; his leaf shall not wither." In comparison, Dr. Johnson, "with all his glory," resembled "an Egyptian king, buried and forgotten in the pyramid of his fame."

Of course a great deal of what Beecher read was not literature; neither was it all connected with the studies of his profession.

> He is a good authority [says Lyman Abbott] on roses, trees—both for shade and fruit—precious stones, soaps, coffee, wall-papers, engravings, various schools of music, . . . the applications of constitutional law to moral reform questions, physiology and hygiene, and I know not what else.

To this formidable list Howard adds organ-building, pottery and porcelains, anatomy and medicine. Abbott was impressed too by "the accuracy [of Beecher's] historical information, the statistical knowledge, the detailed acquaintance with economic and industrial aspects of the slavery question," and his addresses in England, delivered without manuscript and in large part ad libbed, would seem to support this view. We hear stories of his being such an eager reader that he brought Froude to the dinner table with him and devoured him between courses, and there is testimony to his ability to leaf through a book quietly, taking what he wanted from it and ignoring the rest. Yet he and those close to him seem to have agreed that generally speaking he was a slow reader, and one of his Plymouth successors, Newell Dwight Hillis, says he read little after he was fifty-five, relying on others to keep him posted in various areas of interest. Though he says somewhere that he never read for style, this is not strictly true, for he got "power and vigor" out of Milton, "fluency" from Burke, and "exhaustiveness" and "the sense of adjectives" from Borrow. Once he was even found reading Ouida for her "wonderful vocabulary."

Lyman Abbott says that some of Beecher's oral criticism of literature was penetrating, but there is nothing in print that goes beyond a pleasant suggestiveness, as when he compares *Lorna Doone* to "a capital fowl, somewhat overstuffed, and a trifle too long in the oven; otherwise, a dish fit for a king." There are a reasonable number of references to Shakespeare. It is interesting that he should have realized that in Latin countries Iago is sometimes regarded as the hero of *Othello*. He also says that "the Ariels and witches of Shakespeare are charming and striking" when the plays in which they appear are read but ridiculous when they are acted. Ariel and the witches make a strange combination, with "charming" about the last suitable adjective to apply to the latter, and one wonders whether he ever saw these characters acted, and if so in what productions. Once he showed at least passing enthusiasm for a minor Elizabethan poet, Samuel Daniel.

Abbott tells us also that Henry "read and re-read such writers as Homer, Dante, Milton, Thackeray, Scott—the first two in translation." As we have seen elsewhere, Scott was very important in Lyman Beecher's household, and I am sure that for Henry he was the king of novelists. As much as anything he ever wrote, his comments on *The Antiquary* show that he did have certain standards for the evaluation of fiction: "There are two general considerations in estimating a novel. First, has the author been a faithful copyist of nature, even when his effort is of the imagination? And, second, has he made a judicious selection and skilful combination of his material?" When Robert Bonner asked him to write *Norwood,* he hesitated. "A very moderate reader, even, of fictions, I have never studied the mystery of their construction." But he tried to write in the spirit in which Wordsworth "sung the humble aspects of the natural world" or Crabbe "depicted English village-life." He praised Cowper's letters too for their ability to describe trivia in absorbing fashion, and he gave Ruskin credit for sharpening his sensitiveness to nature.

Of course ethical considerations bulk very large in Henry's evaluation of literature, and when he calls Job "the mightiest drama ever written, and one which leaves all other dramas poor and pulseless in the comparison," one cannot but wonder whether he would have placed it quite so high if it had not been part of the Bible. He calls Victor Hugo a religious writer because he creates "a powerful tendency toward humanity and self-sacrifice and purity." Himself he preferred "the reprehensible grossness of Chaucer" to "the perfumed, elaborate brilliancy of Moore's license" and "the downright and often abominable vulgarity of Swift" to "the scoundrel indirections of Sterne." "Embosomed in the midst of Thomson's *Seasons* one finds descriptions unsurpassed by any part of *Don Juan.*" Shakespeare, though "often gross," is "not often covertly impure," but Bulwer, who "made the English novel literature more vile than he found it" (to put him into the hands of a young reader would be a "crime against the first principles of nature"), is "slyly impure, but not often gross." Compared to his contemporaries, Shakespeare "is not more illustrious for his genius than for his purity." Does this mean that Beecher read extensively in the other Elizabethan dramatists? It does not seem very likely, but Harriet says he did, mentioning Ben Jonson, Massinger, Webster, and Ford in particular, and adding that he "wrote out analyses of their principal characters on phrenological principles." Whether or not all Beecher's specific ethical judgments of various writers are sound, it should be understood that his standards of evaluation were not merely pious. He called many Sunday School books and songs "the swill of the house of God."

> The lives of pious and good boys, which enrich the catalogues of great publication societies, resemble a real boy's life about as much as a chicken picked and larded, upon a spit, and ready for delicious eating, resembles a free fowl in the fields.

The comparison is not a very happy one, for the "chicken picked and larded" serves a useful purpose; in fact, it can yield no nutriment at all until after being subjected to this process.

In some ways, Henry Ward's response to the other arts seems warmer and more immediate than his response to literature. He understood the Puritan antagonism to art because for him art was "language," and the art the Puritans knew spoke "all the abominable doctrines of oppression." But there was something physical in his nature which required the stimulation of what he could see and handle. He admits that the artist may have a "calling," and he differs from most of the preachers of his time in his painful awareness of Saint Paul's apparent indifference to "the physical and visible beauty which was developed among the Greek people." It is not surprising that his collecting should have embraced rugs and soaps as well as pictures and engravings, that window shopping in art stores should have been his notion of "going on a spree," that he loved to watch the workmen in Tiffany's atelier and learn as much as possible of their processes, nor even that the precious stones, sometimes borrowed from New York jewelers, that he liked to carry unset in his pockets, should, under the proper light, have produced an almost hypnotic effect upon him, like that of soothing music.

He does not have a great deal on architecture beyond his feeling that a dwelling house should reflect the character of its owner. In *Norwood* Dr. Wentworth criticizes the New England type of mansard roof as producing the effect of "an old woman's cap, with spectacles mounted on it; for two windows projected from the steep double-leaved roof in a manner that invariably suggested a pair of great eyes!" He thought the Grecian style fine for "well-placed public buildings" but "cheerless, pretentious, and frigid for private dwellings." Apparently he did not believe the Gothic type of church building well adapted to modern Protestant worship.

Great painting, on the other hand, was ecstasy, almost intoxication. There was little of it in America in Henry's younger days, and when he first visited the great European galleries, he was "so much affected" that he could not control his nerves but found himself "trembling and laughing and weeping, and almost hysterical." "I had never imagined such a wealth of glory. The sense of exhilaration was so transcendent that I felt as if I could not stay in the body." And he acknowledges freely that he had "never had, under preaching, anything like such a personal feeling of holiness, or such a sense of the nearness and overpowering presence of the other world . . . as through the faculty of ideality." [8]

The ecstasy was modified only by satiety. There were "Murillos, Titians, Caraccis, and others of equal note" in the Louvre, but at first he could see "only a vast wilderness of color, and the sense of beauty, jaded and sated, sinks under the burden." Somewhere or other, he mentions nearly all the great painters, and of course many of his judgments are conventional enough. He appreciated Rubens but disliked his "fat" women. He found Greuze full of "sweetness, innocence, and simplicity of character," but Poussin was "cold and stiff" and Turner "utterly displeasing." "French nakedness" wearied him, but he adds, "I am willing always to see the human form sculptured or painted when it seems to serve a good purpose." Leonardo's Christ was one of the few painted images of the Savior which pleased him; most painters failed to rise to his ideal. He knew, admired, and collected George Inness, and the painter's latest biographer is even inclined to credit Henry with some significant influence upon Inness's work.[9] He gave Hogarth credit as one of the first democratic painters; he had no objection to realism as such but he did want the painter to respect what he was painting. Pictures without "meaning," which pleased through form and color alone, seemed to him, like writing with no attractions except fine language, to belong to the lower branches of art, but they had their place, for he had no patience with artists and critics who were interested only in greatness. The humbler branches of art served many useful and humane purposes, and a man ought to be willing to be used thus.[10]

To Beethoven, the "Shakespeare" and the "Milton" of music, who possessed "those elements which are sure to win all who have a genuine love of nature," Henry Ward has more references than to any other composer. Psalm 73 reminded him of Beethoven's symphonies and these in turn of the tumult of the forest. Beecher praised Beethoven, among other things, for his power to "think" in his symphonies.

In the midst of the grand movement, sweeping on as if it were the sound of winds and birds in some mighty forest, there will suddenly, as it were far away, remotely, come in one single, simple, wailing note, while everything is going on. And then, before you know it, he has modulated the whole symphony; and it follows that one note, and conforms to it, and develops the new theme.

He speaks of Handel also, but he seems to give Mozart much less than his due, possibly because he was shocked by *Don Giovanni.* "Mozart could create the music of the flowing stream, the murmur of the leaves, the song of the birds; Mozart could never rise into the very highest realm of human feeling; it was not in him." He greatly admired Gounod's "Funeral March of a Marionette" and apparently *Faust* also, though he would probably have had to reject the ballet, since he told William A. Hammond that "poetry of motion," as manifested in the dance, meant nothing to him.

Of course his enjoyment and appreciation of opera in general was handicapped and conditioned by his mistrust of the theater. He even disliked professional singers in church because their "unwashed lips" had all week been singing "the disgustful words of glorious music in operas." But, like most of the evangelicals of his time, he praised Jenny Lind, who was as widely known for her Christian virtues as for her art.

Henry sounds like a churchman when he tells the Yale theologues that the finest orchestra on earth is inferior to a great organ. Yet he himself stopped attending the Saturday evening concerts of the Philharmonic because they excited him too much before his Sunday preaching. Music in worship seems to have been something of a problem to him; in one essay, he wondered why the average congregation wanted even an organ "unless it were that other fashionable churches had organs; or, that it formed a cheerful and pleasant interlude to the tediousness of other parts of worship" (can he possibly have meant the preaching?). Yet he sponsored some two hundred organ concerts at Plymouth Church, and he seems also to have had a Steinway in his home. Plymouth placed its heaviest reliance upon congregational singing, and the *Plymouth Collection of Hymns and Tunes* was a pioneering effort which widely influenced other churches.

In his early lecture on "Popular Amusements" (*Lectures to Young Men*), Beecher classifies theater-going as a vice, though he also considers it an expiring evil. Only during one period, he says, was the drama important for literature. Though he speaks with respect of Mrs. Siddons, Ellen Tree, Fanny Kemble, Garrick, and Sheridan, he feels that their influence was outweighed by that of many other undesirable persons. In his later years, as the theater improved and Beecher's own toleration widened, he came to think of actors as "a large-hearted, great-souled, and happy people," and Dion Boucicault, with whom he had crossed swords publicly on the morality of the theater, said that in 1884 he acknowledged he had been wrong in his earlier hostility. In at least one sermon, he referred to Sir Henry Irving, with whom and his great acting partner, Ellen Terry, he enjoyed friendly social relations on both sides of the Atlantic. Apparently he also saw Edwin Booth, Joseph Jefferson, Salvini, and Ada Rehan.[11]

Of course Beecher himself possessed an intensely dramatic imagination. He liked charades and participated in school theatricals, once enacting the tyrant Gessler in *William Tell*. Knox says he acted out whatever he narrated or described even in conversation, often finding it impossible to keep his seat while he did so. But of course most of his acting was done in the pulpit. In the lecture on prostitution in the early Indiana series addressed to young men, he invited his hearers "to enter with me, in imagination, the strange woman's house, where God grant you may never enter in any other way," and there are numbered "scenes" in the printed text of the lecture on gambling. This lecture was so vivid that one "smart" auditor asked Henry how he could describe a gambling hell so vividly if he had never been in one (he had, as a matter of fact, derived his information from a professional gambler), eliciting a characteristically quick rejoinder: how did the challenger know he had been accurate? Sometimes he threw himself into the characters he described in the "illustrations" used in his sermons, with characteristic gestures and grimaces, all of which seem to have come to him spontaneously and without pre-planning or being remembered afterwards.[12]

IV

Yet Henry Ward Beecher took much more from humanity directly than from the expression of humanity in art. He considered himself a very sympathetic person, and he makes a great point of his conversations with omnibus drivers, gate-keepers, deck hands, etc.; some of this was professional, but there was interest in humanity in it too. "My God," he says, "has given me a sympathetic nature, ardent and loving." "Sympathetically," he felt in tune "with the whole universal life and beauty of God's world and with all human life." "With him," he says of Christ, "it was to look and love. He saw, and his soul went out with a gush." It may not have been true of Christ, but it was certainly true of Henry.

> Hundreds and hundreds of times, as I rose to pray and glanced at the congregation, I could not keep back the tears. . . . I had such a sense of compassion for them, my soul so longed for them that it seemed to me as if I could scarcely open my mouth to speak for them.

Yet he could be sharp. Patience was not "a natural gift" for him. He had "as much temper as anybody," and he did not always sufficiently "measure" his words. Perhaps he indulged himself most in journalism, where the contemporary tradition supported and encouraged it, but he did not wholly escape a rather rough self-assertion even in church. Once, when people shouted "Pulpit!" and "Can't hear!" when he started to speak from the floor of a strange church, he retorted, "If you make less noise you will hear me before I get through," but he did not go into the pulpit. In a lecture on "Evolution and Religion," he quotes a definition from Spencer, and then adds, "If you do not understand that, I am sorry for you." He accepted the teaching of Jesus that "a murderous temper is malice," and he never avenged an injury.

But when the president of Dartmouth published a book justifying slavery, he wrote:

> When I see a drabbled woman upon Broadway, when I meet a man who has been wrecked, I feel as if I could lay down my life for them, if necessary, to save them; but when I read a book written by a hoary-headed president of a college, intended to extol an institution that would consign a child like this [one born in slavery] to a life worse than death, I curse him, in the name of my God.

On a somewhat higher level his "Duties of Religious Publication Societies" is a masterpiece of eloquence and invective against the American Tract Society for its refusal to take a stand against slavery. Once a member of Plymouth threatened to leave if Henry supported Cleveland. He replied, "I would only say that having profited so little by my teachings as this arrogant sentence indicates, I should certainly advise you to change your church relations in the hope of better results."

Beecher's conduct in social relations was as individualistic as everything else about him. He himself said that he was afraid of nothing and of nobody when he was on the platform but that he could never enter a room in which he expected to encounter strangers without embarrassment. The only important exception was children, with whom he seems always to have felt at home. He could speak of personal matters in the pulpit, which he rarely did with individuals, so that it was hard even to draw reminiscences from him. In his youth he formed a close friendship with a handsome Greek boy, Constantine Fondolaik, who died very young of cholera; for a time he even adopted his friend's name, signing his initials "H. C. B." In college he seems to have sustained fairly close social relations with his classmates without in any sense compromising or apologizing for his strict temperance and moral principles. One does not gather, however, that he had many very intimate friends during his mature years, nor did he always choose these wisely, as the famous case of Theodore Tilton shows. ("I never knew a person," said Edward Eggleston, "who knew man so well and men so ill as Henry Ward Beecher.") His social behavior varied with his mood. Sometimes he would talk as brilliantly and almost as consecutively as in the pulpit; again he might withdraw into himself, ignoring questions he did not wish to answer, and achieving not only silence but complete impenetrability—"the face of a sphinx." One observer even says he sometimes read in the presence of bores.

Henry had a certain weakness for the expression of noble sentiments, whose utterance he must have known would reflect credit upon himself, but this was in the manner of the time, and as a clergyman he may well have believed that he was only bearing his testimony. Surely his Ugly Duckling boyhood could not have been calculated greatly to inspire self-confidence, and I should not call Beecher arrogant even in the days of his greatest success. Rejecting what many churches would call authority in religion, he "tried to inspire kind feelings and thus lead men to take up their crosses. I have never sought to exert my authority, but to promote the utmost freedom of thought and action." And if this sounds like self-praise, we shall still have the testimony of one of his Plymouth successors that "Nothing pleased Mr. Beecher more than to have his men stand up in the Friday evening meeting and combat him." [13] It is interesting that, like the actor who never musters the nerve to tackle Hamlet, he never preached on the Crucifixion, finding the subject "too awful and sublime" for his powers.

His "independent personal habits" Henry attributed to his "Western training"; in the East he felt himself generally unacceptable outside his own church; consequently he made it a rule never to intrude upon anybody or ask for a favor. He found it hard to bring himself to speak out in England during the Civil War because "my American ways, which are well enough with Americans, may utterly fail here." He almost did not publish his

Lectures to Young Men because he thought Isaac Barrow had covered the same ground so much better than he could, and he spoke of his life of Christ as the poorest of a whole collection on the subject; F. W. Farrar's, he added, was worth all the rest put together. Henry Ward never pretended to a knowledge he did not possess. When he found his own uninstructed judgment of a painting confirmed by an authority, he was greatly pleased, and when he spoke at a public dinner to Herbert Spencer, he expressed his desire to sit down with the guest of honor some quiet evening "and bring up my crude thought, my vagrant imagination, and avail myself of his superior experience and thought." But he was equally modest about his spiritual attainments. "I always feel most for those who are furthest from grace, perhaps because I see in them some likeness to myself," and when he woke up early in the morning and thought over his life and accomplishment, it seemed to him that he had produced so little, with that little "so poorly done," that he felt discouraged about going on. Perhaps he is pulling the humility stop too strongly when he tells the Yale theologues that it is the singing that brings people to Plymouth Church, that and the "loving, cheerful, hopeful courage" of the congregation. "They get a sermon too, but then it is more the singing, I think, that accounts for the throng." Nevertheless he always claimed that he had tried to win men for Christ, not for himself, and that otherwise his work would have been "worse than useless," and I believe he was sincere in this and conducted his ministry accordingly. "My little services will be ground up to make soil for somebody else who will see better things and better thoughts than I have seen. But since I am a pilgrim of the heavenly host, what matters it?" [14]

Beecher liked to think of himself as an apostle of joy. He hated funerals and cemeteries and did not even visit the graves of his children. "I believe they are in heaven, not in Greenwood." He hated black also and those who attempted to make their faces "look like midnight" as evidence of grace.

As a child, I was always merry, sportive, and joyful. I have been so all my life, and I mean to be so all the rest of my days. But I do not attribute my joyfulness to my religious state. . . . I know there are many Christians who are better than I am, who put forth more effort to be good than I do, who are more earnest, more self-denying, and more consistent than I am, but who are not so joyful. With me joy is largely constitutional.

Again he says: "God, in his providence, gave me a temperament and a training which led me to inspire men with courage, with hope, and with consolation; and I have been blessed to an unusual extent as a comforter."

Unfortunately this was not the whole truth. For Henry also inherited "a tendency to sadness, the remains in me of positive hypochondria in my father and grandfather, and in certain moods of reaction the world seems black and I see very despairingly." He adds, "If I were, in such moods, to speak as I feel, I should give false colors and exaggerated proportions of everything."

From one point of view, he was worse than his father had been. "My father," he told Lyman Abbott, "wrote his sermons with the angel of hope looking over his shoulder and inspiring his pen. I have never expected to succeed. Success has come to me always as a surprise." As a divinity student he feared that "I shall not succeed in anything," though even then, if all else failed, he planned not to give up but to go into the Western wilds as a missionary, and he asked Eunice if she would go with him. Even in mid-career he was not incapable of utterances which smack of the sickly melancholy of Romanticism. "There is no unmixed good in this world except dying, which cures all ill and inherits all blessing." "My labor will not run through a great many years more, thank God. I do not know which to be more thankful for, that I have been permitted to labor so long, or that I shall soon be permitted to lay down my labor." "One should go to sleep at night as homesick passengers do, saying, 'Perhaps in the morning we shall see the shore.' " "That we are so near death, is too good to be believed." All in all, the contrast between Henry's cheerfulness and his melancholy seems almost great enough to suggest a divided personality.

V

How much these temperamental problems affected Henry Ward Beecher in his intimate family relationships is uncertain; they certainly did affect his work. Though he said his father was "too busy to be loved," they were certainly not unhappy in their personal relations. Of his brothers and sisters Harriet seems to have been the closest to him, and Harriet almost worshipped him, seeing him as "from childhood of an ideal purity," one who "reverenced his conscience as his king," found his "glory" in "redressing human wrong," and "spake no slander, no, nor listened to it." [15] His mother died when he was only three; he could remember neither her face nor her form but only "the warm pressure" when she took him to her bosom. Yet he gave her the kind of veneration the devout Catholic offers the Blessed Virgin; next to Christ she was the dominant spiritual presence of his life; when he was under accusation, more than sixty years after he had lost her, he declared that since *she* knew he was innocent, all was well. But he did not get much from his stepmother, Harriet Porter Beecher, who "was a woman of profound veneration, rather than of a warm and loving nature." "I was afraid of her. I revered her, but I was not attracted to her."

The controversial figure, inevitably in view of the Tilton scandal, is Henry's wife, Eunice Bullard. She had been brought up by a stock type of the old New England Puritan father, and as she grew older, she looked like a very grim, reserved New England woman herself. So she has been called a "Griffin" and a "Gorgon," and there were rumors, which have been echoed by many writers, that she and Henry were not in sympathy with one another;[16] actually there is no really unambiguous evidence to support this view. To be sure, Beecher once said that "earthly love is a brief and penurious stream, which only flows in spring, with a long summer drought," but he also said that "he that hath dwelt with the woman of his love through a score of years has a thousand memories and associations that are more precious than those of a young man." Certainly he was much in love with her in the beginning: "I could have looked through ten thousand and never have found one so every way suited to me." In Brooklyn she handled his mail and his bank account, and went through his pockets, at his own request, to make proper disposal of both valuable and useless material. She accompanied him on some of his lecture tours and took care of his engagements until Pond became his manager. When Thomas Wentworth Higginson visited the Beechers in Brooklyn, he thought Eunice treated Henry like "a sort of great, happy child." [17] So, I should think, she might, and Henry being what he was, I do not see how this could well have been avoided. So, too, did Olivia Langdon treat Mark Twain and Edith Carow, Theodore Roosevelt, but nobody has ever suggested that there was estrangement between these couples. When, in his essay on "My Pockets," Beecher humorously complains of his wife's trying to limit his purchases, he at once adds that "she is as nearly perfect as it was thought that such a poor sinner as I am could endure." It was noted that when they went out in company, Henry and Eunice always chose each other for partners whenever it was possible to do so, and Ellen Terry, who loved Eunice deeply (and to whom she herself was "my darling Nelly"), got the impression that husband and wife were very close.[18] Certainly no wife could have borne herself in a more exemplary manner than Eunice did at the time of her husband's trouble. Whether he was innocent or guilty, her sufferings must have been profound, but she sat by his side in the courtroom and held his hand whenever he could be present, and when he was not there she came alone.

Financially the Beechers knew poverty and affluence equally well. The bride had to make a ten-dollar ring do for both engagement and wedding, and the poverty in which they both lived in rural Indiana was something most of us would rather not try to imagine. It was very different in later years, when he was probably the highest-salaried clergyman in America and supplemented his salary with large earnings from lecturing and journalism—$240,000, Pond says, from ten years of lecturing. Lyman Abbott insists that he was too radical to attract a really wealthy congregation, but even his admiring kinsman, Lyman Beecher Stowe, speaks of "his town house and his country estate, his collections, his fast horses, precious stones and other luxuries." His farm was a show place, for Beecher was not quite untouched by the affluence of the Gilded Age. He defended luxury as not evil in itself; the only question was: "How much of my wealth given to the public good shall be employed *directly* for the elevation of the ignorant and how much *indirectly?*" But he certainly made no scientific attempt to adjust proportions. In "My Pockets" he humorously described his inability to hold on to money, and generally speaking it seems to have been the interest or the individual which presented itself first that got what was available. Never a mean man, he gave lavishly (and not always intelligently) to whoever asked of him, and he seems to have been equally lavish in buying whatever struck his own fancy, whether he needed it or not.

The Beechers had ten children, of whom only four grew up. Henry Barton Beecher went into the insurance business in Brooklyn; William C. Beecher became a lawyer; Herbert Beecher held public office in the Northwest, living in Portland and Seattle. The surviving daughter married the Reverend Samuel Scoville. This is a comparatively unimpressive record beside Lyman's, and though Mrs. Beecher's account of her husband's grief when one of the children died is very moving, we know much less about Henry as a father than we do about Lyman himself. As a child he had learned "women's work" as well as the chores that commonly fall to a boy, and he seems to have performed in both aspects quite uncomplainingly when occasion arose. As for his children, he helped them when they needed help and played with them when they didn't, much as if he had been a child himself. Though he says ponderously that "a little rubefacience on the skin is sometimes a great help to a child," one gets the impression that he was a gentler father than Lyman. If his father's fondness for practical jokes lived on in him, it was in a much gentler form, and he respected the child's individuality, even in religious matters, as his own had never been respected. Yet he could punish severely when occasion demanded, as when he found the children trying to discover whether or not a kitten could swim under water.

Perhaps the strangest problem in connection with Beecher's sociality or the lack of it is his inability or unwillingness to do pastoral work. Unlike Phillips Brooks, who felt that pastoral work and preaching must be carried on together and that both suffered if either was neglected, he believed that it was impossible, for him at any rate, to be pastor and preacher both. He once told an English questioner that he did not need pastoral visitation to achieve warmth and love toward his parishioners. "I have too much feeling, anyhow too strong, and therefore am very glad not to do some of those things." Since pastoral work is not generally undertaken for the spiritual benefit of the pastor, this seems to be getting it all but the point. Sometimes, in seasons of sorrow, Henry's sympathetic nature seems effectively to have manifested itself.[19] Generally, however, he apparently dodged even the ministry of comfort, and it is quite possible that, his temperament being what it was, he could not have stood the strain of many such close contacts.

As a religious worker, then, Beecher dealt with men in the mass; individuals disarmed him and threw him off the track. He simply was not aggressive enough to be able himself to set the tone for a tête-à-tête but left this to the other party. "I don't wish to push myself upon anybody; to feel that I have pushed myself upon any human being who does not want me is enough to kill me." As a young Christian, he resolved to speak of religion to everyone he met but he soon found that for him this was impossible. In mid-career he could no more have accosted a stranger with Moody's famous question, "Are you a Christian?" than he could have laid the Atlantic cable. Even with those closest to him he was intensely reserved about such matters. "I feel almost a morbid sense of the rights of people. I will not intrude on persons' consciences and personal liberty. I will not invade the rights of others in the church, in the household, or anywhere else."

VI

When D. L. Moody invited Henry Ward to join forces with him in evangelistic work, the pastor of Plymouth Church was flattered, even tempted:

> I should like to go up and down the land preaching the gospel of the love of God in Christ Jesus. But Mr. Moody and I could not possibly work together in such a mission; he believes that the world is lost, and he is seeking to save from the wreck as many individuals as he can; I believe that this world is to be saved, and I am seeking to bring about the Kingdom of God on this earth.

There was another reason, no doubt, which he did not state; he knew that such an enterprise could not possibly have operated successfully under two heads; nevertheless he spells out his own point of view accurately. "I hold that it is a Christian minister's duty not only to preach the Gospel of the New Testament without reservation, but to apply its truths to any question that relates to the welfare of men." Whatever the special limitations and qualifications of his own temperament, he could not, therefore, have failed to recognize the social aspects of religion.

Beecher's attitude toward many of the problems which he—and the nation—faced during his later years seems conservative enough to us, and he is never more trying than when he defends the cutting of railroad workers' wages during the panic year 1877:

> It is true that $1 a day is not enough to support a man and five children if a man would insist on smoking and drinking beer. Was not a dollar a day enough to buy bread? Water costs nothing. Man cannot live by bread, it is true, but the man who cannot live on good bread and water is not fit to live.

This, however, is far from being the whole story.[20] Henry saw no need of Socialism, Communism, or Nihilism in the United States, but he admitted that had he been brought up in Russia, he might have been a Nihilist himself.

Beecher shared the forward-looking but not radical outlook of his time; it will not do to call him a coward simply because he did not agree with us. If he was conciliatory when examined by the Indiana presbytery called to ordain him, he still believed what he said, though he may well have believed some of it differently from the way his examiners believed it. But when he was required to range himself with the Old School party, he flatly refused, and his little church backed him, withdrawing from the presbytery. He played a man's role in fire and riot service in the West, far beyond what was expected of a clergyman.

Whether or not Beecher's Civil War lectures in England exerted the influence upon public opinion once attributed to them does not modify his courage in appearing as he did before audiences which sometimes howled and heckled for the better part of an hour before he was allowed to speak. His lecture appearances in Dixie after the Civil War called for courage too, and even more was required by the tours he undertook with Pond after the Tilton scandal. As the manager writes of Richmond in 1877:

When we got into town the newsboys were selling anti-Beecher poetry and songs on the street. We reached the hotel: Mr. Beecher registered and left the room in the midst of general tittering and sneering. When he went into the dining-room, even the waiters tittered and sneered, and it was hard to get waited on.

Some of the criticism directed against the Beechers for their slowness to enter the anti-slavery fight seems based on the assumption that they ought from the beginning to have been Garrisonian abolitionists. They, of course, acknowledged no such obligation. Henry's political philosophy could have supplied him with no justification for the federal government's overriding the rights of the sovereign states. He respected the rights of slavery under the Constitution and believed in working for reform *within the law*. Generally speaking, he had little confidence in the efficacy of attacking people's prejudices directly; like John Fiske, he thought the thing to do was to put a new idea into the mind with which the old ones could not comfortably keep house; if this were done skilfully and sympathetically, the hearer himself must sooner or later do whatever needed to be done to achieve an adjustment. Beecher's brave early activities in Cincinnati after the Birney riots were inspired less by opposition to slavery than by the necessity of defending civil rights, and he did not really preach against slavery until 1840. Anti-slavery appeared very clearly on his first Sunday in Plymouth however, and he made it clear that he would wear no fetters in Brooklyn and be bound by no precedents but would preach the Gospel as he understood it, whether men accepted it or not. He never defended John Brown, but he once had the chains by which Brown had been bound brought to the platform in Plymouth Church, where he hurled them to the floor and stamped on them. The "slave auctions" which he conducted in the church were highly emotional and sensational also, and the fact that they were built around young and attractive girls has encouraged posterity to discern an unwholesome note of sexuality in them, but it may be that this shows more about posterity than it does about Beecher. Once he promised a slaveholder (or his agent) that either the slave girl who had run away would be returned to New Orleans in ten days or else $2000 would be paid for her freedom. He was pleased that the man trusted his word and he raised the money without any trouble.[21]

It is not surprising that Beecher should occasionally have made a statement which for us carries unpleasant racial overtones, as when, speaking of a hungry child, he says, "Anybody would feel pity for such a child—even if it were a negro's!" This was not typical, however. Henry did not think the ultimate capabilities of the American Negro could be fairly evaluated in his time, but he was sure that the American destiny was bound up with that of the Negro nevertheless. He boldly declared that Southerners dislike "amalgamation," as the nineteenth century called miscegenation, only when it "has been made lawful." He refused to patronize a Brooklyn omnibus which would not carry Negroes and urged others to boycott it too, so that the rule had to be changed. Plymouth Church was always open to Negroes, but Beecher did not pretend that he thought all members would welcome them.

He spoke up for the Indians also and for the Jews, in Germany and in the United States, and opposed "nativism" of all varieties, being willing to admit Orientals to American citizenship. In one passage he speaks of Jews as having become "a by-word and a hissing to the earth" because of their rejection of Christ, but he also says that "for everything that constitutes superior religion we are indebted to the great Hebrew stock." He had much more faith in the melting pot and especially in the public school than many of his contemporaries. Consequently, though he wanted immigrants Americanized, and Christianized too if they needed it, he was willing to accept them as they came and put his trust for the future in the validity of American institutions.

Henry Ward's social conscience seems weakest and his logic shakiest when he comes to war. Primarily this is because on other issues he was likely to take up an ethical absolutist position. The Christian had no right to choose between evils or to do evil that good might come; he should obey the law even when it oppresses him, but he must refuse obedience "to every law that commands [him] to sin." It was upon such grounds that Henry opposed "any counsels that lead to insurrection, servile insurrection, and bloodshed during the period of anti-slavery agitation," and once at least he insisted quixotically that the truth must always be told even to sick or irresponsible people. But he never applies ethical absolutist reasoning to war as such.

This does not mean that he was a militarist. He respected the Quaker point of view on war and peace; in *Norwood* the Quakers who give shelter to Pete and Barton are admiringly presented, and when Dr. Wentworth opposes them, it is not on the war issue but on what seems to him their refusal to use art and the imagination in their religion. In his personal life, too, Henry, sharp though he could be, often used non-resistance on his adversaries more successfully than many of those who professed it as a principle.

"Patriotism in our day," Henry once said, "is made an argument for all public wrong, and all private meanness. For the sake of country a man is told to yield every thing that makes the land honorable." And he added, "There never was a man so unpatriotic as Christ was." When he read his Bible, he could not justify such incidents as the revenge of Moses upon the Amalekites: "I am not satisfied with the theory that God has the same 'right' to exterminate nations by the hands of other nations that he has to destroy men by earthquakes and pestilence." No power above naked, conscienceless might could be invoked to justify the deeds of England in India or those of "the confederated nations of Europe" in Poland. And the United States was no better, employing her "gigantic strength with no moral restrictions" against Mexicans and Indians, "making treaty after treaty, violating one almost before another is formed."

In such utterances Beecher was not far from the pacifist kingdom, yet he never really goes in through the door.[22] Temperamentally he apparently had considerable interest in military matters. Once he was greatly interested in the lore of the Peninsular War. He called Napier's work "one of the noblest monuments of military history ever given to the world" and once told Lyman Abbott, who thought he would have made one of the worst on record, that if he had not been a clergyman, he would have liked to be a general! "In the history of the world," he declares absurdly, "military training is for civilization next to moral training," and he skilfully begs every moral question involved when he says: "The New Testament declares that malign revenge or hatred are not to be felt toward an enemy. We do not think it touches at all the question of what kind of instruments men may employ." The best one can say for Henry in this connection is that there were times when he himself seems to have felt that there was an uncomfortable contrast between such utterances and his profession and commitments, but the closest he comes to recognizing this is when he remarks, at the cornerstone laying of the Brooklyn City Armory, that "I was a man before I was a minister. Whatever a man should feel, I feel. Whatever any man should say, I ought to speak; I am a citizen, a Christian citizen." Even in his mid-sixties he was a chaplain of the National Guard in New York and participated in their parades.

One day during the riots produced by anti-slavery agitation in Cincinnati, Harriet found her brother making bullets, and when she asked him what they were for, he replied, "To kill men."

When Kansas became the background for the slavery struggle, Plymouth Church took a prominent role in fitting out the anti-slavery men who went to settle there. This was the period when Sharp's rifles were called "Beecher's Bibles" and Plymouth itself "the Church of the Holy Rifles." Perhaps this was not quite so bad as it sounds, for Henry and those like-minded honestly believed that a show of firmness in Kansas would avert bloodshed, and they were not wholly unjustified by the event. But they were not facing the problem in quite the spirit in which Christ confronted his final adversaries.

As for the Civil War, as late as 1859, in his address before the Boston American Tract Society, Henry was asking why "those causes which in other lands break out into wars, with us produce only discussions." He had no more fear of disunion, he said, than that the continent would break in two. At times he even seemed willing to let the South go. But his Thanksgiving Day sermon in 1860 was "Against a Compromise of Principle," and as time went on, his mood hardened. Still describing "the wretchedness and wickedness and monstrosity of war," he began to feel that in this case it was not "unmixed evil," as "eighty years of unexampled prosperity have gone far toward making us a people that judge of moral questions by their relation to our convenience and ease." "I am for war," he once declared, "just so far as it is necessary to vindicate a great moral truth. But one particle of violence beyond that is a flagrant treason against the law of love." Unfortunately he did not explain just how that vindication was to be effected nor how the "one particle" could be prevented once the war was under way. In describing the Battle of Gettysburg at the climax of his novel *Norwood*, he does not blink the suffering, but the emphasis falls elsewhere:

> As the midwife in the throes and groans of the mother, heeds not the pain, but waits for the child that shall bring joy out of woe, so we must needs think the Merciful heeds not the forms of suffering, but looks beyond at the blessings wrought by them!

But the analogy does not hold. A battle is neither mother nor midwife. The first endures pain; the latter strives to relieve it. Neither inflicts it.

It would not be fair to call Henry Ward Beecher a bloodthirsty patriot as the war advanced, but he came pretty close. "I would denounce my own brother, I would denounce my own father," he says, "if he were ranged on the side of these enemies of their country and of freedom." Since neither was thus arrayed, such magniloquence could have no higher effect than inflaming egotism and unsettling weak minds. When Beecher's own son asked permission to enlist, his father replied, "If you don't, I'll disown you." The boy went and promptly proceeded to prove that army camps are not Sunday Schools and that their influence sometimes outweighs that of the Sunday School even with ministers' sons. During the early days of the war, Beecher's public criticisms of Lincoln were very severe: "The President seems to be a man without any sense of the value of time." "Not a spark of genius has he; not an element for leadership. Not one particle of heroic enthusiasm." Later he was much more sympathetic, but the best authorities do not give much support to the popular belief that he and Lincoln became intimate, though he did undoubtedly keep in close touch with Secretary of War Stanton.[23] Plymouth Church became an active and passionate center of war activities, and Henry Ward himself fitted out a regiment. When Grant was called a butcher, he defended him on the ground that "war is not created for the purpose of saving life, but by a noble spending of blood to save the Commonwealth." When England rubbed American feelings the wrong way in the *Trent* affair and other matters, Beecher can hardly be said to have played a conciliatory role; though he thought conflict between the mother and daughter nations would be a tragedy, he still left the impression that we could take the old lady on if we had to, though he did not explain how this was to be done. Later, when the war was long over, he made a suggestion which, as we in these latter days have learned at bitter cost, carried far more horrible implications than anybody in his time could have imagined: England and America together, he thought, were "bound to take care of the world"! All in all, the most attractively Christian part of Beecher's Civil War record was his temperate, wise, just, and forgiving attitude toward the South after hostilities had ceased. This was far indeed from the program of reconstruction which the Radical Republicans engineered, but we may be sure it was pretty close to what Lincoln would have favored if he had lived.

VII

When all was said and done, however, Henry Ward Beecher was first of all a preacher. "I have worked," he says, "from three considerations—the love that I have for God, the love that I have for my fellow-men, and because I could not help myself. It was in me, and it had to come out. I was made to be a preacher, and I have preached just as fountains run."

"The Divine Abundance" was a suitable title for one of Henry's sermons, but though most of his discourses were reported stenographically, I find little to indicate any of the old-fashioned "spell-binding" or "flannel-mouth" characteristics which some persons imagine to have found their final exemplification in him. He was certainly not an untrained preacher. Early in his ministry he read diligently in South, Barrow, Howe, Sherlock, Butler, and Edwards. He also subjected himself to considerable formal exercise in voice training and rhetoric, walking the woods with his brother Charles and, as he says, making the night hideous by "exploding all the vowels, from the bottom to the very top of our voices," according to "Dr. Barber's System."

Nobody would claim that Henry Ward was a doctrinal preacher in the old Puritan sense. Primarily he addressed himself not to the intellect but to the *consciousness* of men, the will. He did not try to prove too much or to argue much, for he knew men were not sufficiently governed by their minds to be greatly moved by argument, and he had no desire to raise doubts where none had appeared before. H. C. Howard was probably right when he called him "more persuasive than convincing," "an artist in language but not exact," with "no close coherence of thought in his sermons," but this language is not necessarily pejorative. The beginning of his sermons was often quiet, casual, and hard to hear; indeed Oliver Wendell Holmes described his speech in general as "pointed, staccatoed," "short-gaited; the movement of his thoughts is that of a chopping sea, rather than the long, rhythmical wave-procession of phrase-balancing rhetoricians." It was only when he was extraordinarily roused that he would express himself in what another hearer calls "passionate outbursts in which the words came like a torrent," and many found him most effective not in the Sunday services where he "preached" to thousands but in the Friday night "lecture room talks," when he sat on the platform surrounded by those who were closest to him and most in sympathy with him and spoke simply and informally of the matters which lay closest to his heart. I am well aware that there are those who gag at this picture of the guru surrounded by adoring disciples, but I wonder if a more sympathetic judgment is not in order here. I find little self-exploitation in such of the lecture room talks as have been printed, and if Henry Ward is to be rejected out of hand in this aspect and dismissed as a fakir rather than a father in Israel, I fear most of the religious teachers of the world must go into the discard with him.[24]

There was extraordinary variety in Henry's preaching. "The sermon," says Lyman Abbott, "might be a Biblical exposition, or a devotional meditation, or a philosophical essay, or a chapter in ethics, but, whatever it might be in form, in its spirit it was always true to himself." Abbott finds three distinct periods in

Beecher's preaching. In the first he is "largely pictorial, imaginative, emotional"; in the second "the emotions and the imagination have been brought into subjection"; in the last he is first of all a teacher.

> The sermons are expositions; he is an interpreter of faith; he is attempting to show men that the spiritual experience, into which he has before been endeavoring to carry them by all the forces of his nature, is an experience consistent with the highest exercise of reason; he preaches less for conversion, and more for instruction and edification.

His sermons have considerably less style than those of Phillips Brooks, and he was not a literary preacher in the sense of quoting much poetry in them.[25] Indeed he used few quotations of any kind, except from the Bible; his poor verbal memory made this impossible for him. He emphatically rejected the idea that one must preach "nothing but the literal, textual Christ, or the literal, textual four Gospels, or the literal, textural Epistles; for all of life is open to you." And he asks: "Are we wiser than the Apostles?" and replies, "I hope so. I should be ashamed if we were not. 'Are we better preachers in our time than they would be?' Yes, we ought to be."

What Henry hated most in this world was the old "swallow's nest" pulpit, stuck up on the wall at one side of the chancel, leaving nothing but the preacher's head and shoulders visible. Our old churches, he said, were "constructed on the principle of isolation or wide separation,—as though a man should sit on one side of a river and try to win a mistress on the other side, bawling out his love at the top of his voice." For him "a man's whole form" was "part of his public speaking. His feet speak and so his hands." When Plymouth was rebuilt he had the platform extend out so that he was thrust into the midst of his hearers, with a table made of olive wood from Jerusalem instead of a pulpit, and when the ladies wanted to put up a silk screen covering for his legs and feet, he agreed only on the condition that "whenever I make a pastoral call at your houses you will have a green silk bag into which I may put my legs."

Obviously such an arrangement could have served only a man who extemporized in the pulpit. Henry began writing his sermons in the traditional New England manner, but after he had found his stride, he never took anything into the pulpit with him but a page or two of very cryptic notes. He made the plan for his first Yale lecture on preaching while shaving himself before going to the hall. On the way to deliver his oration at Fort Sumter, he seemed so little concerned with what lay before him that his son-in-law even remonstrated, to which Beecher replied, "What do you mean by coming around trying to scare a man to death? I'll have something to say when the time comes," and he did. One Sunday afternoon, Calvin Stowe suggested that he ought sometime to preach on the eighth of Romans. He replied that he might as well do it that evening. He went to bed as usual for his afternoon nap and slept until nearly six. Then he went to his study and prepared what Stowe and others thought a magnificent sermon. Such feats require a well-stored, highly disciplined mind which has assimilated everything that is usable in all that has ever been thought or experienced or read and can bring it all to bear on the spur of the moment wherever it happens to be needed. No wonder interruptions stimulated him. "There is nothing in the world," he says, "that is such a stimulus to me as an audience. It wakes up the power of thinking and wakes up the power of imagination in me." Once the sermon had been preached, he had no interest in it nor even in the printed report of it. "I never look after a bullet when once it is fired."

Beecher himself is largely to blame for the widespread impression that he had no theology. "I study everything except theology," he says, and once when a young man told him he was studying theology, he replied, "No objection to that if you don't believe it." Sometimes he was less brash about it and more wistful, as when he says he has been told so often he is no theologian that he has come to believe it. In his early preaching he sometimes used the systematic theology he had learned in the seminary, but in time it all "slipped away." "It did not do me any good. It was like an armor which had lost its buckles and would not stick on."

Yet so high an authority as John Wright Buckham says that "there was as much theology in Beecher's little finger as in the loins of the average popular preacher." [26] Certainly he did not lack theological training. Nor did he wait until he reached the seminary to acquire it. In Lyman Beecher's household, theology was served at every meal, and the children spoke as freely as their father in discussions that sometimes continued for two or three hours. "When I was a boy eight years old and upward," he once said, "I knew as much about decrees, foreordination, election, reprobation, as you do now."

Lyman Beecher, as we have seen, undercut Calvinism. His son repudiated it, for Calvinism illustrated "the monarchical idea rather than the idea of fatherhood" and "concentered in God the barbaric authority to which men had wearily and long submitted in magistrates and masters." "My father," he says, "was what is called a Low Calvinist, but he was a good deal too high for me, for we had many valiant battles over the breakfast-table together, and I found so much trouble with Calvinism that I concluded I would get along without it." If he remained Calvinistic in any sense, it was in believing "what John Calvin would have believed if he had lived in my time and seen things as I see them. My first desire is to know what is true; and then I am very glad if John Calvin agrees with me, but if he don't, so much the worse for him." He felt very much the same way about Jonathan Edwards, thinking that reading "Sinners in the Hands of an Angry God" might well drive a man mad. "There was never anything that so nearly killed me as trying to be Jonathan Edwards." Calvinism, he thought, made "as strong men as are ever met on the face of this earth," but it killed five hundred for every five it matured.

Henry rejected out of hand the notion that the whole human race fell with Adam ("Where is the text? Where is the teaching? What prophet, what evangelist, what Lord and Savior Jesus Christ ever taught that?") and believed that a God who continued to turn "the crank of creation" after the race had fallen into total corruption would be worse than a doctor who went about "in-oculating men with mad-dogism." He rejected too the term "total depravity," including his father's specialized interpretation of it, though without mentioning his father. "We do not feel called upon to give the mischievous phrase any respect. We do not believe in it, nor in the thing which it obviously signifies. It is an unscriptural, monstrous, and unredeemable lie." For him the Eden story was "an allegory or parabolic poem," and he replaced the Fall with the evolution hypothesis. As for election, "the elect are whosoever will, and the non-elect whosoever won't." But he never stopped his study of theology; one winter he traveled with Stanley's commentary on Corinthians, which he annotated from beginning to end. Neither did he cease facing vital questions in his own mind. "Do you think because I preach so positively that I have no doubts? Oh! what nights I have gone through! What uncertainties! What jeopardies!" He never doubted that a man must "believe right" about "those truths that are connected with godliness, with purity of thought, purity of motive, purity of disposition," though he had little interest in church ordinances or the doctrines upon which denominations have split. "There is one thing," he told a young pastor, "you cannot doubt, and it is this, that men need building up in spiritual manhood, and the New Testament is of all books the one best fitted for that work"; when the young man expressed his admiration for Beecher's own certainty, he replied, "That is a thing that grows." Certainly the "Theological Statement" which he prepared in 1882, when he withdrew, upon his own initiative, for fear of embarrassing them, from the New York and Brooklyn

Association of Congregational Ministers[27] would not alienate many of the orthodox nowadays.

Yet entirely orthodox he was not. He believed in the Personality of God (Matthew Arnold might satisfy himself with "a tendency in the universe," but Beecher would rather "chew thistle-down all summer"). He accepted the Trinity ("I can conceive that in a higher range of being unity may be comprised of persons as in the lower it is made up of groups of faculties"), though he did not pretend to be able to understand it, and he had no interest in Nicene or Athanasian creeds. He carried his belief in the Deity of Christ to a length which orthodoxy itself has not achieved. He accepted the Atonement, though he disliked the word as not belonging to the New Testament (Beecher was sure that God saves men but was inclined to think that *how* He does it was His "look-out" rather than theirs). Certainly he performed valiant service in breaking down the still popular notion that the Father is Justice and that only the Son is Love. "Any view of atonement is false that makes God so vengeful that there had to be a propitiation, a placation." If he was anything, Henry was the prophet of God's undying, unconquerable love, but there are times when he seems to allow all His other attributes to be swallowed up in this one, and his own conversion experience was essentially a commitment to the thesis that it was God's nature

> to love a man in his sins for the sake of helping him out of them; . . . that He was a Being not made mad by sin, but sorry; that He was not furious with wrath toward the sinner, but pitied him—in short, that He felt toward me as my mother felt toward me, to whose eyes my wrong-doing brought tears, who never pressed me so close to her as when I had done wrong, and who would fain with her yearning love lift me out of trouble.

Even a human being can love a person who is physically diseased; why cannot God love one morally diseased? He does not want man to come before Him trembling like a slave. He is a father.

He says, "I have nothing in the universe to which you are not heir—joint heir with Christ, your elder brother." If you hold back from Him because you are conscious of your sins, He replies:

> *On that very account come*, come boldly, come to Me; it is my nature, it is my business in the eternal sphere; I love to take hold of those that are filled with infirmities, and whose infirmities break out into transgression, and after transgression into the sense of guilt.

If this seems more like the Motherhood than the Fatherhood of God, Henry stresses the feminine element in religion even more when he says,

> I marvel how a woman, with her need of love, with her sensitive, yearning, clasping nature, can look into the face of the Lord Jesus, and not put her arms about his neck, and tell him, with gushing love, that she commits herself, body and soul, into his sacred keeping!

Actually, however, he did not believe the religious experience essentially different for men: "No man ever excogitated God; no man ever came to Him by philosophical analysis. If any man has come to the realization of God, it is heart that has done it. . . ." As for himself, "There is no flower in all the field that owes so much to the sun as I do to the Lord Jesus Christ." And he tries to sum everything up categorically:

> From the beginning, now, and to the end, I affirm that the central ruling power of the universe is love; not love for loveliness, not love for beauty, not love for that which is complete, symmetrical and strong; but the other way—for littleness, for weakness, for poverty, for want, for suffering, for sin and sinfulness.

But if God's love swallows up His justice and righteousness, then the Son, for Henry Ward, swallowed up both Father and Spirit.

All that there is of God to me is bound up in that name [Christ Jesus]. A dim and shadowy effluence rises from Christ, and that I am taught to call the Father. A yet more tenuous and invisible film of thought arises, and that is the Holy Spirit. But neither are to me aught tangible, restful, accessible. . . . [Christ] is my *manifest* God. All that I know is of him, and in him. I put my soul into his arms, as, when I was born, my father put me into my mother's arms. I draw all my life from him. I bear him in my thoughts hourly, as I humbly believe that he also bears me.

When Unitarians told Henry that they could not pray to Christ, he replied that they were praying to Christ without knowing it, and that all they knew of God had been made real to them through Christ. "Oh, take away my Jehovah," he cries, "but do not take away my Jesus!"

Henry believed that Christ was "God manifest in the flesh." And he asks, "Is the whole of God in Christ?" To which he replies, "Well, that is asking me, Can infinity be inclosed in the finite? What I understand by His laying aside His glory is that Christ, when He came under the limitations of time and space and flesh was limited by them." But he goes further than this. His Christ was "a being that came down from heaven into the world to shed the light of moral truths upon it." "The Bible teaches just this, that the Divine mind was pleased to take upon itself a human body. We have no warrant in Scripture for attributing to Christ any other part of human nature than simply a body." [28] So even Henry's admirers call him Sabellian and Patripassionist, and Lyman Abbott thinks he finds the influence of Swedenborg in him.

Henry was reared on the orthodox Calvinistic notions of conversion, and in a sense he conformed to them. As late as his Yale lectures, we find him defining three stages: renunciation, adhesion, and construction. He knew that life in general did not flow as on an even keel; there were crises and developments in secular life too, and he tended to believe that at some point the Christian must make a decision, "although the circumstances which led to it, and the results which follow from it, may be long-drawn and gradual." He even had "no objection" to conversion's occurring twice (and in his own case this seems to have happened), but he found little warrant in Scripture for the orthodox formulations and believed that if he had had "the influence of a discreet, sympathetic Christian person" available, he himself might have escaped much agony and been a Christian from his mother's lap. "I know that many persons are converted," he says, "without feeling the need of the blood of atonement." For the Jews, the blood symbolized the life, but when Christians who did not know this babbled about being "saved" or "washed" by the blood, their materialism sickened him. To be a Christian meant "to obey Christ, no matter how you feel." If you experience ecstasy afterwards, this is something to be grateful for, but it is non-essential and secondary. Moreover, conversion did not alter a man's essential character and personality or prevent him from being himself; it simply helped him to develop the highest powers of the person God had created in him. "I remember how I tried to do impossible things, and how I thought God had given me up to eternal reprobation because I did not succeed."

By modern standards, Beecher was not very radical in his attitude toward the Bible. Not only did he believe that the Fourth Gospel was written by the Apostle John but he had no doubt that "the substantial basis" of the Pentateuch was written by Moses or by some clerk or Levite under his direction! But he declares uncompromisingly that the theory of plenary inspiration "has no warrant in the Bible itself, and is contrary to the known history and structure of the book." In *Norwood* Dr. Wentworth calls this "the extreme reactionary Protestant doctrine."

Since he was, during his later years, an avowed evolutionist, Henry had no difficulty accepting the idea that there is a development within the Bible itself. "The Old Testament has a great deal of straw on which the wheat grew"; he accepted or rejected its teachings "according as they agree or disagree with the moral judgments formed in the school of Jesus Christ." Prayers larded with references to the patriarchs made him shiver; only one or two of them could have lived outside of Sing Sing in modern society—"unless they went into politics." [29]

On miracles and on prayer Henry perhaps shows a certain tendency to have his cake and eat it too. As an evolutionist, he found no evidence "that God created any part of the organic world by an instantaneous inthrusting of Divine power," but he still saw natural law as something "administered" by God. Thus a miracle is not "the setting aside of a law of nature" but rather "the exhibition of the supremacy of a higher law of nature in a sphere where men have been accustomed to see the operation of the lower natural laws alone." From the same point of view, prayer becomes "asking God to use the enginery of Nature, the enginery of society, and above all, the enginery of our souls in our behalf." He accepted many Bible miracles which his posterity is not much concerned about, such as assuming that Christ was in actual contact with Satan during his temptation.

Henry disliked Dante's hell, Michelangelo's picture of the Last Judgment, and Jonathan Edwards' sermon on damnation, which he tends to lump together. In his life of Christ he inclines to treat the New Testament account of the Last Judgment as a parable. But though he knew that "the vast majority of the human race have at death been unfit for any such heaven as is revealed in the New Testament," he did not believe "that any one of God's creatures will exist in eternal suffering." If he were to believe that, Henry could never violate his own nature by calling God "Father" or even mentioning His name again. But he was not a universalist because he could not believe that God would force salvation upon anybody; "he will not clear the guilty unless they suffer themselves to be drawn to him." He was not dogmatic about such matters, but he did not completely rule out either annihilation or a species of conditional immortality.

Beecher was a most unprofessional churchman. "I am not in sympathy with the Church alone but with the whole human family." Here he saw himself following the example of Christ, who may "almost be said to have neglected the external forms which truth must put on" and "left the externalities of religion to take care of themselves." A man may live a Christian life outside the church, just as he may acquire an education outside the schools; all such institutions are mere means and contrivances, and when you make them an end in themselves, you turn them to evil. As the world stands, he admits frankly that the church has done harm as well as good.

> There is scarcely one single perversion of civil government, and there is scarcely one single persecution of men, there is scarcely a single one of the great wars that have depopulated the globe, there is scarcely one great heresy developed out of the tyranny of the church, that has not been the fruit of institutional religion.

He believed in Christian unity, not church union, and the modern ecumenical movement, as it is practiced, would leave him cold. He wanted as much religious variety in a community as possible, and in his view all denominations could contribute to this; he had no desire to put them all through a common mangle and turn their bright colors to a uniform and nondescript gray. As for the sacraments, they were symbols of an inner spiritual condition and of no value save as they ministered to it.

Naturally he believed in religious toleration, but there were certain limitations upon his sympathies. Though he rejected the damnation of the virtuous "heathen," he still inclined to judge all the peoples of the ancient world, even the Greeks, by Jewish standards. (In the famous lecture to young men on "The Strange Woman" he even excoriated modern French standards; one wonders how much he knew about them.) At first he inherited his father's distrust of the Catholic Church, and though he grew away from this as he grew older, he was never able to find anything of value in Cardinal Newman. He opposed spiritualism as likely to "weaken the hold of the Bible upon conscience [and] the affections," and he seems equivocal toward the Mormons even at the very end: "They have a right to their own opinion; they have a right to liberty of speech and conscience; but they have no right to liberty of conduct when it goes against the Law and the Constitution."

Professor McLoughlin's view that there is a noteworthy affinity between Henry Ward's thinking and that of "the 'Father-Mother God' of Christian Science, and its positive thinking approach which sublimates all suffering" [30] seems ill-advised. Though they are philosophical idealists, Christian Scientists are often accused of making religion a mere matter of mending bodily woes. Actually this is an imperceptive judgment. Mark Twain is not usually regarded as an apologist for Christian Science, but he did understand that for its devotees the Spirit of God, which is life and love, "pervades the universe like an atmosphere," and that he who establishes a vital connection with it is made whole throughout his entire being. As "a vicious creation of the gross human mind," disease "cannot continue to exist in the presence of the Immortal Mind, the renewing Spirit of God." Mrs. Eddy did not invent the Motherhood of God; there is warrant for it in both the Old Testament and the New. And Beecher's attitude toward suffering represents a trend in religious thinking which is antithetical to Christian Science.

The reader who runs through the anthology called *Comforting Thoughts* will see at once how often Henry returns to this matter, and I for one have not been greatly comforted. If he does not glorify suffering, he does see it as something consciously and deliberately inflicted upon human beings for purposes of spiritual discipline. "No one has suffered enough until he is patient of suffering." "Not when God is lifting men up, but when He is pressing them down, is He blessing them most." What could be more naïve—or more horrible—than this? "When God comes into the family and takes away one child, instead of complaining because he has taken one, it would be wiser to thank him that he has left the rest"! This, in contrast to other passages in which Henry perceives that it is not God who is responsible for the death of children but the unsanitary conditions in which greedy men have forced them to live! This from a man who recognized elsewhere that "health, and occupation, and association of ideas" must be employed, as well as recourse to "the means of grace," by those who would feel Christ's presence, and, indeed, that they themselves are "means of grace."

If I stress this matter, it is less to clear up confusion or put Henry right on a particular issue than because his very error (if such it be judged) helps clear him from oft-levelled assertions that he preached a soft or easy-going religion. Experimental, do-it-yourself religion is never easy; it requires far more self-discipline than either assent to a system or an ecstatic self-surrender in a moment of overwhelming emotion, followed by the conviction that the religious problem is now solved once and forevermore. Beecher relied heavily upon intuition, and, as McLoughlin says, "he wished to be a Christian transcendentalist." Under the influence of his religious intuitions and experiences, he perceived various aspects of the truth and expressed them, but he thought of his religion in terms of a conscious union between himself and Christ, and he was never so foolish as to believe that this could be achieved without a total, self-abnegating, yet completely fulfilling surrender to God. I am not saying he achieved this; I greatly doubt that anybody has ever quite done that. Certainly Beecher never thought or spoke of himself as one who had attained. But he did speak as one who aspires; he knew the sinfulness of human nature and always took it into consideration; he insisted upon religious and moral obligation even when addressing those whom many have thought of as in need only of Christian comfort. "To preach the Gospel to the poor was to awaken the mind of the poor. It was to teach the poor: 'Take up your cross, and deny yourselves, and follow me.' "

Of course it was not roses all the way for him even as a preacher. When Thoreau and Bronson Alcott visited Plymouth Church together, Thoreau called it pagan but Alcott found it very good, though he thought Beecher as much player as parson.[31] Some found his bluntness of expression coarse, and Bristow speaks of his "sometimes almost homiletic lawlessness, approximating the grotesque." Samuel Bowles found no reverence in him. Of course he did not always satisfy himself. "Abbott," he once said, "the thing I wanted to say, I didn't say, and the thing I didn't want to say, I did say, and I don't know how to preach anyhow." But there were other times when he "felt up to a sovereign height of inspiration," so that it was not himself who was speaking, "when I am caught up and carried away so that I know not whether I am in the body or out of the body, when I think things in the pulpit that I never could think in the study." At such times he could perhaps have understood and accepted George W. Cable's testimony that Beecher had "reshaped" his whole life, "when I had reached years where not many lives are reshaped." The Plymouth pastor achieved that for many, but he could not have done it for one had he not in some measure realized his own ideal of the preacher as "a large nature filled with enthusiasm for God, but even more for man, and caring for men as the chief care of his own life more than for the Church, more than for the law, more than for theology." Before it can become operative in a man's life the truth must exist in him as "a living experience, a glowing enthusiasm, an intense reality." He must "take the great truths of the Lord Jesus Christ's teachings, and the love of God to the human race, and make them a part of his own personal experience, so that when he speaks to men it shall not be he alone that speaks, but God in him."

4

PHILLIPS BROOKS

The Lord Our God Is a Sun

I

Phillips Brooks was Protestant Episcopal Bishop of Massachusetts for only fifteen months, but he had been the unofficial Bishop of Boston before that for many years. When the news of his death came, people greeted each other with lamentations as if a head of state had been taken, and the spirit of mourning which took possession of the city on the day of his funeral was more spontaneous than official. In his engagement book, William Lawrence, who was to be one of Brooks's episcopal successors, wrote "The Light is gone out of life," and the next morning, while conducting a service, he broke down for the first and only time in his career.[1] Today, nearly eighty years later, a "Phillips Brooks Calendar" is still published in Boston every year.

Izaak Walton described John Donne in the pulpit as "preaching to himself like an angel from a cloud." Whatever may have been true of Donne, and whatever Walton may have meant by the expression, Brooks certainly never preached "to himself"; he was too much on fire to bring others to share in the warm, personal relationship with Christ which was the essence of his own life and the most precious thing he knew. But he must often have seemed to his auditors as if he were speaking like an angel from a cloud. The avalanche of words engulfed them in the great church like the music from the great organ itself; intellect, art, and love were blended to produce an echo from a world which many of them had never glimpsed save with him as a guide. But the angel was substantial enough to tip the scales finally at three hundred pounds, and he realized the need of having good solid earth under his feet. Brooks was as great a pastor as a preacher. There was nobody in Boston who wanted to see him that he did not want to see, and he would go to anybody who sent for him, white or black, of the Trinity parish or of no parish, wherever and whenever he might be asked.

Phillips Brooks was born in Boston on December 15, 1835 (just three days before Lyman Abbott came into the world at nearby Roxbury), the son of William Gray Brooks, a hardware merchant, and Mary Ann Phillips, his wife. There were six "Brooks boys," of whom four became clergymen. Phillips Exeter and Phillips Andover were both founded by members of the family. Wendell Phillips was a kinsman, and there were connections with the Everetts, Frothinghams, and Adamses. There were many clergymen on the mother's side of the family, running back to early Puritan days, but it was through his father that Phillips Brooks was related to John Cotton.

The First Church of Boston was the family temple, but the increasing turning of this pulpit toward Unitarianism displeased Mrs. Brooks, and when Phillips was four years old, she took her children with her into the Episcopal church. Her husband, however, was not confirmed until 1847.

Phillips' preparatory school was Boston Latin, and in 1855 he was graduated from Harvard College. His first idea was to be a teacher, but though he received an appointment at Boston Latin, the class of hellions assigned to him there were more than he could cope with; he was the fourth teacher they were permitted to drive from the school. "Old Gardiner" made his contribution to the happy situation by assuring Brooks that he had rarely known anyone who failed as a teacher to succeed at anything else. It does not seem to have occurred to him that he himself had failed as head master.

In 1856 the young man entered the Episcopal Theological Seminary at Alexandria, Virginia, where he was graduated three years later, after which he became rector of the Church of the Advent, in Philadelphia; in 1862 he transferred to Holy Trinity in the same city. On July 21, 1865, he offered the prayer at the same Harvard service in honor of her Civil War heroes at which James Russell Lowell read his "Commemoration Ode." It does not seem good taste to speak of a man as having created a sensation through a prayer, but there is no denying that Brooks's prayer impressed many of his hearers as the event of the exercises; Thomas Wentworth Higginson felt "that I had never heard living prayer before." This was Boston's first opportunity to hear Phillips Brooks in a state of inspiration which later, at Trinity, was to become almost normal with him, and the forces were activated which, in 1869, finally brought him to his Boston parish.

This was the old Trinity, on Summer Street, near Washington. Location-wise and otherwise, it was already inadequate for the needs of the congregation it served, and it must have been vacated soon even if it had not burned in the great Boston Fire of November 1872. The new church in Copley Square, designed by H. H. Richardson, though begun in 1873, was not dedicated until February 1877. It seems odd that during the crucial years of his establishment in Boston, Brooks should have had to deliver his sermons in the secularized surroundings of the Institute of Technology's Huntington Hall on Boylston Street, where the only decorations were pictures of scientists in their laboratories! Though this apparently did not cramp Brooks's style, all must have recognized that the new church, one of the masterpieces of ecclesiastical architecture in America, at last gave him the setting that had always been predestined for him.

Meanwhile, however, a good deal had happened. As early as 1865–66, Brooks made the first of his many long journeys abroad. In 1870 he became an overseer of Harvard College, and in 1877 she gave him an S.T.D. In 1882 he regretfully declined the Plummer Professorship, but in 1886 he accepted an appointment to the Board of University Preachers, which post he held until 1891. In 1871 he delivered at Yale a series of very successful lectures on preaching. In 1879 he gave the Bohlen Lectures on "The Influence of Jesus" before the Philadelphia Divinity School, and in 1885–86 he discussed "Tolerance" before more than one group of theologues.

In 1886 Brooks was elected assistant bishop of Pennsylvania and declined, but when in 1891 he was chosen Bishop of Massachusetts, he felt bound to accept. The overwhelming administrative duties which he then undertook with zeal would have been difficult for a man in his physical prime, and by this time Brooks was not that. The situation was rendered even more difficult by the fact that he found himself preaching as frequently after his consecration as before it. On January 23, 1893, he died of diphtheria, after a brief illness, a little more than a month past his fifty-seventh birthday.

II

Brooks was a giant of a man, about six feet, three and one-half inches tall, who weighed 160 pounds by the time he was sixteen. People used to stop to stare after him in the street, as they did after Edwin Booth, but Booth's was a frail, spirituel kind of beauty, while Brooks overwhelmed with an irresistible, though benevolent, power. "Clad in a voluminous ulster," writes one Harvardian, "with a large, broad-brimmed silk hat back a little on his head, and usually with a big walking-stick under his arm,

Dr. Brooks strode along in Brobdingnagian ease, looking like a walking tower." One admirer speakes of his "somewhat Luther-like face," but surely he was better looking than Luther, despite such habits as often leaving his mouth open or dropping his head upon his breast so that one could not tell whether he was bored or asleep or lost in his own thoughts. Indeed there were those who called him beautiful—"his great wonderful eyes looked down upon one with pathos and power indescribable," writes Edward Abbott—and when he was at his height, his photographs were as much in demand as those of a popular film star at a later period.

Though he had a highly nervous constitution, Brooks's health during most of his life was excellent, and he might well have lasted longer than he did if he had not imposed such strain upon himself as no human constitution could have been expected to withstand. He hated sickness and shied from it, finding no "grace" in it. "It seems to me terrible, the whole idea of suffering, but even more of weakness and weariness." It is remarkable that, feeling thus, he should still have been so skilled as he was in ministering to the sick in his parish.[2] In later years, his knee threatened to give way under the enormous weight it now had to support, and the railroad accident of 1888 from which he so narrowly escaped with his life was a great shock to him. The severest pain he ever experienced had come just before this, when he had to have his thumb lanced for a felon, and he made this worse than necessary first by insanely delaying to call a doctor until it was almost too late and then by refusing chloroform and instead puffing a cigar through the operation.

In college Brooks paid no attention to sports and exercises; neither did he do much walking; his classmates considered him physically lazy. His health was the gift of God, and he seems to have done little to build it up or conserve it. It would not be accurate, however, to say that he never took any exercise; sometimes he even turned to the gymnasium as an emergency measure. We hear from time to time of fishing, bathing, boating, horseback riding, billiards, and bowling, but he would not shoot, for he did not wish to kill even an insect. Like D. L. Moody, he enjoyed driving fast horses, but this is hardly exercise. Oddly enough, he was fond of mountain climbing, which he pursued to and beyond the point of danger, both at home and abroad, which must have been a considerable strain for a man of his bulk. As we have seen, he was devoted to travel, but evidently this meant strain also, for he always lost weight under it. He was not indifferent to the pleasures of the table, and in 1886 he described a "beautiful luncheon" he had had in Victoria—"rice, salmon, lamb chops, baked beans, and cherry-pie." Though not a teetotaler, he drank little; in Germany he got a bottle of good Rhine wine for a quarter but he would rather have given a dollar for a pitcher of ice water.[3] Coffee was another matter, and in the early days at least his idea of a good cup was one that had been poured into a vessel filled with lump sugar! Yet the only beverage about which he was passionate seems to have been lemonade, and he drank it on his deathbed. As to his pipe- and cigar-smoking, it may be, as has been suggested, that his frequent references to it suggest that he was a heavier smoker than he actually was, but the habit cannot have been helpful to his physical well-being in any case.

Though Brooks was not unresponsive to the beauties of nature, he was never seduced by the popular nineteenth-century tendency to permit nature worship to take the place of religion.[4] "The Bible shows how the world progresses. It begins with a garden, but ends with a holy city." It was not the holy city he saw when he looked out the window from Boston's Hotel Brunswick, yet he once declared that he preferred this to anything the country had to show. His college essay on "September" characteristically passes over all the charms of the season to concentrate on the persons who were born or who died in that month. Probably it is not his love of nature which speaks in his attribution of blame to one who unnecessarily pulls a leaf from a tree but rather his gentleness, his horror of destruction, and his respect for all living things. The same point of view appears in his attitude toward vivisection. He was not an extremist, but he thought much of the suffering inflicted upon animals for experimental purposes both useless and unnecessary.

Brooks was always careful not to overestimate the value of aesthetic sensibility; perhaps he was influenced here by the fact that he could not find it in Christ. "Nature is as much more beautiful as she is more free than art." Yet he himself possessed this sensibility in a high degree. He passionately loved color (especially red) and shared Henry Ward Beecher's feeling for gems. He rejected "the carving on house-fronts which is meant merely to look pretty, and so fails of even that," but he almost literally covered his walls with pictures, and he also wanted his friends' portraits around him. In ecclesiastical architecture, he definitely preferred the tower to the spire and the rounded to the pointed arch, and he contended successfully for these Romanesque features both at Holy Trinity in Philadelphia and at Trinity in Boston.[5] He sacrificed the symbol of

> aspiration towards ideal ends, the predominant mood of the American people, more particularly in New England, where Puritanism has prevailed. . . . But the tower without the spire is in itself complete as a religious symbol, bespeaking the sense of protection in God, the need of God as a defence and shield; as in the words of Luther's hymn, "A strong tower is our God."

This seemed to him to express a more fundamentally modern conception of religion, involving "the consecration of the world that now is, the recognition of the sacredness of earth and of the secular life," to secure which he was willing to tone down "the ideas of solemnity and devotion,—spire and arches mounting upwards to express the soul of religious aspiration pointing forever away from earth to heaven."[6] He says little of significance about sculpture, rejecting the Venus de Medici as "too little, physically, morally, and mentally." He seems to have seen most of the great paintings on exhibition during his time in American and European museums, and he commented upon them intelligently, though untechnically: the Rembrandts, "which get, more than any others, the total conception of the man they portray"; the Vandykes, "so full of refinement, gentlemen and ladies always, appealing to the part of us which always feels the power of good taste"; Titian, who had "the sumptuousness of Venice," yet was able "to portray the sensitive and delicate and shy." But it was the Sistine Madonna at Dresden which stood "to all pictures . . . what the Bible is to all books." [7]

With music Brooks had a kind of professional relationship in his church work, and he seems to have done a reasonable amount of concert-going for a man as busy as he was. He liked to sing, but he was not always on key, and we are told that though he admitted he knew nothing about music, he did not like this to be taken literally. He wanted tunes in church that people could sing, and he was fond of "Holy, Holy, Holy" and "Jerusalem the Golden." As a Harvard student he took part in Hasty Pudding theatricals, and once, when he and Fanny Kemble were living in the same boarding house in Philadelphia, they took their meals together. In Europe he met Charlotte Cushman, whom he considered a "lady of genius." But though he admired Edwin Booth and was much impressed by Greek tragedy, he was as shy of the theater in general as his Puritan ancestors had been and advised people not to attend it because of its "dreadful indiscriminateness." He was not wholly consistent about this, however, especially when he was in Europe, where the German theater in particular impressed him by both its aesthetic excellence and its respectability. And he seems to have visited the Eden Musée in New York, including the Chamber of Horrors, without batting an eye.

Majoring as he did in college in English literature and the

classics, Brooks read enormously, both in literature and, a little later, in the theological field.[8] Though he was never obscurantist in his attitude towards it, science meant little to him. He once conversed in Latin for two hours with a Spanish priest. He also gave considerable attention to the modern languages, and he was trying to improve his German as late as 1882. One would think that he must have read less in later years when there were a dozen demands upon his time for every hour in the day, yet he was a member of the Examining Committee of the Boston Public Library. When travelling he read incessantly, and we are told that when he finished a book, he threw it out the window, which seems an even more eccentric habit than Theodore Roosevelt's tearing the pages out of the magazines he read on the train and dropping them on the floor. Brooks seems never to have outgrown a romantic respect for authors rare in a person of his sophistication; as he once wrote S. Weir Mitchell:

> I have not had enough to do with great people to have ceased to feel a thrill at an author's gift of his own book. An author, the man who can wave his wand and summon all these people and make them behave themselves like folks for four hundred pages, is a mystery and a marvel to me.

Brooks himself wrote a good deal of poetry, his special devotion being to the sonnet, and though the general reader now knows him only as the author of "O Little Town of Bethlehem," much of his work was creditable.[9]

His tastes in literature and his convictions concerning it were moderately conservative. Though he was not pig-headed about the classics, he saw in "the large and simple types of human life and character" presented in them a light which he compared to "the calm moon" shining "upon the vexed and broken waters of the seas," and he did not want "the old classical culture" dropped "till some substitute far more satisfactory than has yet appeared is found to take its place." He had a great feeling for the seventeenth century, which he thought of as the beginning of the modern period, but this apparently was about as far back in English history as his imagination could reach, for he tells us that "the men and women of Tudor times are different and distant from us. They are as little modern in their character as in their dress and houses." Yet he refers to and quotes from Shakespeare with reasonable frequency.

Like everybody else in his time, he loved the "brave, healthy, life-loving Sir Walter." Among the Romantic poets, I should say Coleridge touched him more deeply than any of the others, though he says of Shelley that he "tried so hard to be heathen and would still be Christian in his own despite." Browning he admired in his work and quite as much, though differently, in person—"a clear-headed and particularly clear-eyed man of the world, devoted to society, one of the greatest diners-out in London, cordial and hearty as a dear old uncle"—and Tennyson, whom he knew better, was even dearer to him. He praises Thackeray and George Eliot, but though he sometimes quotes Dickens, he greatly disliked the first volume of Forster's *Life* and thought its hero "a disagreeable person." He had no use for the "foolish realism" that was coming into vogue during his later years—"wherever the background is lost, the foreground grows false and thin"—and he did not care much more for "the vagueness of the whole impressionist school of fiction and of poetry, which tries to do with a few broad sweeps of the brush what it despairs of working out in clear, minute, intelligent detail." [10]

Brooks's passionate interest in biography,[11] dating from his college days, shows his intense absorption in the study and problems of human character. As Charles W. Eliot once pointed out, "any spark of genius in man or boy delighted him so much that he would believe no evil of its possessor, unless the evidence was overwhelming." [12] To him human beings were more interesting than art and art itself of interest primarily as it reflected and illuminated them. Consequently he believed that if the necessary material could be made available, the life of any human being, "simply and sympathetically put in words," would interest his fellow men, and once at least he expressed a Whitmanesque kind of hunger for union with his kind.[13] He had many friends who loved him, and it does not seem that many men can have enjoyed (or been pestered by) more intensive and extensive contacts with the greatest and the least of their time than he. Within two months of coming to Holy Trinity in Philadelphia, he made six hundred new acquaintances.

Yet Brooks was far from being completely at home in social relations. He came of a large, close-knit family—"one of the happiest homes the world can show"—whose members were devoted to each other but not much given to society and totally indifferent to it in a formal sense. His social manners were varied. "It was a dull rainy day, when things looked dark and lowering," wrote one observer, "but Phillips Brooks came down through Newspaper Row and all was bright." Yet Edward Abbott found that "he loomed up as we passed him on the street, overhung us, swept by us like a visitor from another sphere. He was not a man of numerous personal sympathies but had rather a generic sympathy with man." Church committees and conferences and conventions he frankly and unashamedly loathed. We are told that there were times when he sat through a whole dinner without saying a word, and that though he had a way of passing with ease into the secret places of your life, he could never admit you into his. Children he loved to such an extent that he was known to sit down on the nursery floor to play with them when he should have been eating dinner downstairs, yet he admits that he was afraid of even the boys in his confirmation class.[14]

When it came to pastoral work, however, Brooks's humanity and heavenly charity were never doubted. "The priest should be, above all things, a man with an intense and live humanity," he said, and there was nobody whose practice accorded better with his preaching. He would not have Divinity itself infringe upon human rights. "The needs of human nature are supreme, and have a right to the divinest help. The little tasks need divinest impulses. The secular woes are only relieved by God." He always answered his letters in longhand, in his notably clear, elegant, and handsome handwriting.[15] Office hours he would not set, believing that people came to see him when their need was greatest; "God save the day," he said, "when they won't come to me." When Leighton Parks stayed with him on Clarendon Street, the rectory bell rang an average of once every five minutes all day long. Calling on a mother with a sick baby, Brooks sent her out for a break while he tended the child. One man, totally unknown to him, facing a dangerous operation, wished to spend the evening before in his company, and Brooks took his right to do this quite as a matter of course. Once he arrived for an important evening appointment at eleven o'clock because he had been sent for by a Negro who had been injured in a street affray; when he was asked why he had not sent his assistant, he replied simply that the man had sent for *him*. When he became one of the Harvard preachers, the Harvard boys became de facto members of his own parish, and when one of them needed to be straightened out on a religious problem, he was quite willing to spend a whole afternoon at it.

Brooks's attitude toward women and marriage is something of a puzzle. About the only certain thing is that he did not plan to lead a celibate life. From seminary days on he looked forward to marriage and parenthood, and when he was in his early twenties, he listed his requirements: the girl must be small and beautiful and (as a kind of afterthought) good, and she must not know too much! As late as 1867 he thought he was growing more rather than less susceptible and "shouldn't wonder if it came to matrimony pretty soon." He congratulated his married friends—"life is a poor imperfect thing unless a man is married"

—and looked forward to sharing their happiness, and as time went on, he felt his singleness more and more. "Life is pretty lonely, after all," and if anybody knew it, he thought he did. He told Bishop McVickar that it was the mistake of his life not to have married. "The trouble with you married men," he once said, "is that you think no one has been in love but yourselves; I know what love is; I have been in love myself."

Brooks was very much a man's man, and some have thought him indifferent to women. He would not have a surpliced female choir at Trinity, thinking the church already quite young-ladylike enough; when he visited Chicago, he reported liking the men he came in contact with but not the women. There were even those who thought Brooks greatest as a preacher to men, especially young men. It is no doubt true that, in a day when the church was becoming more and more feminized, Brooks felt it important to present the challenge of the Gospel to men. As a pastor, however, he was quite as diligent, skilful, and sympathetic in his ministry to women and girls. He thought the religious impulse itself more essentially feminine than masculine, and he believed women more likely to be unified beings than men. When, in the eighties, he served as vice-president for the Woman Suffrage Festival and Bazaar, he drew a stern rebuke from that arch anti-feminist, Francis Parkman, and at least one observer thought him more communicative with women and more dependent upon their friendship. In the course of his life, he seems to have been specifically interested in a number of women—Jenny Fairfax in seminary days in Virginia, a girl named MacBurney in Philadelphia, and, most of all, Sara Gemma Timmins in the eighties. She, at least, he might have married if she had lived.[16]

It may be that too much of a mystery has been made of this matter. Perhaps the right girl just did not happen to come along at the right time; if she had, there could have been a wedding, and then all these speculations would be beside the point. Yet there are considerations on the other side. Brooks was more interested than most men are in achieving a unified life, and this, for him, involved the reconciliation of everything that is human with everything that is divine. I am not saying that he consciously agreed (in prospect) with Bernard Shaw that "you cannot devote your life to two divinities—God and the person you are married to," yet one must feel that he may have been "better accommodated than with a wife" in a sense far different from the Falstaffian. His preaching, his pastoral work, and finally his administrative duties absorbed him and wore him out before his time to such an extent that even the reading upon which the health of his soul so largely depended was crowded into odd moments and corners of time. One cannot but wonder what he might have done with a wife or she with him.

III

Brooks was the rhapsodic type of preacher. The theme of his sermons was "life," "full," "rich" life; they were crammed with passion and thought together, and the words "abundant" and "abundance" occur in them again and again. He was not dramatic, certainly not anecdotal, and though he referred to Shakespeare with reasonable frequency, and quoted occasionally from standard English poetry, he was, on the whole, sparing in his literary references and quotations. He talked at the rate of 190 to 214 words per minute, sometimes making an effort to slow down his pace but never succeeding for long.

> He often began his morning prayer in Appleton Chapel [writes President Eliot], with some familiar collect of his Church, which he recited rapidly and monotonously; then, with a characteristic backward

movement of the head and shoulders, he would burst into extemporaneous prayer like a strong stream which has broken through a barrier.

The Scottish preacher Alexander Bruce of Glasgow compared Brooks to "a great water main attached to the everlasting reservoir of God's grace and truth."

Sometimes it was difficult to hear him at the beginning of a sermon, but his enunciation was clear, and he gained power as he proceeded, making few gestures[17] except when he stumbled over a word or got himself tangled up in a sentence, when he would toss his head impatiently, dropping his pince-nez to the end of their long cord and being obliged to retrieve them before he could continue his reading. His voice was breathy and not unusually beautiful in itself, and there were those who said he spoke in a monotone. It seems clear that he never learned how to use his voice properly and occasionally it failed him. He impressed partly by overwhelming his auditory, and it would seem that there was a certain strain involved in listening to him. It seems clear that the preacher himself experienced considerable strain also. When he was young, "his face grew pale and his whole countenance straitened with a look of agony in the moment before he turned to mount the pulpit." It seems odd that at this period many thought Brooks personally impassive, like a medium through whom a revelation is "given"; when he was older the emotional force of his sermons was greatly reinforced by the fact that the preacher's own being seemed shaken and overwhelmed by it.

Brooks was a phenomenally "successful" preacher from the beginning, and "calls" from churches and colleges alike—one from as far away as San Francisco—came raining in upon him before he had fairly got settled in his first parish, yet he complains that "I myself never get any idea whether I hit them or not." He often thought himself superficial, and even as late as the eighties, he would have liked to "go to Leipsic and stay there till I knew something, so that no scholar in the world could puzzle me." Yet he needed a good audience "for inspiration"; when it was too small, he saw the individuals in it and this threw him out. He wanted, and thought he needed, and sometimes ordered built, a reading desk of a certain height; in Harvard's Appleton Chapel he once broke off the brass desk in the large pulpit by leaning on it too hard. Yet when he tried to reach the unchurched at Faneuil Hall, he stood in the middle of the platform and performed convincingly without notes or pulpit of any kind.

By this time, however, he was speaking more and more extemporaneously, which was an increasing necessity for a man who gave two Sunday sermons, a Wednesday night lecture,[18] and a Saturday night Bible class in his own church, and who, for many years, averaged two sermons a day from autumn until spring. In the early days everything was written out in longhand on exactly thirty pages, each eight inches by six and three-quarters. Ideally the preparation of a sermon was spread out over the better part of a week;[19] later, of course, this would have been impossible. This does not mean that the extemporaneous sermon was not prepared, but its preparation consumed less time, and as he grew older, the extemporaneous method of delivery seemed more congenial to his temperament. Apparently, then, he became more of a speaker than he had been earlier and less of a writer. He never at any period ruled "inspiration" out of his sermons, but in the early days he sometimes thought he was more inspired when writing the sermon than when he was delivering it.[20]

Many persons, distinguished and otherwise, have attempted to describe the manner and the effect of Brooks's sermons; among them all, none is better worth hearing than George A. Gordon, the pastor of Old South Church, across Copley Square from Trinity, himself often called, in his prime, the greatest preacher in America. Says Gordon:

> I can see him now, in an afternoon service in the sombre light of Trinity Church, in his black robe, and while his figure retained all its colossal proportions, standing out against the dusk of the coming evening, with his glowing face increasing to radiance as the light faded, and his inspired presence swaying under the inward power; and I can imagine something of the strange being that Jacob met in the gathering darkness so long ago, in whom the life and strength of God were manifested, and who threw his arms about the troubled man in that divine night-wrestle.[21]

I have quoted this statement for an ulterior purpose; from it we can learn that Brooks's personality was an important element in his success. In fact, Gordon describes him in terms which would hardly need to be modified to apply to a great actor in the climactic moment of one of his great interpretations. In itself Brooks would not have objected to this. To his way of thinking, it would not have been at all desirable that the Gospel should have been "written on the sky, or committed merely to an almost impersonal book." "All truth must be brought, in order to be effective, through a personal medium," and it was the essence of the Christian religion that it should have called for faith not in a series of theological propositions but in Christ. Therefore Brooks attacked such otherwise useful books as Francis Ellingwood Abbott's *Scientific Theism* and *The Idea of God* by John Fiske for leaving out this aspect. "All the great teachers of religion who have done the most Christlike work have always been those whose personality has been the most complete, and who have been in truest human relationship to the souls they taught."

From another point of view, however, Brooks was not at all a personal preacher. His sermons were rich in content far beyond that of most preachers, and he concentrated upon his theme absolutely. "The listeners never thought of style or manner," says James Bryce, "but only of the substance of the thoughts," and one clerical admirer pronounced him "nearly as impersonal as Shakespeare." It is interesting to remember that neither his name nor the subjects of his sermons ever appeared on the sign-board before Trinity Church while he was in charge there, but only "Services at 10:30 and 4." In a deeper sense, to be sure, Brooks *did* reveal his personality in his sermons, and it would hardly be an exaggeration to say that he revealed it nowhere else. He says:

> I have known shy, reserved men, who, standing in their pulpits, have drawn back before a thousand eyes veils that were sacredly closed when only one's friends could see. You might talk with them a hundred times, and you would not learn so much of what they were as if you once heard them preach.

Assuredly he was one of these men.

IV

Phillips Brooks was not greatly interested in the formulation of theological belief for its own sake. He saw the Athanasian Creed as "the very spirit of a settled, unprogressive, and exclusive theology" and sympathized with the criticism Duns Scotus made of Aquinas. Once he complained that it was too close to Christmas to "feel theological," since Christmas "upsets theology entirely." But this does not in the least mean that he did not hold definite beliefs or know why he held them, or that they were not important to him. "Preach doctrine," he cries, "preach all the doctrine that you know, and learn forever more and more; but preach it always not that men may believe it, but that men may be saved by believing it."

He shows the influence of many philosophers and theologians, though he was no slavish follower of any of them. Says A. V. G. Allen:

He was an idealist with Plato. With Kant he lived in the human consciousness. He felt the force of the transcendental philosophy. There are hints of the Berkeleian principle, as well as reminders of Hegel's ruling idea. Yet on the other hand he retained his youthful devotion to Bacon in the idealization of the world of outward nature, while in Lotze he found a healthful check for the extravagance or one-sidedness of a transcendental idealism,—the purely intellectual estimate of things.

Hooker and Butler had some influence upon him, and, in some aspects, even Schopenhauer. He was touched by Horace Bushnell, by Schleiermacher, and, among his English contemporaries, by Robertson, Stanley, and Maurice.

His basic conviction was that "man is the child of God by nature although ignorant and rebellious." God manifests, and has always manifested, Himself to every man and to every nation, up to the utmost limits that can be grasped, but His supreme revelation of Himself was made through Jesus Christ. Through Christ men learned how to free themselves from sin and identify their wills with that of God. Faith does not mean believing something *about* Christ but trusting Him and trying to obey Him, and "the eternal part of us is not that which God shall choose at some future day to endow with everlasting life" but that which has within itself "the essence of its immortality." The church is the body of those who have been saved and are themselves laboring to save the world. As for the Bible, it is "not properly a Revelation," for revelation can only be achieved through a person, but "the History of a Revelation." "The Bible is a temporary expedient; the oneness of the soul with God is an essential and eternal necessity." And though Brooks was, even for his time, conservative in some things—he seems to have assumed the Davidic authorship of the entire Psalter—he was not greatly impressed by Messianic prophecy in the Old Testament. "There is an evidence of Christianity there; but it is not the great evidence. The human soul learns to believe in Jesus because of the way in which His presence comes to the immediate needs of the human soul."

And what and who is Jesus Christ? In reverence and humility let us give our answer. He is the meeting of the Divine and Human,—the presence of God in humanity, the perfection of humanity in God; the divine made human, the human shown to be capable of union with the divine; the utterance, therefore, of the nearness and the love of God, and of the possibility of man. Once in the ages came the wondrous life, once in the stretch of history the face of Jesus shone in Palestine, and His feet left their blessed impress upon earth; but what that made manifest had been forever true. Its truth was timeless, the truth of all eternity. The love of God, the possibility of man, —these two which made the Christhood,—these two, not two but one, had been the element in which all life was lived, all knowledge known, all growth attained. Oh, how little men have made it, and how great it is! Around all life which ever has been lived there has been poured forever the life of the loving deity and the ideal humanity. All partial excellence, all learning, all brotherhood, all hope, has been bosomed on this changeless, this unchanging Being which has stretched from the forgotten beginning to the unguessed end. It is because God has been always, and been always good, and because man has been always the son of God, capable in the very substance of his nature of likeness to and union with his Father,—it is because of this that nobleness has never died, that truth has been sought and found, that struggle and hope have always sprung anew, and that the life of man has always reached to larger and larger things.

Brooks himself once said, during his later years, that he had but one sermon, and Allen defines it as an exposition of "the sacredness, the beauty, the glory of life, and that because all men were children of God, and Christ was the eternal Son." His adherence to the Evangelical party in the Episcopal Church nowhere shows more clearly than in the stress he placed upon conversion, which was sufficient to cause some to think he behaved more like an old Puritan parson than an Episcopal priest, while others fancied they found him resembling D. L. Moody. Says one observer:

> The attitude of Phillips Brooks was calculated to deter all who had not gone through a real "religious experience" in the Evangelical sense of the expression, no matter how innocent, how manly, womanly, sound, affectionate, true-hearted boys and girls they might be, no matter how unreservedly they were willing to make their vows "to renounce the devil and all his works". . . .

He expressed his own understanding of the change that occurs in the convert's life in one of his memoranda: "His [the convert's] heart is like that stable at Bethlehem, eighteen hundred Christmases ago, one day a place for beasts to dwell in, the next changed to a holy place forever, by the new hope and salvation that has found its birthplace there." But if Brooks was right about all this, then it is clear that he spent much of his life in a parlous state, for he apparently gave no thought to conversion until after he had entered the theological seminary, and he was not confirmed until July 12, 1857, a little less than three years before his ordination. "God," he said, "is first to the world, and to some extent to every man, a Working Hypothesis." He made no commitment to the ministry upon entering the seminary; he was willing to give it a trial and that was all.

He thought there were enough sins in the world without men taking pains to make sins, as they have often done, out of perfectly innocent acts.

> The Church so easily forgets her ends in her means. We are too apt to speak in church to artificial sins which the great universal Christian conscience does not recognize, to rebuke the improprieties that are not wrong, and to denounce the honest errors which good men may hold, and yet be good, as if they were the first enemies with which we and our Gospel had to fight.

With this he had as little patience as with outworn creeds, "doctrinal statements, which once were true and did vast good and yet were only temporary aspects of the truth." God wanted us to be men and women, not misty angels; our bodies were temples of the Spirit, and Christ, living a human life, had sanctified all that belonged to them. It is true that Brooks believed, or sometimes professed to believe, in a personal devil, on the somewhat pragmatic ground that this belief personalized the fight against evil and thus strengthened man's hand,[22] but his Second Advent was purely spiritual, not a "fantastic idea of a new incarnation and of a visible Christ in Palestine" but simply "a power of Christ over the destinies and institutions and hearts of men more real and spiritual than any that any age has seen yet." As to future probation, "every period of existence is probationary with reference to the times which follow it," but it ends not in "a fixed decree, but in a more strongly assured character." On the other hand, Brooks had no use for the kind of modernism that seemed to have been designed merely to make religion easy; neither did he go along with those who seemed determined to believe as little as they possibly could believe and still call themselves Christians.

We ought to be afraid of any theology which tampers with the sacredness of duty and the awfulness of life. I would far rather be a believer in the most material notions of eternal penalty, and get out of that belief the hard and frightened solemnity and scrupulousness which it has to give, than to hold all the sweet broad truth to which God is now leading us, and have it make life seem a playtime and the world a game.

V

Modern readers have been most inclined to criticize Brooks for his alleged weakness in preaching the Social Gospel. In Philadelphia he alarmed his father by crusading in the pulpit for the causes in which he believed; after coming to Boston, he did not conceal his views, but his sermons were devoted to "spiritual" things. He parted from the Socialists when he refused to believe that a man might be redeemed by redeeming his environment. He did become a member of the Society of Friends of Russian Freedom, however, and when he was asked to give an address to "workingmen," he gladly agreed but stipulated that this label must not be used. "Workingmen" were men, human beings; he would not set them apart as a separate race or seem to obscure the fact that whatever was valid for them also held good for humanity at large. After the Civil War, Brooks helped organize the violently Republican Union League Club, and though he refused to vote for Blaine, he did not join the Mugwumps in voting for Cleveland. He criticized the church for going to rich men's doors, cap in hand, and flattering them because she wanted their money, but his discussion of such passages as "Sell all thou hast," [23] sensible as they are, could not be expected to please an egalitarian.

As a Social Gospeller, Brooks probably did best by the Negroes. He was committed to their cause from his seminary days in Virginia, and when the war was over, he wanted to give them both the ballot and the education they needed to use it intelligently. As a matter of fact, he was committed to what is now called desegregation while the war was still on.

> If the negro is a man, and we have freed him in virtue of his manhood, what consistency or honor is it which still objects to his riding down the street in the same car with us if he is tired, or sitting in the same pew if he wants to worship God?

"To many," he adds, such things "might seem like radicalism, but Christianity is the radicalism of the world."

In Civil War times, interest in the Negro was not calculated to awaken a Northerner's conscience to the sinfulness of war itself, nor did it have this effect with Brooks. He became a patriotic orator even when writing to his brothers, addressing them as Queen Victoria said Gladstone always addressed her—like a public meeting:

> The war is inevitable, and let it come. I repeat it, sir, let it come. It is in vain, sir, to extenuate the matter. Gentlemen may cry, Peace! Peace! but there is no Peace! the war is actually begun . . . The excitement is intense. Several young men of my congregation have enlisted and are going on high religious motives. Who dare say that it isn't his duty to go when the duty is so urgent and the cause so sacred?

And again, "What of the war? Isn't it grand?" He considered entering the service himself, either as a chaplain or in the ranks, and for a brief time he was in the service of the Sanitary Commission.

Aside from his disgust over finding war glorified in Robertson's printed sermons, I find nothing to indicate that he really changed his mind about it in later years. He always places great soldiers along with other great men as exemplars of the best in mankind.[24] He liked the Germans and sympathized with them in 1870 but was antagonized by the military spirit which they seemed to develop. In the early days, he was very critical of England; later he became much more sympathetic. Like many in his time, he thought it was America that must carry the torch of progress. In 1889, however, Japan was "the prettiest and brightest" of all "bright, merry, pretty places," and he doubted that there could be "a grim spot in all the islands." Once he gave a series of weekly lectures on the "Four Services of Membership," comparing baptism to "The Enrollment," catechism to "The Instruction," confirmation to "The Marching Orders," and communion to "The Life in the Field."

For a churchman, Brooks was amazingly cognizant of the faults and dangers of organized religion:

If a Church in any way hinders the free play of human thoughtfulness upon religious things by clothing with mysterious reverence, and so shutting out from the region of thought and study, acts and truths which can be thoroughly used only as they are growingly understood, by limiting within hard and minute and invariable doctrinal statements the variety of the relations of the human experience to God,—if in any such way a church hinders at all the free inflow of every new light which God is waiting to give to the souls of men as fast as they are ready to receive it, just so far she binds and wrongs her children's intelligence and weakens her own vitality. This is the suicide of Dogmatism.

Or if a Church lets any technical command of hers stand across the path, that a command of God cannot get free access to the will of any of the least of all God's people—a system of ecclesiastical morality, different from the eternal morality which lies above the Church, between the soul and God, a morality which hides some eternal duties and winks at some eternal sins,—just so far the Church wrongs her children's conscience and weakens her own vitality. This is the suicide of Corruption.

Or yet again, if the symbols of the Church, which ought to convey God's love to man, become so hard that the love does not find its way through them and they stand as splendid screens between the Soul and Love, or have such a positive character of their own, so far forget their simple duty of pure transparency and mere transmission, that they send the Love down to the soul colored with themselves, formalized and artificial; if the Church dares either to limit into certain channels or to bind to certain forms of expression that love of God which is as spiritual and as free as God, then yet again she is false to her duty, she binds and wrongs her children's loving hearts, and once again weakens her own vitality. This is the suicide of Formalism.

There was no reasonable foundation for the widespread contemporary suspicion that Brooks was Unitarian in his theology, but he was a kind of one-man ecumenical movement. He was "Mr. Brooks," who refused to wear clerical garb even after he had become a bishop, preached at Moody's tabernacle, shared in union services at Old South, and took part in Lyman Abbott's installation at Plymouth Church. After some hesitation, he came out for the abolition of compulsory chapel at Harvard (Emerson had wished to retain it), and the change would probably not have come when it did without him.

Brooks rejected the Apostolical Succession and practiced open communion. "The accident of formal ordination is a trifle." When he baptized a dying child, the act had nothing to do with saving a soul. "The child dying unbaptized goes to the same loving care and education which awaits the child baptized. But the baptism is the solemn, grateful, tender recognition, during the brief moments of that infant's life on earth, of the deep meanings of his humanity." In the eighties, when the exclusivists proposed calling the Episcopal Church "The Catholic Church" or "The American Church," he was ready to withdraw if necessary rather than be party to such an enormity.

Though he was far from seeing the religion of the future in syncretistic terms, Brooks carefully studied non-Christian religions, longing to see Christianity come to India "not merely for what it will do for India but for what India will do for it. Here it must find again the lost oriental side of its brain and heart, and be no longer the occidental European religion it has so strangely become."

"As a principle of action or a standard of belief," Brooks thought orthodoxy "obsolete and dead"; its very principle had been disowned. Orthodoxy was "an attempt to carry truth over life on a safe bridge," being "the treatment of the imperfect as if it were perfect," and standing to the church much like prejudice to the single mind. No longer could truth be regarded as "a deposit, fixed and limited"; it was rather

> an infinite domain wherein the soul is bidden to range with insatiable desire, guarded only by the care of God above it and the spirit of God within it, educated by its mistakes, and attaining larger knowledge . . . as it attains complete purity of purpose and thoroughness of devotion and energy and hope.

"Personal judgment," in other words, was "on the throne," and, except for those who still held to "the authority of the infallible Church, the ecclesiastical conception of the sin of heresy" was no longer possible.

Heresy itself remained, but only in terms of "personal and wilful obstinacy," as the New Testament conceives it. God can punish only wickedness. Error is not guilt and therefore cannot be justly punished. "The guilt of error is the fallacy and fiction which has haunted good men's minds," and until this fallacy has faded away, the danger of persecution is always present.[25]

VI

There is one other aspect of Phillips Brooks's (in the larger sense) religious life that calls for consideration in conclusion. And this consideration must proceed in a curiously indirect way.

Brooks once spoke of the contrast between the seriousness and profundity of Browning's poetry and his light, bantering social manner. He might have cited himself in the same connection. As a social being he was gay and unclerical in the extreme, so that his friends speak of his mirth, gayety, hilarity, buoyancy, and exuberance, and of his incessant joking, chaffering, and bantering. Moreover, he could pass from the clerical to the social being in the twinkling of an eye and with such apparent ease that many found themselves wondering which was the real man. "So deep was the inward contradiction in the man," says Allen suggestively, "that there are moments when it might seem as if the two sides of his being were not thoroughly fused together."

Except in this playful, friendly, but superficial manner, Brooks did not make conversation easily; meeting him socially, it was difficult to get him to talk seriously about anything, and quite impossible to persuade him to talk about himself. "None of us," wrote George A. Gordon, "has a right to say that he was intimate with Phillips Brooks." Like Longfellow, he never discussed his personal concerns with others; unlike him, he even kept them out of his private memoranda. Even within the family circle, this reserve set up barriers. "Somehow I have never been quite frank with you," he wrote his brother William in 1858; "as much with you as anybody, but not thoroughly with any one, I think."

Part of this, beyond question, was sensitiveness, modesty, native New England reserve; part of it too was a certain moodiness. If Brooks could be hilarious, he could also suffer from depression: "it *shall* be a happy new year" sounds a little like Stevenson on the "duty" of being happy. Brooks was so sensitive to weather that he had to give up writing a sermon because he was depressed by the rain. There was a conflict in him too between his desire for a quiet, scholarly life and his need for the crowded and multitudinous contacts which such a life could not have provided. His natural inclination was always to agree with those who conversed with him rather than to disagree, yet we are told that "it was easy to rouse him to tremendous explosions of wrath," and Bishop Lawrence says, "No meddler ever meddled with him twice." Certainly he had a quick, nervous temper, and if he was not often involved in controversies, the reason is not that he had no gifts along this line but rather that he recognized his aptness and took care to keep himself in hand.

There are, however, other, more basic considerations involved. Most devout Evangelicals in Brooks's time presented Christianity in somewhat negativistic terms. This Brooks could not accept, and his own commitment to the religious life was delayed in consequence.

> The conventional denunciation of the intellect as a dangerous guide [says Allen], and of wealth as a thing to be avoided, the condemnation of the natural joy in life and its innocent amusements, the schism between religion and life,—against all this he inwardly protested.[26]

He believed in the centrality of Christ to all human concerns and activities—this was the theme of his very first sermon, "The Simplicity That Is in Christ"—and he wanted all other interests subsumed in this. As he himself puts it, "We may not always be consciously thinking of God, only we must think of all things through and in Him, as we do not always look at the sun and yet see all things we know only by the sun's shining."

Subsumed, not suppressed. "You do not make life simple by making it meagre." In the world of the spirit, the divine has no more right to suppress the human than the human to turn away from the divine. God's work must not return upon itself. The Christian brings *himself* into God's Kingdom, with all his gifts and powers consecrated to God, but with the integrity of his personality recognized, and no obligation resting upon him to squeeze himself into a standard pattern which another had predetermined. Being converted was not bathing in Lethe. "Never let your Christian life disown its past." He saw the Christian graces as "the natural virtues held up into the light of Christ." He who would lead others to Christ must have "the broadest mental outline, and the deepest moral truth, and the purest spiritual faith." If Brooks seems to overstress the mind, it is only because this aspect had so often been neglected by others. If we love God with heart and strength but not mind, the resulting affection is "a crippled thing." The Christian must recognize "how Christian truth is bound up with all the truth of which the world is full." Brooks believed with Paul that the wise man must become a fool in Christ, but in the last analysis his reason for becoming a fool must be to become wise.

There is nothing whatever to be said against this ideal except what must be said of all ideals—that they are never completely achieved. Gamaliel Bradford once tried to do a psychograph of Brooks but gave it up because he said he could not get hold of him. Once he had got past the preacher, there did not seem to be any man there. I would not put it that way, but I know what Bradford meant. He meant what Mary Garden meant when, in her autobiography, she told us that her creativity expressed itself so completely in her operatic characterizations that her private life was empty. At the same time it is a bit disconcerting to find one of the greatest of preachers living for his next vacation. "Only three Sundays more, and then I shall be out of the harness." "Have only two sermons more to write, and you will see me." In 1886 he writes that what he is "most longing for and looking forward to in life" is retiring to North Andover in a few years.

He never did this, nor would he have done it had he lived longer until the time came when he had to do it, and then he would not have been contented. I believe Phillips Brooks to have been completely sincere both as a preacher and as a man. But he could never have stood the strain of living twenty-four hours a day on the pulpit level; Christ did not advise his disciples to build tabernacles on the Mount of Transfiguration. Brooks stayed there longer than most preachers do, and if some preachers do not feel the strain of breathing the rarefied air so strongly as he did, perhaps we ought also to remember that the Mount of Transfiguration is not the only place where a pulpit may be erected.

5

D. L. MOODY

Whosoever Will May Come

I

Moody was "one of the most forceful and interesting Americans of his time. He established soul-saving as a Big Business just as surely as John D. Rockefeller established oil-refining, or old Phil Armour the assassination of hogs, or Pillsbury the milling of flour."

The judgment is that of H. L. Mencken, who has been accused of many things but never of being too enthusiastic about religious leaders. Mencken continues, describing Moody as "a man of parts, and perhaps the greatest evangelist since John Wesley. Whitefield, Charles G. Finney, Alexander Campbell and other such performers were puny compared to him. . . . Nor are any of his successors in his class." [1]

Most of Moody's books and articles were ghost-written,[2] and his printed sermons, utterly devoid of both thought power and literary charm, give no adequate idea of the power he must have possessed. Obviously the preacher's presence must have added much—the quiet confidence that exuded from him, the charisma which enveloped him, the genuine passion that so obviously possessed him. It is said that when a thunderstorm burst while Whitefield was preaching, he used it with tremendous effect to illustrate the Judgment, but that when he was asked to print the discourse he refused unless the thunderstorm could be printed with it. Moody's contemporary Joseph Jefferson proved with *Rip Van Winkle* that though a play can be good literature, it does not need to be. Moody himself had no use for the theater, but he often achieved highly dramatic effects, and a sermon resembles a play in that what it needs most of all is a theme which deeply enlists the emotions of the audience and a man before them who understands it and can present it with power.

There are so many good stories about Moody that one is tempted to revel in anecdotage for its own sake, and it may well be that more of the real Moody can be apprehended thus than in a more formal or analytical way. He won young Wilfred Grenfell, who was just about to slip out of a meeting which a long-winded brother was praying to death, by announcing that while Brother So-and-So was finishing his prayer, the congregation would sing a hymn. Rebuked for the infelicities of his style, he admitted—and sincerely regretted—his shortcomings, then added that he was doing his best for God with the powers he had: "Are you?" A heckler told him that the man who invented the use of illuminating gas did more for the world than Christ, only to be asked whether he planned to send for the gas-fitter when he lay dying, and an admirer who professed to have achieved sanctification was invited to return the next night bringing his wife with him to testify as to his condition. Challenged to quote a verse in the Bible which condemns smoking, he offered instead one which favors it: "He that is filthy, let him be filthy still."

Dwight Lyman Moody (he hated his given names and never used either of them) was born at Northfield, Massachusetts, on February 5, 1837. On his mother's side, his English forebears ran back to the foundation of the town. His father, Edwin Moody, was a mason who died at the age of forty-one, when D. L. was only four years old, leaving his widow with seven children to rear and twins on the way. Though Moody never alluded to it, alcohol seems to have been involved in his father's decline. The family background was Unitarian, and the Moodys were not notably religious.

The mother, Betsy Holton Moody, showed herself a person of character by holding her farm and her family together, paying off the mortgage, and seeing her children settled in life. Under the circumstances, it would not have been fair to expect her to be always a charming or amiable figure. In later years, Paul Moody believed that his grandmother enjoyed being uncomfortable "and found a degree of virtue in it." She drank her tea out of a marmalade jar long after the need for such parsimony had passed, and when her son gave her china she refused to use it. Nor did she ever "make a fuss" over her grandchildren. "There was no cookie jar nor any sweets to reward good grandchildren and she seemed to be afraid of spoiling us, for she was certainly never remarkably demonstrative and, I always felt, suffered our filial kisses with a sort of grim resignation."

One of Moody's friends later estimated that his schooling was about the equivalent of a fifth-grade education, but Findlay thinks this an overestimate. His schoolmates later remembered him "as more remarkable for mischief than for close application to study." He used "ain't" and "he don't" even in the pulpit, his spelling was atrocious, and, like Sarah Bernhardt, he never had time to finish his words. Paul says he had a "certain deafness to shades of sound," and that when in Europe he tried to say "*Bon jour*" to an elderly lady, it sounded like "*Mon chèr*"! In any event, the schooldays of this man who afterwards refused several honorary degrees ended when he was thirteen.

In 1854 Moody went to Boston, where he was employed as a salesman in a shoe store kept by an uncle, which stood close to what was afterwards to be notorious as Scollay Square. He joined the YMCA, presumably as an associate member, since only those who belonged to evangelical churches were eligible for full mem-

Lyman Beecher

William Ellery Channing, from a painting attributed to Washington Allston. By courtesy of The Colonial Society of Massachusetts

Henry Ward Beecher, about 1851

Phillips Brooks

Trinity Church in Copley Square, Boston, with insert showing the architect H. H. Richardson, from Harper's Weekly, *1886*

Plymouth Church, Brooklyn, showing the size of the auditorium and the way the platform thrust Beecher into the audience

D. L. Moody preaching, as the Chicago Tribune *saw him in 1898*

Washington Gladden

Lyman Abbott

bership; he may already have been attending Mount Vernon Congregational Church, but he was still nominally a Unitarian. On April 21, 1855, while he was wrapping up a package at the store, he was converted by his Sunday School teacher, Samuel Holton, who had stopped in to talk to him about his soul; he thereupon applied for membership at Mount Vernon, but because of his phenomenal ignorance of Christian doctrine, acceptance was delayed for a year. Asked what Christ had done for us, he could not reply. He was sure Christ had done a good deal, but just what it was he found himself unable to particularize.

Moody's real beginning as a Christian worker came in Chicago (where he settled in 1856) and took the form of YMCA and Sunday School work and of relief work under the auspices of the United States Christian Commission, during and just after the Civil War. In the Y, of which he became president, he headed an aggressive campaign for evangelical Christianity among young Chicago businessmen and an ambitious building program;[3] his Sunday School work established a national reputation for him as a convention speaker. At first all this was carried on along with Moody's work in the shoe business (by this time in the wholesale end), where he intended to earn $100,000, and seemed in a fair way to do so. (Once at least he loaned out money at an interest rate of seventeen percent per day!) But in 1860 he decided that he could no longer divide himself and that he must give up business for Christian work. The responsibility for his success or failure he decided to place squarely before the Lord. He had enough savings to carry him through the period of transition; if, when this was gone, he had not yet been able to establish himself, he would take it as a sign that he had been rejected in this new capacity.

Moody's most wonderful achievements during his Chicago period were made in his Sunday School work in "The Sands," the notorious North Side red-light district, on the lake shore just north of the Chicago River. In the beginning all he wanted to do was to teach Sunday School, but when he applied he was told that all classes were provided for, and that if he wanted a class, he must bring it with him. He proceeded to do just that, and the children were such derelicts as most of us have never encountered except in *Oliver Twist* and sociological reports. He dug them out of the homes—or holes—inhabited by saloon keepers and prostitutes, sometimes literally dragging them out from under the bed, emptying out the whiskey jugs of their elders, and escaping getting his head knocked off by dropping on his knees to pray for them. He filled his pockets full of "missionary sugar," fed the hungry and clothed the naked—one boy was quite that except for his overcoat—and gradually the children came to love him and to draw their parents in. Moody risked his life in cholera epidemics and established a bureau for tracing lost boys who had disappeared into the underworld. By 1864 all this had led to the establishment of the Illinois Street Church, with Moody as its never-to-be-ordained pastor. He had no desire to set up rival establishments to other churches, but when he faced a group who would come to him but trusted nobody else, what could he do? He made good citizens and good Christians—in a surprisingly large number of cases he even made Christian workers—out of some of the most unpromising material on the North American continent.

William R. Moody remarks justly that the Christian Commission was a kind of combination of Red Cross and YMCA work. Moody went to the front a number of times and was one of the first representatives of the Commission to enter Richmond after the fall of the Confederacy. But for himself and his own career, it may well be that the primary importance of his Civil War service was that it helped bridge the gap between his Sunday School work and his mature evangelism. D. L. Moody was not often accused of diffidence. Hardly anybody has ever written about him without making use of the term "brusque." Yet it was no accident that he began his soul-winning with children.

Without the war he might not have been able to make the transition to adults as early as he did.

By this time Moody had both married and become allied with his evangelistic partner, the singer and song writer Ira D. Sankey. Emma C. Revell came of a Huguenot family from England; she and Moody were married in Chicago on August 28, 1862. Emma was her husband's equal in character and spiritual development, and she was greatly his superior in refinement, tact, and appreciation of the delicacies of life.[4] Sankey, a Pennsylvanian, Moody met and heard in Indianapolis in 1870. "Where are you from?" he asked. "Are you married? What is your business?" Sankey was married and had two children, and he was in the Federal revenue service. "You will have to give that up," said Moody, "to come to Chicago and help me in my work. I have been looking for you for the last eight years." It is Findlay's opinion that "without Sankey's assistance, Moody's triumphs in England from 1873 to 1875 and in the great revivals which followed, might never have occurred."

In October 1871 the Moodys were burned out in the Chicago Fire; it is interesting that the only story we have about them in this connection should be a humorous one. Their most valuable possession was a portrait of Moody by Healy. Mrs. Moody wanted her husband to take it, but he positively refused to travel through the streets of the burning city cherishing his own portrait, whereupon his wife, nothing daunted, cut the canvas out of its frame, rolled it up, and carried it herself.

Without the Fire, Moody might not have left Chicago when he did. He had been in England in 1867, when he had come under the influence of the Plymouth Brethren, engaged in Christian work on a small, unpublicized scale, and established a noon prayer meeting in London. Now, in 1873, he went again, with Sankey, thinking of undertaking an evangelistic campaign there. The venture could not have begun more inauspiciously, for when Moody and Sankey arrived, they found that both their promised sponsors had died. They began in Yorkshire, moved into Scotland and Ireland, where they met rather astonishing success, and opened a four-months campaign in London in March 1875, in a specially constructed tabernacle called Victoria Hall, which was capable of accommodating seven thousand people. All of this was prominently reported, praised, attacked, and spectacularly fought over not only in the religious but also in the secular press. When the evangelist returned to America in 1875 he was in very much the position of a young American prima donna who, having earned her reputation in European opera houses, has now returned to undertake the conquest of her native land. Nor did the career falter, for mass revivals followed in Brooklyn, Philadelphia, New York, Chicago, and Boston.

Yet it might have faltered had he not again resembled the rarely creative artist in other lines in the ability he manifested to achieve a new and freshly interesting expression of himself whenever the old had begun to pall. It is true that towards the end of his life Moody sometimes felt out of touch with his times, at the same time averring that he was too old to change. It would not be true to say that he ever gave up mass evangelism, for he died when a Kansas City campaign that he ought never to have undertaken in his state of health was just getting under way. He preached again in England in 1881, 1884, and 1892, and he engineered a literally gigantic campaign in Chicago at the time of the World's Columbian Exposition, with meetings going on all over the city, at times in as many as 125 places. What was amazing was that so much of his later energy should go into educational work. Immediately upon returning from England after his first campaign, Moody made it clear that Northfield and no other place on earth was home, and it was here that he established the Northfield Seminary (for girls) and the Mount Hermon School (for boys), both near the beginning of the eighties, and, about a decade later, the Northfield Training School for girls who desired to become Christian workers. The first two institutions now enjoy a fine scholastic rating; the third has never been as well known as the Bible Institute in Chicago, possibly because it has not been so involved in controversy.[5] Despite a very rough reception when he first preached at Oxford and at Cambridge, Moody's courage and sincerity finally won him a hearing as a college preacher also, and there were summer conferences at Northfield which involved many college men and enlisted many recruits for foreign missionary service.

By the nineties, however, Moody's once superb health had broken down. In the early days he seems to have had no particular weakness but seasickness, and Paul says of him that he was the worst sailor he ever encountered, beginning to feel sick even while going up the gangplank! "I only remember his being housed with a cold once, and then I recall more vividly his dreadful impatience at being housed than anything else. He wasn't equipped by nature to be a good invalid." There may have been a psychosomatic element in the seasickness, though Moody does not seem to have been much given to that sort of thing. But there was a demonic element in his energy. He believed that "the devil tempts most men, but a lazy man tempts the devil"; indeed he even says that the slaves of all other vices are redeemable but that he has never known a lazy man to be redeemed! We are told that he perspired so freely while preaching that he would have to change all his clothes afterwards (he bathed three or four times a day, in the coldest water he could find), and Sankey is supposed to have prayed, "O God, do tire Moody, or give the rest of us superhuman strength!"[6] This was zeal for the Lord but it was temperament too, for Moody had manifested the same tendencies when he was only selling shoes. When customers did not come into the shop, he went out on the sidewalk to look for them, and his fellow clerks compared him to the spider waiting for the fly.[7]

Of course Moody neither drank nor smoked, and his habits were completely hygienic, except perhaps in one aspect. In the early days he worked so hard that he would fall asleep over his prayers; he thought at the time that this was because he was a sinner; later he decided it was only because he was a fool. "God is not a hard taskmaster, and in later years I have learned that to do your best work you cannot afford to neglect the common laws of health." Thereafter he religiously observed one day of rest in seven. Paul says too that he always took a nap after lunch, and he seems to have walked and worked in his garden until the condition of his heart made it dangerous for him to do so. By this time his weight had climbed to the dizzy height of 280 pounds, and the jokesters said he had a built-in shelf to hold the Bible he liked to keep in his hand while he preached. ("He was no more an ascetic than a sybarite," said his son. "And he loved good food.") The heart condition did not become dangerous until very late, but as early as 1891 he was warned that if he went to India, he might have a stroke. In London, Sir Andrew Clark examined him and, hearing his work schedule, called him a fool and told him he was killing himself, a statement no less true because, as Moody pointed out, the doctor himself was an even bigger fool and would die first, which he did. Moody's own death occurred, after a classical death-bed scene, on December 22, 1899. "I was born of the flesh in 1837. I was born of the Spirit in 1856. That which is born of the flesh may die. That which is born of the Spirit will live forever."

II

Moody's method of preparing his sermons was highly individual:

He prepared outlines [writes Paul Moody], writing them in his large hand on the four sides of ordinary correspondence paper. These he kept in blue linen envelopes on the outside of which were written the dates and places where they were used. Into these envelopes he would thrust anything which was related to the subject until they were often very full.

He left over four hundred of these envelopes, and some of the sermons had been given more than one hundred times. "If I find a sword effective, why shouldn't I use it often?" Yet because his sermons were not given from manuscript, and because he was constantly changing them to make them applicable to the particular situation which existed at the moment of delivery, they were never twice the same. Thus while he thought nothing of opening a big revival with, say, the sermon on "Sowing and Reaping," which had already been given scores of times, it was, in a sense, a new creation every time he gave it. Sankey was often compared not to a standard concert singer but rather to a music hall artist. By the same token, it might have been said of Moody that instead of touring, like a standard tragedian, with an unchanged and unchanging classical repertoire, he was more like the vaudeville or revue headliner who has only the general outline of his act prepared in advance and who fills in and omits and ad libs to his heart's content every time he appears.

In all this the need for self-expression must have been very important, for Moody's mother tells us that when he was a little boy he would go up into the attic and make a speech all by himself, and this habit apparently antedated his interest in religion itself. Moody always preferred to "talk" rather than "preach"; he detested "people that have a religious tone—a religious voice—who always change their tone when they begin to talk to you on the subject of religion, and have a particular whine that makes you think of cant." Like Phillips Brooks he spoke two hundred words a minute or more, colloquially, often incorrectly, but quite without the vulgarity that was later to distinguish Billy Sunday. His vocabulary was simple, largely Anglo-Saxon, and rich in verbs. Nobody ever claimed that his voice was beautiful, but it had great carrying power, and nobody seems to have been repelled by it. The sermons he preached were brief, without logical development, but rich in emotional appeal. The many stories with which they were studded came, some from the Bible, some from Moody's own experience, some from the common stock-in-trade upon which orators and evangelists drew. The Earl of Shaftesbury found everything as wrong with Moody and his meetings as there could possibly have been, but the very "imperfection of the whole thing" was deeply impressive. The preacher reached "the inmost soul" and carried it into the presence of a loving Christ.

To literature and art Moody's sermons naturally owed nothing, for neither really existed for him. How sensitive he was to the charms of nature I cannot say. It is clear that the country around Northfield had a strong hold upon him, but many elements besides natural beauty were involved in this. He tells us that after his conversion he fell in love with the birds on Boston Common: "I never cared for them before; it seemed to me that I was in love with all creation." But a good many people can achieve that much without being "saved."

As a boy Moody had his share in the sports and games cherished by the youngsters of his region, and he did not altogether leave these things behind him when he grew up. Gamaliel Bradford seems considerably to have underestimated his interest in outdoor sports. Indoor games he was predisposed to dislike because they so often took on gambling associations, but he was one of the boys at Northfield long after most men of Moody's bulk would have considered themselves ruled out. He owned an abundance of animals, some of them fairly exotic, and indeed his horses and cattle were always more for pleasure than for profit. Moody lived a little too early to kill himself with a motor car, but he drove his buggy like a madman, across the fields as well as down the road, driving "sanely and with care," says his son, only when his wife went with him.

About the only work of art I have found him particularizing is a picture he saw at the Paris Exhibition of 1867, depicting the sower of the tares with a hideous expression on his face and the planting coming up in the form of reptiles. This was "sacred" art, of course, but he did not always approve even of that, wondering whether it might not be idol-making to paint pictures of Christ, especially since nobody could know what he really looked like. Naturally "secular" art did not fare better. Once he tells us of visiting Louis Prang's Boston studio to follow the process of chromolithography, but this was technology rather than art. Once, in one of his very rare errors of judgment, he foolishly allowed himself to be drawn into publicly denouncing nude paintings in a newspaper article. The paper printed the article in the Sunday issue and illustrated it with reproductions of the pictures he considered immoral.

He said nothing against literature as such, but it obviously meant nothing to him. If you were "saved," you did not need it, and if you were not, neither it nor anything else was of any value to you. He could not have quoted poetry in his sermons, for his verbal memory was so poor that he could not recite the Lord's Prayer without following a text. Novels were always "trashy" or "flashy"; there is no indication that he ever heard of either Scott or Dickens. How could he have missed the death of Little Paul and of Nell, so like in kind to his own countless *Kindertotenlieder* but so much better done? and would he have failed to see the redemptive Christ figure in Florence Dombey? He was interested in Kipling when the latter lived at Brattleboro and considered inviting him to lunch, but nothing came of this.[8]

Moody advertised his meetings in the amusement columns because he wanted people to see the advertisements, and once he accosted Richard Croker at the Murray Hill Hotel, urging him to oppose a bill which would permit New York theaters to operate on Sunday. But oddly enough, he went, at least once, to Madame Tussaud's and spoke of it without embarrassment in a sermon. There are only a very few references to Shakespeare in his sermons, though once, in his youth, he recited Mark Antony's oration, having Caesar's coffin brought in so that a cat could jump out of it at the climactic moment.

Bible stories Moody dramatized all his preaching life. Robert Morss Lovett says his description of the woman who had lost the piece of silver was as good as *Gammer Gurton's Needle*, and Charles Goss tells us that once, during his Elijah sermon in Detroit,

> it appeared to me that supernatural things were actually occurring in the room. . . . In the final outburst we actually beheld the chariot swoop down from heaven, the old man ascend, the blazing car borne through the still air; and when the impassioned orator uttered that piercing cry, "My father, my father, the chariot of Israel the horsemen thereof!" the excitement was almost unendurable.

This comes very close indeed to Walter Prichard Eaton's statement that when Peer Gynt's mother died, in Richard Mansfield's production of Ibsen's play, "the reindeer bells rang in the air [of the imagination], the roof disappeared, and through happy tears you saw the poor old mother reach the gates of Paradise." And this again, I suppose, suggests what Sarah Bernhardt meant when she described a rare, perfect performance by saying that "God was there." For all great platform artists are alike in one thing—that the audience sees what the artist wishes them to see.

The great mystery and the great paradox in Moody's aesthetic world was music. "The Bible and music," he says, "have moved the world more than any other two agencies." You could not have expected more of Milton or Browning. Yet the man was tone-deaf, could not carry a tune nor tell one tune from another, and he is said once to have been greatly elevated by "Yankee Doodle" because he had been told it was "Rock of Ages." For all that, nobody ever used music more effectively for religious purposes than he did; he even used it in the inquiry room, both for its emotional appeal and to create a greater degree of privacy than could otherwise have been obtained. Sankey had distinct musical limitations (he has even been called a musical reciter rather than a singer), but his contribution to the Moody and Sankey meetings was nevertheless very great, and when he improvised "The Ninety and Nine" one evening, Moody was quite as overcome as the audience. If he was not sensitive to music himself, he must have been phenomenally sensitive to its effect upon those around him.

III

Taking so little, comparatively speaking, as he did from books meant that Moody had to take more from life and therefore from his direct contacts with human beings. He was an intensely emotional man. When he first learned just what was involved in a Roman scourging, he wept for days, begging forgiveness for not having loved Christ more. Yet his attitude towards human nature and the principles upon which he regulated his intercourse with his fellow beings were not simple and are difficult to sum up in a phrase.

To begin with, his natural heartiness and sympathy found itself at war with the pessimistic aspects of his religious belief. "Everything human in this world fails. Every man, the moment he takes his eyes off from God, has failed." Reform is useless. "Men are all naturally bad and cannot reform until the Redeemer gets into their hearts." At times this conviction even causes Moody to deny human brotherhood: "Show me a man that will lie and steal and get drunk and ruin a woman—do you tell me that he is my brother? Not a bit of it. He must be born again into the household of faith before he becomes my brother again."

Just how a thoroughly bad creature can make the decision by which he is saved is never very thoroughly explained, and it is clear that Moody seldom allowed his theology to get in the way of simple human kindness. He was not prepared to say that no man had ever committed the unpardonable sin against the Holy Ghost, but he was sure he had never met such a man. He would stop work to hitch up his buggy and drive a stranger passing his door with a heavy valise to the railroad station, though he admits frankly that he did not wish to do so. When the Moodys had house guests, family prayers followed breakfast instead of preceding it; Moody knew that the spirit of devotion was not fostered in hungry people by tormenting them with the smell of food. How charming were his relations with the old Frenchman Paul who acted as a kind of retainer at Northfield! Between master and man there was a true, deep bond of affection; Moody never spoke a word about Paul's drinking habits until the man turned away from them himself; neither did he ever try to win him away from his inherited Catholicism.[9]

Paul Moody thought his father a less competent judge of character than he was generally rated, for he saw only the best in people and consequently was often disappointed in their performance of the tasks he had entrusted to them. Certainly there was no toadying in his social relations and no Pharisaism either. "Glad to meet you, Lord. Just get two chairs for those old ladies over there, will you?" His Christ, who could overmatch all earthly glories, was also equal to any problem which human degradation might present, and Moody, as His servant, turned away because of no sin on the part of those whom he sought to save. If his charity failed anywhere, it was with "cranks"—short-haired women and long-haired men he calls them—who brought their axes to him and expected him to grind them. "He kept himself always somewhat mysterious," says R. L. Duffus. "He never let himself be pawed over. He never let gushing women make a fool of him." He would not see such people if he could avoid it, and if they penetrated his barriers he disposed of them as briefly as possible. Once, when he could do nothing else, he lay down and calmly went to sleep. Even in the inquiry room, he simply dropped those who had obviously come back to argue with him. But basically none of this was a matter of "keeping himself" at all. He was simply being true to D. L. Moody. There were some things he could not do.

Moody's own intensities were relieved by his ability to relax socially. During his later years he was never satisfied except when he had the house full of guests, and we have references to his regaling them with story after story until they literally held their sides. His memory for names and faces was miraculous; perhaps he had more room in his head for such things than some of us have simply because he did not burden himself with so much material taken at second hand. Yet he was never a "familiar" man, and it was very difficult to reach a first-name basis with him. Neither in youth nor in age did he form many intimacies outside his own family. He loved the poor sinners whose souls he tried to save, yet one feels at times that he thought of them primarily as raw material for the spirit of God to work on. Again, though there was no hint of insincerity in the tributes he paid his co-workers and other religious leaders on memorial and other occasions, he generally seemed to be thinking of what they meant to the Kingdom of God rather than what they meant to D. L. Moody.[10]

To the family, of course, none of this applied. Mrs. Moody was about as perfect a wife and mother as it is given to mortal woman to be, and her husband thought his winning her a miracle comparable to God's ability to use him as He did in spite of all his obvious limitations. "My mother," says Paul, "was the buffer between him and the world. She was the 'shock-absorber.' She stood between him and things." Once at least he dared to speak in a sermon of "how I loved her the first year we were married and how happy I was then." He had no need to limit it to the first or to any other particular year. And whatever else the Moodys were prepared to sacrifice to do the Lord's work, apparently the thought of being separated from each other for any extended period was never entertained. If the Lord wanted Moody to do His work, He had to provide enough to take them both in.

He loved his three children with equal devotion, delighted in bringing them presents, always remembered birthdays, and wrote or telegraphed when he had to be away from home. Paul, who thought him "the greatest and best man I have ever known," makes it a special point that "he never . . . talked down to me, but flattered me with the constant assumption that my opinion was sought and that he was interested in what I thought or had to say." Once he walked the floor over Paul's difficulty with a school assignment, and once, when the boy undertook to build a useless and impossible barn at Northfield, Moody put on a ceremony of dedication when it was finished, with Henry Drummond reading imaginary telegrams of regret over their inability to be present from Grover Cleveland, Queen Victoria, and others. Moody displeased some of his more narrow-minded admirers by sending his sons to Yale rather than to a more evangelical school, and though he himself believed in and observed all the prohibitions generally observed by devout Christians, he seldom preached about these things and asked no pledges of the boys when they went away. The one piece of advice he gave Paul in which the latter "saw no sense" was that he should grow sideburns because his face was long and narrow. He returned to this many times, "urging it strongly. But I was adamant." The same spirit carried over into his relations with his grandchildren (Irene's death may well have hastened his own), and other children too, first in his slum Sunday school in Chicago and much later at Northfield.[11]

The only aspect in which Moody can be thought of as having left anything to be desired as a father was one of the many in which he suggests a strong resemblance to Theodore Roosevelt. "For heaven's sake, don't put it into Theodore's head to go too," said Mrs. Roosevelt on one occasion: "I should have another child to take care of." A huge cauliflower, a huge cabbage, and a doughnut were among Moody's gifts to infants. It was all to his credit that when he thought he had been wrong or unjust in his dealings with a child, he should come to his bed to beg forgiveness afterwards, but I am not sure that the strain of seeing him in tears was not worse than the original injury inflicted, and he can hardly have helped a convalescent much when he lowered his great body to the side of his bed—and broke it down. Roosevelt did not serve his guests rubber eggs and potato chips made of pine shavings from the joke shop, nor can I imagine him rolling on the ground in laughter as Moody did when Paul was stung by bees.

Was there a bit of the old Adam left in Moody here? He is supposed to have been able to achieve what he did by giving himself up completely to another—and that other Jesus Christ. "If the Lord wanted me to go to Africa I would start this afternoon. I'd rather a thousand times be in Africa with God than to be in America without Him." He would seem to have made this self-surrender about as completely as any man can, but who can doubt that he found a fuller expression of his powers and a richer self-satisfaction in this life of surrender than he could possibly have found in any other human pursuit or any form of obvious self-indulgence? Does the religious leader, when he is as successful as Moody, really live a more selfless life than the artist or the scientist or the great statesman or even the technologist or businessman? There is no suggestion that Moody ever pondered these matters. He does say that "it is the greatest pleasure of living to win souls to Christ," and when two hundred people rise together in one of his meetings to indicate their desire to make a decision for Christ, he murmurs, "My God, this is enough to live for." He loved "to influence a man's will," a will which has been "set against God," so that it may be "broken and brought into subjection to God's will." But he was not an analytical man in any sense, and only during the storm and stress which preceded his "second conversion" does he seem to have gone through any protracted spiritual struggle. It was not that he was self-satisfied or that he ever felt "safe." "I never did anything in my life, I never addressed an audience that I didn't think I could have done better." He never wanted his name perpetuated or his life written. "My lack of education has always been a great disadvantage to me; I shall suffer from it as long as I live." That is why it took him so long to get up his courage to address a college audience; when he visited Harvard and was told that professors there lectured daily throughout the college year, he said, "Emma, this is no place for us; I only last three weeks." Nor did he ever feel immune against temptation. "You know I'm not afraid to die but there are times when I am almost afraid of living." Horrified and frightened when the life of a man of standing suddenly fell into ruins, he cried, "In one brief moment I can undo what I have taken a lifetime to build up." But though he might regret his limitations, he accepted them, as in larger matters he accepted God's promises. If the Lord could keep him alive to do the work to which he had committed himself, no doubt He could be trusted for spiritual salvation also.

Nevertheless he was always the captain of the ship. Few questioned it, and those who did came out badly. Moreover, this did not apply only to the ship that he was sailing; it is interesting that his uncle in Chicago at first seriously hesitated to employ him, thinking that if he did, Moody would soon be running the shoe store. Once a mother slapped a fractious child in a railway station; Moody first ordered her not to do it again, then turned to a guard and directed him to open for her the gate before a restricted area, so that she and the child might sit down. Once, having left something he needed at his hotel, he commanded the conductor of a transcontinental train to hold it for him while he went back and retrieved it. Once he took charge in a street accident involving two horses and gave all the orders necessary to straighten things out. And once, in a strange church, where the ushers had overlooked some pews in passing Communion, he rose, went to the Communion table in the rubber boots he chanced to be wearing, served the communicants, and took his seat again. "Intentionally he never wounded any one," writes one of his admirers; "he simply lacked perception, and did not put himself in the other man's place."

If this was his manner with strangers, one can easily imagine how he would handle intimates and subordinates. Guests in his house might expect to have a letter tossed across to the table to them with "Answer that!" and if they asked, "What shall I say?" Moody might reply that he did not intend to hire a dog and then do the barking himself. He was capable of singling out individuals for comment in his huge audiences, if they were doing something they should not be doing, or even if they were not; once in London he called up a deacon from Boston's Mount Vernon in order to tell the audience that this man had kept him from joining the church because he thought he did not know enough. Once he demanded—and got—50,000 tickets printed on a Saturday afternoon by simply insisting that he needed them and that it must be done. And once he asked a friend to talk to a prospect in the inquiry room. "You will have to excuse me, Mr. Moody; that is something I never do." "Either sit down and talk to that man," said Moody, "or else sit down and let some one talk to you."

To be sure, when he was convinced he was wrong, Moody always admitted his fault and, sometimes publicly, begged forgiveness. He did that, very early in his career, one night in Chicago, after he had impulsively knocked a man down the stairs for insulting him, and once, seeing an acquaintance with whom he was not on good terms in one of his audiences, he left the platform and went out with the man, and they came back reconciled. I do not question Moody's complete sincerity in any of these encounters. But I submit that he could not have failed to realize that, in every such acknowledgement, he was giving a pretty good account of himself. Sankey made a much greater sacrifice than Moody did when he gave up his share of the song book royalties, partly because he, not Moody, had created the material, and partly because he had a lower earning potential. I have no reason to suppose that there was any more question in Sankey's mind as to how the royalties should be handled than there was in Moody's. But I cannot help wondering what Moody's attitude would have been if Sankey had not been willing to go along with the proposed relinquishment.[12]

IV

Moody's strength lay in his humanity and his complete religious devotion; his weaknesses as a religious leader were on the intellectual side. When his theology was objected to, he was likely to reply that he didn't have any, and in a sense this was true. He told one inquirer that his creed might be found in print in Isaiah 53, and his Chicago church, which embraced members from a number of different communions, cannily framed no confession except in the words of the Bible itself. Moody might declare that salvation "had nothing more to do with election than with the laws of China," yet his Calvinist supporters could declare that there was nothing in his preaching incompatible with their beliefs. Certainly there is a trace of Calvinism in his discussion of the New Birth—"God may well restrict those who are to dwell in His holy presence to whomsoever he will"—and this is a late utterance.[13] Occasionally, too, he would permit himself to express an idea which seemed inconsistent with anything he might be expected to believe: "Jesus Christ lived for thirty years without preaching—almost unheard of; it was only when the Spirit of God came upon Him that He began to preach."

James Findlay has argued[14] that Moody's utterances on the Atonement bring him closer to the Moral Influence Theory than we might have expected him to come. The Moral Influence

Theory is the only one that stresses God's love and the influence of its appeal to the human conscience, and insofar as he deals with these matters at all, Moody stands not untouched by its influence.

A great many people have a wrong idea of Christ. They think He only saves us from hell, but He keeps us from sin day by day. God knew a great deal better what the world needed than ourselves. Therefore He gave us Christ, not only to save us from death, but to free us from sin.

Yet I doubt that Horace Bushnell would have recognized a true disciple in Moody. He tells us that "the Atonement was a transaction which took place between God the Father and God the Son nineteen hundred years ago."

Why, people say, "I don't believe in the doctrine of substitution." Well then, if you don't believe in that, you don't believe in the Bible. I tell you, take the doctrine of substitution out of that Bible, and I would not carry it home with me. If it does not teach that, it teaches nothing.

He also advised any hearer whose pastor had "covered up this doctrine of blood" to fly from his ministry "as those who flew from Sodom."

Many people say, "I wish I was as good as that woman who has been ministering to the sick for the last fifty years. I would feel sure of heaven." My friends, if you have the blood behind you, you are as safe as anybody on this earth. . . . It is not our life of good deeds or our righteousness that will take us into heaven, but the atonement. And the question ought to come to every one tonight, "Are we sheltered behind the blood?"

Certainly this is as unmoral as anything any Calvinistic believer in election ever preached. Moody's faith in a physical Second

Coming of Christ is alloyed with materialism too, and his description of "The Resurrection" in the sermon so entitled [15] reads like the work of an engineer.[16]

Moody's Sabbatarianism was extreme, though sometimes strikingly modified by his basically tolerant nature. He did not want even religious newspapers read on Sunday (the secular ones were of course beyond the pale); the day should be devoted entirely to church-going and Bible study. In the early days in Chicago, when he was holding services in quarters which were employed for anything but religious purposes on Saturday nights, he himself cleaned out the filth the celebrants had left behind them because he would not hire somebody else to work on the Sabbath, and he was a famous man when, in the same city, he walked sixteen miles on Sunday from one hall to another because "I want no hackman to rise up in judgment against me." Yet when many of his supporters were urging that the World's Columbian Exposition be closed on Sundays, he took no part in the debate, but devoted himself exclusively to the work he was doing and allowed it to speak for itself.

He often speaks of the devil, and there is no reason to suppose that this was a mere figure of speech. He "will move earth and sky to keep us from Christ" and "seek to keep us in 'Doubting Castle.'" Once, when a high wind threatened to unroof Mody's tabernacle, he told his audience that "the devil don't want you to hear this story of Jesus' dying for you," which would seem to give Satan powers similar to those attributed to him in the witchcraft trials.

He believed in hell too, and in the early days Mrs. Moody used to cringe when he preached about it. Later, threats were replaced by "a passionate note of tender appeal," and some of his critics actually complained that he did not preach repentance. The change was due partly to his own maturing and partly to the influence of "the little Lancashire lad," Harry Moorhouse, who, beyond anybody else, taught Moody that there were no limits to God's love. R. W. Dale says that when he did talk of hell, it was "with tears in his voice." But he did not talk of it often, for he did not want to "scare" people into the Kingdom. Sometimes there is even a hint that hell is not a place but a state of mind: "God will not punish us. We shall punish ourselves. When we come before God He will turn us over to ourselves. 'Go and read the book of your memory,' He will say." Yet his sermons are full of stories about people who were converted shortly before dying, and in spite of the fact that many of them were living perfectly decent lives, Moody seems to intend us to believe that without conversion they would have gone straight to hell. There is a nasty threat involved in the alternative presented in at least one invitation to penitents: "It is to have Him for our Saviour now, or at some future day to have Him for our judge." And the sermon called "A Man Who Lacked Moral Courage" tells a terrible story of attempted conversion which failed, in the clear conviction that the poor man was damned forever; no allowance is made for his being in an abnormal, irresponsible state; neither is it suggested that the Christians who drove him more than half crazy by working on him as they did must in any measure be blamed. When Robert Ingersoll died and Moody was asked for a comment, he showed his true gentlemanliness by speaking of the beauty of the great infidel's home life and of the sadness of dying without hope for the future. He was less tolerant, however, when he called unbelief not a misfortune but "the damning sin of the world today." Murder, swearing, and lying are not the root sins. "God condemns the world because they believe not on Him; that is the root of all evil." It should be declared with emphasis that Moody could never have wished to persecute anybody for unbelief. But many others, adhering to his point of view, have done so.

Everything Moody believed was based upon the Bible, or claimed to be, and the Bible, which contained God's promises to mankind, had to be taken, even in its English version, absolutely at face value. Now in Moody's time the authority of the Bible was being undermined both by the scientists, who saw the whole process of creation in different terms from those postulated in Genesis, and by the Higher Critics, who introduced new methods of Biblical scholarship and interpretation. Moody did not pay much attention to science; with the Higher Criticism he grappled much more valiantly. There were moments when he seemed on the verge of becoming a Higher Critic himself: "Thus, in the tenth chapter of Hebrews, we find Paul, if he wrote this, just taking up the very thought. . . ." More suggestively still, he once declared that in reading any Bible book, we must keep in mind the place, date, and purpose of composition and the readers the writer had in mind. This, of course, is exactly what the Higher Critic does. But Moody never gets far along this road, and the question he asked Sir George Adam Smith—why it was necessary to teach people that there were two Isaiahs when most of them had not heard of one—shows how profound his understanding of such matters was.

"That the Bible contains passages that I do not understand," said Moody, "is to me a strong proof of its Divine origin." He was reasonable enough when he thanked God "that in His Word I find heights I cannot reach, depths that I cannot fathom, breadths that I cannot measure." It was much less reasonable, however, to conclude from this that "the Bible was not made to understand." [17] Neither did Moody's methods conduce to understanding. He once said that if he had to choose between zeal without knowledge or knowledge without power, he would choose the former; the choice was about as desperate as that which Moody the practical joker liked to pose with such questions as "Would you rather be a bigger fool than you look or look a bigger fool than you are?" (His comment on either of the two expected answers was "Impossible!") When he was asked to recommend a good life of Christ he recommended four—the Four Gospels. "A man had better spend a year over those four Gospels than to run over the whole Bible." Certainly his recommendation that the Christian go direct to the Bible itself, not getting stranded on the commentaries, was excellent, open-minded advice, but it can only work for those who have enough background knowledge to read the Bible without help.

Often Moody recommended "running over" the whole Bible —that is, taking great key words like "Faith" and "Blood," looking them up with the aid of a concordance, and thus allowing one passage to explain another. The assumption here was that the Bible is all of a piece. No allowance is made for differences between the various books, or for religious development within the period of Biblical history. "The Old Testament was written only to teach us who Christ was. . . . You take Christ out of the Old Testament and it is a sealed book to you." On the other hand, if you get the key to Genesis (or to any other book), "you get the key to the whole Bible." When he tells us that the Book of Leviticus "is one of the most valuable, because it relates all about the worship of God," he is inconsistent on more than one score, for Moody certainly did not worship God according to Leviticus, and if everything in the Bible is equally inspired, how can any one book be either more or less valuable? The sermon on "The Precious Blood" contains a hideously impercipient account of Abraham's attempt to sacrifice Isaac, with no attempt to place it with reference to an outgrown aspect of primitive culture, and no question raised as to the actuality of God's command or Abraham's duty to obey it. Similarly, he ignores the change from the pastoral to the agricultural economy reflected in the Cain and Abel story, and elsewhere he seems to think that God really did command Saul to slay the Amalekites. He also foolishly plays into the hands of the infidel by insisting that Jesus vouched for the historicity of Jonah and the "whale" (as Moody here calls him), Lot's wife, Sodom and Gomorrah, and more besides.

Moody's admirers have made much of his good relations with Christian liberals, and if we compare him with some of the

Fundamentalist spokesmen with whom we have been blessed since his time, he certainly deserves this. A. P. Fitt says that he once dismissed a woman teacher from a summer conference at Northfield for teaching that Genesis contained myths and legends, but he was on the best of terms, there and elsewhere, with such men as Washington Gladden, Lyman Abbott, Henry Drummond, and Sir George Adam Smith. Late in life he listened with great interest to Bible expositions by Dr. Henry Weston of Crozier Theological Seminary. In an article he ghost-wrote for his father to sign, Paul Moody once declared that the Higher Criticism was less dangerous than un-Christian attacks upon it. Moody stopped and pondered the statement carefully, but he signed the article. "I believe," he said, "the Church has less to fear from heresy than from animosity," and he was consumed with shame when a conservative allowed a liberal to outdo him in charity. At the time of the World's Columbian Exposition, he displeased some of his admirers by his sympathy with the Parliament of Religions that was being held in connection with it. His relations with Roman Catholics were far more cordial than those of many Protestants of his time, and he contributed liberally to the building fund of the Catholic church at Northfield. On the other hand, he was hysterical about spiritualism, regarding the "spirits" as devils from hell and taking up a strictly Old Testament attitude toward them.

There is not a thing that I need to know, there is not a thing that I ought to know but the Spirit of God will reveal it to me through the Word of God, and if I turn my back upon the Holy Spirit, I am dishonoring the Spirit of God, I am committing a grievous sin.

Some may feel that Moody's bibliolatry had a depressing effect upon his prayer life. His dislike of long prayers in public services is well known, and the brevity of his private devotions sometimes shocked his friends. "When I go to God I tell Him what I want, and that is the end of it." "Prayer is not praise," he says again; "it is asking God for something," which is surely a partial and inadequate definition. Prayer is talking to God, but when we read the Bible, God talks to us, and "I think it is often more important that God should speak to me than that I should speak to Him." Though this point of view might a priori be expected to inspire a dogmatic, authoritarian rather than a mystical or spontaneous type of religion, we must not suppose that prayer was not important to Moody. Once he reproached his son for having sent out a batch of letters containing financial appeals without having prayed over them—how could he expect to get results? Many will feel that this smacks too much of using prayer as an incantation, yet I doubt that anyone who knows Moody could think of him in that way. He was a child of God who had enough faith and trust in his Father—and who was sufficiently in harmony with His will—not to think it necessary to wheedle Him. Toward the end of his life Moody was on a wrecked ship in grave danger of sinking, and he was as frightened as any man would be in this predicament. But after he had prayed,

> Sweet peace came into my heart. I went to bed, fell asleep almost immediately, and never slept more soundly in my life. Out of the depths I cried unto the Lord and He heard me and delivered me from all my fears. I can no more doubt that God gave answer to my prayer for relief than I can doubt my own existence.

Moody's prayers were brusque and matter-of-fact, like his sermons and his appearance in the pulpit, but, like his sermons again, they seem to have worked.

V

Moody has also been accused of an indifference to social Christianity. "His preaching," says Bernard Weisberger, "froze a part of American Christianity into nostalgia and created a ready-made body of listeners for some men who without his charity, were as sounding brass and a tinkling cymbal." [18] Basically I think this just, but it must not be assumed that Moody wanted it that way. His personal concern for the underprivileged compares very favorably with that of some of his more forward-looking contemporaries. Everyman, however low he sank, had a soul to be saved, but he had a body to be fed and clothed also, and in many cases a family that needed to be taken care of, and Moody made a pretty good job of doing all these things. Only, his overwhelming emphasis upon personal salvation, and his assumption that once this had been achieved everything else would follow, inevitably caused a good many other things to be crowded to one side. In one sermon he actually classifies those who are "mad over politics" with those who live for money or for pleasure. "I have heard of reform, reform, until I am tired and sick of the whole thing. It is regeneration by the power of the Holy Ghost that we need."

Moody varied from time to time in the recognition he was willing to give to social forces as an influence upon character ("it must not be supposed that all prisoners are hardened criminals"), but when he did speak out on a social issue, his rich Republican supporters were not often disappointed, nor were they wrong in regarding his kind of evangelism as bolstering the existent order.[19] When some one appeared at a meeting with a petition to the President about the Armenian massacres, he turned it off by advocating prayer as the better way. "I always believe in approaching any difficulty by way of the throne of God."

Moody endorsed the six-day week and denounced the department store magnate A. T. Stewart because he did not assist a sick clerk. Yet he thought it would be a good thing if the people who begged for twelve months a year instead of working were to die off, and he praised the Prodigal Son for feeding swine rather than begging. If a man needed money, he should work—work at anything.

If it is for fifteen hours a day, all the better, for while you are at work Satan does not have so much chance to tempt you. If you cannot earn more than a dollar a week, earn that. That is better than nothing and you can pray to God for more."

He acknowledged that there was great suffering in New York, but this was due to people having drifted away from God. "When they are close to him, under His protection, they are always provided for." "I never found a person true to Christ but what the Lord would take care of them." If you "let atheism and pantheism and deism and infidelity go stalking through this land . . . property won't be safe." In one sermon Moody even described all the horrible fates encountered by those who had a share in sending Christ to the cross. But all this is neither religion nor economics nor syntax nor decent human sympathy nor common sense. It is rank materialism which reeks of the Gilded Age.

On one subject of social concern Moody seems more enlightened than many of his contemporaries, and this is war. (Nowadays the admonition to turn the other cheek seems to be about the only command in the New Testament which Fundamentalists do not take literally.) When Moody visited the Holy Land, "the sight of Moslem guards at the Holy Sepulchre and at the Church of the Nativity in Bethlehem to keep Christians from fighting wounded him deeply." He even disapproved of the military organization of the Salvation Army and the discipline involved. "It seemed to him," says W. R. Moody, "that the system precluded the immediate guidance of the spirit of God and the dictates of conscience." He did not fight in the Civil War because "I felt that I could not take a gun and shoot down a fellow being. In this respect I am a Quaker." Nor would he shoot a man who struck him down or use a sword in order to defend his rights. "I don't think a man gains much by loading himself down with weapons to defend himself. There has been life enough sacrificed in this country to teach a lesson in this regard. The Word of God is a much better protection than the revolver."

For all that, Moody's pacifism was far from being absolute. One sermon contains a story about a boy who wanted to fight in the Mexican War but whose mother was not willing to let him go until after he had become a Christian! If he did not fight in the Civil War himself, his work for the Christian Commission still brought him perilously close to recruiting. Mount Hermon had a "Military Company" in uniform as far back as the eighties. Paul says his father's sympathies were with the Boers against England, but he does not seem to have opposed America's first false step in foreign relations, in what came to be called the "splendid little war" with Spain.

It may be, as his son believed, that though his own time knew Moody best as an evangelist, the future will think of him first of all as an educator. He himself said of the Northfield schools: "They are the best pieces of work I have ever done." Once he even said he thought "more teaching and less preaching was needed," or if not less preaching, certainly more teaching. Yet the London *Times* objected that he spoke "of deep and mysterious problems as he would of buying so many pieces of cotton" and Professor McLoughlin feels that he "reduced Christianity to a sentimental personal relationship with a personal God." In the early days, he flung his question "Are you a Christian?" at high and low, friend and stranger alike, and if you were not, you were supposed to become one then and there.

Moody's meetings were not sensational by nineteenth-century standards. A master of crowd psychology, he created an atmosphere of warm and friendly camaraderie, but everything that was said and done remained under his absolute control at all times. Shouts of "Hallelujah!" from the "Amen corner" were squelched with a decided "Never mind, my friend, I can do all the hollering." If a noisy prayer was offered, out of tune with the mood he was trying to create, he would skilfully undo its effect by calling for a few minutes of *silent* prayer, and he was known to dismiss a meeting when somebody tried to talk with tongues or go into a trance. He abolished the "mourners' bench" and interviewed his prospects separately and quietly in an adjoining room. Whether it was a crying baby or the danger of a stampede motivated by fear, he was equal to any emergency, and for the most part he handled these crises with both courtesy and efficiency.

There had been nothing sensational about his own conversion, and he was never inclined to insist upon technicolor or strontian lights. He granted that it was possible, especially for the children of Christian homes, to come into the Kingdom without being able to tell just when the change took place; it came not "like a flash of lightning" but like "the gradual rise of the morning light." Both Moody and his wife showed great tact and patience in their dealings with their son William, who was a long time making up his mind to come in. In later years, as his commitment to educational work shows, Moody no longer thought it safe to rely upon the revival meeting for Christian recruitment and training, and he deliberately stopped keeping statistics of conversions. Early in life he made up his mind that he would speak to somebody about his salvation every day, but as he grew older, he became much more tactful, and Paul says he got on famously with the Yale boys Paul brought home from college and never embarrassed them or himself.

As to just what conversion accomplishes, his emphasis and interpretation differed from time to time. "By the second birth," he says, "there is given to man a nature which is Divine in its desires, and unselfish in its character." "It is so easy to serve him after you have taken your stand." Elsewhere, however, he denies the second statement.

I thought when I was converted that my temper was gone . . . but I soon found that I had a battle on hand. I had got to overcome sin, or sin would overcome me. I'd got to fight the world, the flesh, and the devil all the while—and I think, after all these years, that the flesh is the meanest of the lot. . . . I am to reckon myself crucified with

> Jesus Christ—I am to reckon that I stand on resurrection ground . . . but at the same time I am down here in the flesh yet, and if I don't watch the flesh and don't keep myself under—keep the body under—then he is going to get the victory over me.

Actually, he did not really know the meaning of spiritual struggle until *after* he was converted. "I had a pretty good opinion of myself." Later he came to believe that it is *after* a man has been born of God and his higher nature awakened that the real conflict between higher and lower appears.

Nevertheless there must be some moment somewhere when the soul, through conscious choice, has passed from darkness to light. You could be "vile as hell itself one moment and saved the next." Any person in the tabernacle could be saved then and there "without lifting their hands, without moving an eyelash." Moody can hardly be said to have defined what he meant by this nor to have explained how a corrupted and as yet unredeemed human nature could be capable of making such a choice. "You are to believe God's Word; you are to take God at His word and trust Him for salvation." "Christ is God's gift. If you receive Him you are saved, if not, you perish." You "accept" Christ as your "personal" Savior and give yourself to him. But what does all this mean, and how is it achieved? Certainly Moody himself did not know when he was converted in the shoe store, for at that time he could not tell what Christ had done for humanity. And there are times when one sympathizes with the Scottish friend who remarked after hearing one of his sermons, "My friend, what! did ye expect to tell what Christ is in half an hour? Ye need never to tell it in all eternity; ye would never get through with it."

Despite these objections, however, there can be no question that Moody did achieve many lasting conversions, or, if you prefer, transformed many lives. Nor were they all, by any means, those of ignorant or degraded people. Some of his converts had social position; some became distinguished men and distinguished public servants. Doubtless there were many backsliders of whom we hear nothing, and there is a good deal of evidence to indicate that Moody was not notably successful in reaching the unchurched, and that often church membership did not grow as the result of one of his campaigns. Nevertheless his achievments were considerable. How did he manage to do so much with so little?

Part of the answer lies in Lovett's observation that in Moody's time "the core of Protestant belief was still intact." Most of his listeners were not hearing something new and strange; they were hearing something they had been hearing all their lives but had chosen to disregard; now it was being presented to them with power by a man who convinced them that this very neglect had made them the miserable failures they knew they had become. Moody himself must have recognized this, for in his later years he lamented the decline in the old uniformity of belief. Once, he said, his work had been to bring people to decide

> to do what they already knew they ought to do. But it is all different now. The question mark is raised everywhere, and there is need for teachers who shall teach and show the people what the gospel is. I believe that God will raise up a teaching evangelism through which this work shall be done.

The other great element in his appeal was Moody's own personality, which combined power and gentleness to an extent that has rarely been surpassed. He won the derelicts in the Sands because they were overcome with wonder by the strange revelation that there was one man on earth who was not trying to get something out of them but who instead cared enough for them to bring something to them; indeed one of the little boys in that notorious district, asked why he went to Moody's Sunday School when there were others so much nearer, put the case in a nutshell when he replied he went to Moody's "because they love a fella there." Years later the Boston *Evening Transcript* remarked that "the most skeptical must respect such honesty pure and simple, such unadulterated zeal to do good," and a well-known Catholic paper could not find it in its heart to say that the evangelist had not come from God.

It may be objected that when I say Moody wanted nothing from his converts, I ought, in all honesty, to add "except their souls." But they all knew—or sensed—that Moody wanted their souls not for himself but for his Christ, that this Christ was intimately tied up with the best in themselves, and that they could no more satisfy themselves than they could satisfy Moody estranged from Him. It is one of the tragedies of our time that we can still believe in what it is now fashionable to call "charisma" in connection with some men and women while many of us have lost faith in the supreme charisma which is of God. "Don't praise me," cried Moody, "bruise me, rather; but if you love me, love Christ for my sake." It was his word to his contemporaries. It would be his word to us also.

6

WASHINGTON GLADDEN

Where Does the Sky Begin?

I

In 1966 Oxford University Press published in their "Library of Protestant Thought" series a book by Robert T. Handy called *The Social Gospel in America, 1870–1920,* which was made up of selections from the writings of Washington Gladden, Richard T. Ely, and Walter Rauschenbusch. Though he had been dead since 1918, the name of "The Father of the Social Gospel" still led all the rest.

The three named were not of course the only heralds of the "Social Gospel." In a sense, the author of *Applied Christianity* was not even the first. But his importance in the movement was unquestioned.

Gladden was also an important herald of the "New Theology." He helped to break down the old Calvinistic orthodoxy and thus became one of the founders of Liberal Protestantism or Modernism. But in his eyes "applied Christianity" and the New Theology were but opposite faces of the same coin. The old orthodoxy had thought of the Gospel as a means of saving individuals out of a damned race; the New Theology functioned in terms of building a Kingdom of God in this world. Basically it conceived of Deity not as Sovereign but as Father. "Where the truth of the Fatherhood of God is fully set forth," said Gladden, "there, to my thinking, is the whole Gospel." Under the old dispensation, you could think of the non-elect, and of all those who failed to accept Christ in this life in the precise terms defined by the theologians, as "aliens and strangers, subjects of his law, indeed, but in no wise sharing in his parental love"; once you began to think of God in familial terms this was impossible.

This did not at all mean that "the discord between the selfish soul and the Father whose name is love" was a less terrible thing in modern times than it had formerly been. But it did mean that many of the artificial barriers that had formerly been set up between God and man had fallen. Fatherhood and brotherhood are essentially and necessarily social conditions; neither can exist in isolation. "If God is the Father of us all, if we are the sons of God there can be no contrariety between our nature and his," and Christ himself becomes "more, and not *other*."

None of this implies a Unitarian way of thinking, for though the old conflicts between Unitarianism and Trinitarianism held no interest for Gladden, he could not think of God as love unless there was something in the universe toward which that love could be directed; the Son might, therefore, have been a logical necessity long before the creation of man, and the existence, as well as the manifestation, of God in Trinitarian terms might well rest upon more basic considerations than the rival proponents of *homoousion* and *homoiousion* had ever concerned themselves with.[1]

How characteristic of Gladden's whole outlook is his answer to the question "Where does the sky begin?" in the volume he rightly recognized as his best, which bears that title. "We are all dwellers in the sky." The sky is the atmosphere. "We have lived in it all our lives, and could not live anywhere else." This is "the simple, solid, scientific fact."

This had always been true, but it was not until Christ had wrought his great work of Atonement that men realized its truth.

He removed the "imaginary and unreal boundary line which separated the sky from our world"; with him "time does not end, neither does eternity begin." So long as morality carried a distinctively different meaning for God than it did for man, it was not possible that there should be any vital moral relations between them. We know now that there is no such dichotomy, and the results of the realization are far-reaching. We know, for example, that nothing can be right in God which would be wrong in man, and this knowledge has scrapped more than one theory of the Atonement. Christ has always been the head of the church, but now he can also be recognized as the head of humanity, which somehow undercuts all the silly old debates about whether or not the "heathen" are damned. Finally, "social teaching and social service is no longer something outside of religion"; it means "religion coming to reality in everyday life; the divine ideal descending upon human society and transforming it from glory to glory, even as by the spirit of the Lord."

> Faith is no fabric by logicians wrought,
> No sublimate of metaphysic thought,
> No trap of dialectic, shrewdly set
> To catch incautious souls in error's net,
> Nor any skeleton with bound hands
> That here today across our pathway stands;
> Nay, 'tis a Spirit, the soul of trust and truth,
> Of loyalty and honor, grace and ruth,
> Through whom we know God near, and not afar,
> And that in him we live and move and are;
> This is "Our Father's Faith," their living faith,
> That kept them whole, in loss and pain and scathe.[2]

II

Solomon Washington Gladden was born in Pottsville, Pennsylvania, February 11, 1836. He dropped the "Solomon" early; the "Washington" is supposed to have been derived from his grandfather's service as one of General Washington's bodyguard. The family may have descended from John Gladding, who came to Plymouth in 1640, and afterwards settled in Bristol, Rhode Island. Both Washington Gladden's parents were country schoolteachers, but his father was also a Methodist local preacher. Though he had been reared a Congregationalist, there were no Congregational churches in his vicinity, and the Presbyterian churches were too Calvinistic to be congenial to him.

The elder Gladden died in his son's sixth year, whereupon the mother took her two sons and returned to her native heath at Owego, New York. For nearly a year Washington Gladden lived with grandparents near Southampton, Massachusetts, within sight of Mount Tom. He attended Bedlam schoolhouse and worked in the fields. After his mother had married again, he was apprenticed as a farm worker to an uncle near Owego, where he again attended country school. Gladden gave Horace Lee Andrews, a medical student, credit for his intellectual awakening: "He found me a listless and lazy pupil; he left me with a zest for study and a firm purpose of self-improvement. It was a clear case of conversion; and when any one tells me that character cannot be changed through the operation of spiritual forces, I know better."

The uncle was a perceptive man, however, for it was he who steered young Washington away from farming into the office of the Owego *Gazette;* here he began his writing. "The artistic side of the work attracted me; I liked to experiment with display type, and to study pleasing effects in cards and title-pages and advertisements." All in all, he seems to have profited in the print shop almost as much as Mark Twain and William Dean Howells.

In 1855 he entered Owego Academy and made up his mind to prepare for the ministry. The next year he became a member of the sophomore class at Williams College, where he greatly admired the president, Mark Hopkins, and was strongly influenced by John Bascom. James A. Garfield was a senior when he was a sophomore; Henry M. Alden and Horace E. Scudder, the great future editors for Harper and Brothers and Houghton Mifflin Company respectively, were fellow students. During the long winter vacations Gladden taught country school. He made the acquaintance of Samuel Bowles and J. G. Holland, through whom he was invited to write for the Springfield *Republican.* After graduating from Williams in 1859, Gladden taught school in Owego but did not like it, categorizing his 125 pupils more or less evenly as "Afric's sable sons, . . . children of the Emerald Isle, . . . idiots, and . . . children of the wicked one."

He preached his first sermon from the pulpit of the Owego Congregational Church by invitation of its pastor, the future historian Moses Coit Tyler, and at Tyler's suggestion he was licensed to preach by the Susquehanna Association of Congregational Ministers. Gladden always thought he could never have made it if the moderator had not been the liberal and highly unconventional Thomas K. Beecher.[3]

In January 1860, Gladden conducted eight weeks of special services at a run-down church in Le Raysville, just over the Pennsylvania line; then, at the beginning of May, he went to a waif which oddly called itself the "First Congregational Methodist Church of Brooklyn." Here, in November, he was ordained, and on December 5 he married Jennie O. Cohoon, who had been a schoolmate at Owego and now lived in Brooklyn. The Brooklyn post was a difficult one, and Gladden, who had not yet learned how to conserve his energies, promptly brought himself to the verge of a breakdown. The next year he moved into quieter pastures provided by the Congregational church at Morrisiana, two miles north of the Harlem River, where he stayed until

1866, when he was called to his first important charge at North Adams, Massachusetts. The only theological training he was ever to acquire he picked up rather casually by attending some lectures at Union Theological Seminary.

For four years (1871–75) Gladden relinquished the pastorate to work on *The Independent*, where his functions were wider than his title "Religious Editor" would itself indicate. He was happy and successful in this work but resigned it out of conscientious scruples over a question of business and editorial ethics.[4] In 1875 he began his eight-year pastorate at North Congregational Church, Springfield, Massachusetts, and for a few years beginning in 1878 he also edited a magazine first called *Sunday Afternoon*, then *Good Company*.

In 1882 he went to the First Congregational Church of Columbus, Ohio, where he remained until his death—becoming pastor emeritus in 1914 but continuing to do considerable preaching. As a matter of civic duty he served on the Columbus City Council from 1900 to 1902. He was on the Harvard University preaching staff in 1892–94, and again in 1902–3, and might have had further appointments had he been willing to take the time from his church duties. He delivered the Lyman Beecher Lectures at Yale in 1889 and again in 1902. At one time he was considered as a successor to David Swing at Central Church, Chicago; he also came within sight of three college presidencies—Western Reserve,[5] Ohio State, and the University of Illinois. From 1904 to 1907 he was Moderator of the National Council of Congregational Churches; this was the period when he challenged the American Board on their solicitation and acceptance of John D. Rockefeller's "tainted money" (the phrase was Gladden's) for missionary work. He received honorary doctorates from Wisconsin, Notre Dame, and Roanoke College. Mrs. Gladden died on May 8, 1909; her husband lived nine years longer, until July 2, 1918. All creeds in Columbus paid homage at his funeral.[6]

III

Gladden was one of the most reserved of men; few who have written so much have told us so little about themselves. In appearance he was comparatively short, bearded but bald-headed, his eyes peering through narrow, old-fashioned rimmed spectacles, his stocky, rather stiff-looking figure seeming both tightly buttoned up and closely packed. When Charles R. Brown first saw him enter the pulpit at Harvard, he thought he looked like a prosperous businessman or bank president rather than a clergyman. The appearance was misleading. Accomplished though he was as writer and preacher, Gladden was also a pastor and fearless civic leader, and though it is clear that even in this aspect he maintained a certain reserve and dignity,[7] he was deeply loved. Gaius Glenn Atkins speaks of the warmth and passion of his mediatorial prayers in the Sunday morning service as perhaps marking the high point of achievement. Nor are his many books in any sense lacking in warmth and feeling.

In spite of the malaria which he picked up doing relief work in Civil War times, Gladden's health seems to have been excellent. After the early breakdown which he brought on by recklessly overworking himself to the extent of sometimes getting only ten hours sleep in six days, he always disciplined his forces sensibly, but the immense amount which he accomplished must still amaze the observer. So completely was the failing corrected that it is hard to believe him when he tells us that at the beginning of his ministry he was always late, even for services, and that he had to take himself sternly in hand to avoid this. Commenting on the work of miners he once remarked that "it seems almost a crime that a man should be obliged to spend his days in severe toil, where air is tainted and sunshine never comes." Yet he spent his own life in a First Church tower study where the only natural light which reached him had to be filtered through heavy stained-glass windows, the facilities for artificial light were grossly inadequate, and in winter a burning coal fire in the grate poisoned the air.[8] When he wrote his *Recollections* (1909), he said he would like seventy more years of life; in *Commencement Days* (1916), he reported that he was working longer hours than at the beginning of his ministry and that his powers of endurance were now superior to what they had been thirty to forty years before. Two years before he died, he acknowledged "some creeping infirmities of age; limbs not quite so supple or muscles so elastic as once; some impairment of the memory of names and faces," but thanked God for "the goodness and loving kindness that have followed me all the days of my life," and specifically for "sight undimmed and hearing not much dulled; powers of locomotion still fairly good. . . ."[9] When, in his last year, his right side was paralyzed by a stroke, he accomplished the miraculous feat, for a man in his eighties, of learning how to write with his left hand, but his reward was not great, for a second stroke followed hard upon and took him.

Though Gladden often seems over-optimistic to a less hopeful age than the one he lived in, he was not often sentimental.[10] Because he believed that Christ's primary purpose was not to relieve suffering but to save men from sin, he was never guilty of praising indiscriminate almsgiving or anything else that made the donor feel "good." "The indulgence of humane and compassionate feelings is, no doubt, a luxury to some natures. And there are those who suppose that the indulgence of such feelings makes up the greater part of human virtue." He poured scorn upon the kind of sentimentalism represented by John Hay's Pike County ballad, "Jim Bludso": "Just how a man could have two wives at the same time without lying to one or both of them the poet does not tell us." But because Jim was "kind hearted and self sacrificing," the poet creates the impression that such things were not important. And "sentimentalism of this kind is not only sickly, it is nauseating."

Yet Gladden admitted that if he had to choose he would place benevolence ahead of holiness (which would have disgusted a Puritan divine quite as much as "Jim Bludso" disgusted him). A strong hero-worshipper, he surrounded himself, in his study, with pictures of the people he admired, and in *Witnesses of the Light* and elsewhere some of his indulgences for human failings are immense. Thus Victor Hugo had "a natural religiousness in him, which readily responded to the deeper verities of the spirit," and Richard Wagner was possessed of "the same spirit which animated Luther . . . —fidelity to the highest that he knew; readiness to suffer the loss of all things rather than be false to his ideals." Indeed, Gladden's respect for personality was so great that he would not even force the Christian convert to make a public declaration of his intention of discipleship unless he chose to do so. He would not probe the conscience of a sick person; he neither refused nor exhorted unknown couples who came to him to be married. What he did do was try to help them understand the seriousness of their situation by the way he conducted the service.

In all things, Washington Gladden was a man of strong will and personality. He would have agreed perfectly with the little girl who objected to being told to live for others because if everybody did that, there would be nobody left for the others to live for. The Christian law is not "sheer altruism—Thou shalt love thy neighbor and *not* thyself; it is the union of self-love and goodwill—Thou shalt love they neighbor *as* thyself." Both selfishness and sentimentalism are "very simple," but "right conduct sets for us many intricate problems. To refer all human action to one motive makes the calculation easy, but is not always correct." It was not surprising that a man of his temperament should be careful in money matters; he could not recall ever having gone into installment buying. When he died he left an estate of nearly $40,000.[11]

There can be no question about either his courage as a preacher or his efficiency as a church administrator. He gave up an editorial post out of conscientious scruples; he lost the offer of one, possibly two, college presidencies because of his refusal to conceal his views on a controversial public issue. Perhaps Gladden did not greatly wish to be president of Ohio State, but he did wish to be pastor of his church in Columbus, yet he gave the lectures on Biblical criticism which became *Who Wrote the Bible?* though he believed there was a very good chance they might lose him his pulpit. He always insisted upon his rights as a clergyman, both in the church and in the denomination, sturdily defending his freedom of belief when he disagreed with his more conservative brethren. I doubt that any lines in his most famous poem can have been more deeply felt than these, which never appear in our hymnals:

> O Master, let me walk with Thee
> Before the taunting Pharisee,
> Help me to bear the sting of spite,
> The hate of men who hide Thy light,
> The sore distrust of souls sincere
> Who cannot read Thy judgments clear,
> The dullness of the multitude
> Who dimly guess that Thou art good.

I may add that when Gladden disagreed with one of his subordinates in his Columbus church, there was never any serious question as to who was master.[12] Many would say, too, that he was not wise, nor wholly fair to his successor, by remaining in the congregation, and sometimes occupying the pulpit, after he had formally turned over the reins to Carl S. Patton.

Gladden was never a castigating moralist—still less was he unsympathetic toward young people—but there is some pretty straight uncompromising talk about their weaknesses to both sexes in *Myrrh and Cassia*, and this can be duplicated in relation to other groups elsewhere. When an unknown schoolboy wrote asking Gladden to furnish him with a subject for a debate, likely to be popular with judges, he did not ignore the impertinence, as most of us would have done; instead he explained, carefully and politely, why he could not honor this request, after which he added that "if your main object in speaking is to please the judges and win the victory, you ought to fail, and you probably will."

Above all, I think we must realize that no clergyman could have entered into so many public crusades as Gladden did without having a certain gift for controversy. When Tweed asked New York, "What are you going to do about it?" Gladden's answer, in *The Independent*,[13] was one of the most biting and prophetic:

> We are going to turn you and all your creatures out of your offices. That we can do, and shall do, please God, before the new year is a week old.
>
> We are going to get back as much as we can of the booty you have stolen. We know the job will not be an easy one; but you may depend upon us not to give it up without a fair trial.
>
> We are going to use our best endeavors to send you to your own place, the penitentiary. You have been guilty of the most staring and stupendous frauds; and we do not intend to admit, until we are compelled to do so, that men in office can commit such frauds without incurring the vengeance of the law.
>
> At any rate, we are going to make this city and the whole country too hot for you. There is some conscience left in this land yet, and you will find it out before you die. Upon you shall rest, heavy and immobile, the load of a nation's curse! You have trafficked in injustice. You have perverted our laws. You have corrupted our young men. You have done what in you lay to destroy our government. There are some sins that a nation may never forgive, and yours is among them. It is our solemn charge to hold you up while you live to the scorn and contempt of mankind. God may have mercy upon you; but as for us, we promise you that your ill-gotten booty shall be but a poor compensation for the inheritance of shame which shall be yours forever.

He was even bolder when he attacked John D. Rockefeller and the American Board in the "tainted money" controversy, many years later, nor was he at all moved by the arguments of those who urged that as the current Moderator of the National Council, he had no right to raise such a question. He seems to be hitting at William Rainey Harper and The University of Chicago when he declares that a college president who is offered money "which has been notoriously gotten by fraud and rapine" ought to reply:

> Certainly we will take your money, if you choose to give it to us; but you must give it with the distinct understanding that we shall teach our young men that it is a shameful thing to get wealth in the way that you have gotten yours, and that giving a part of it away in charity does not take off the curse.[14]

In his *Recollections*, Gladden wrote of the Tweed encounter that "it was one of the times of my life when I have come across something that needed to be hit and have had a chance to strike hard. Such opportunities make life worth living." There is an essay too in which we are told that temptations destroy peace and integrity only for weaklings. "There is no exercise more exhilarating than kicking the devil down stairs and slamming the door behind him." The only note of doubt I have encountered comes in a late sermon called "Blessing and Banning":

> I have had some fighting to do in my time, and may have more to do before I die; and if I had to live my life over I would by no means agree to keep silent about abuses and to shut my mouth in the presence of iniquities and oppressions; but of this I am sure,—I would put a great deal more of my strength into the promotion and cherishing of the good that is in the world, and just that much less into the warfare with the evil that is in the world.

One reason why Gladden's frankness failed to give offence was that he had humor. Another was that he made no claim to omniscience or superiority. "Do I speak to you as one who has fully entered into this great inheritance?" he asks, in a sermon on "How To Be Sure of God." "Nay, I make no such claim."

Often I am timid and despondent and more anxious than I ought to be; often small things vex me, and the judgment of men irks me, and I am afraid of losses and reverses; the whole trouble is that I am not nearly as sure of God as I ought to be. I am not standing on some eminence above you and calling down to you. I am standing with you, on the common plane of our humanity, but I am lifting my eyes to the hills from which our help must come, and trying to get you to look in the same direction.

When he was dealing with factual matters, he always took pains to be accurate.[15] He never had any doubt that it was possible for a Christian to be a blockhead too, and he speaks of the Biblical literalists as disputing "over the question whether Jonah did really compose that psalm in the belly of the fish, with his head festooned with seaweed." Having quoted the denunciation of Abelard by Bernard of Clairvaux on the charge of having disputed traditional doctrine, he adds, "And then, I suppose, after the hand-clapping ceased, the listening assembly joined in the ancient version of the song, the substance of which has been sung in every generation:

> 'Tis the old time religion,
> And it's good enough for me."

Ask him whether it is right to pray for political victories, and he will tell you, "Yes, if you belong to a party that is not past praying for." And he himself quotes the promise of heaven in the Doddridge hymn—

> No midnight shade, no clouded sun,
> But sacred, high, eternal noon.

"Let us hope," he says, "that it will not be as bad as that; that there will be cool shadows, and soft twilights, and even grateful darkness in which we may sometimes bathe our weary eyelids."

But not all Gladden's shafts were directed against the conservatives. He thought the *Zeitgeist* had been "somewhat out of his head for the last generation or so, having got hold of some crazy and incomplete theories of evolution, and being inclined to regard the environment as the sole and decisive factor in the development of life." He also believed that people who classify Christ with other religious leaders "do certainly succeed in classing themselves, and not among great thinkers." And he made brilliant fun[16] of Thomas Henry Huxley's silly statement that by referring to Jonah, Jesus Christ had affirmed his belief in the historicity of that character, from which it must follow that Christ could not be accepted as an authority on anything else either. Gladden had no difficulty in showing from Huxley's own writings that the scientist himself had made similar references to literary characters in whose historicity he could not possibly have believed.

IV

When his successor in First Church pulpit told Gladden that his interest in the ministry was largely confined to the cultivation of personal religion and the application of religious principles to social problems, the old man gazed at him, dropped one eyelid in the way he was famous for, and inquired, "Well, what else is there?" For him these things made up the heart and meaning not only of religion but of life itself, but it must not be supposed that his range of interests was narrow. A country boy, he loved nature passionately, especially the Berkshires ("there were few heights to which I had not climbed; there were not many trout-brooks whose length I had not measured"), which he ached for after he had left Massachusetts for that flat Middle West. One of his first books, *From the Hub to the Hudson*, came out of his explorations of the Connecticut Valley, and he greatly enjoyed writing it. Lest it should seem unprofessional, he had originally intended to publish it anonymously, but he decided against this in the conviction that such a book would "be likely to do less harm than a book about the Mode of Baptism or the Origin of Evil."

If possible, however, the world within interested Gladden even more than the world without. Science was less important educationally in his time than it is today. Gladden recognized its importance, fought for its fredom, and always acknowledged its claims where they had been established, but he was happiest when he could find religious significance in it, as when he defines heredity as God working in us and environment as God working around us. Languages he loved, not only Greek and Latin but also German and French, both of which he quotes in *The Christian Pastor and the Working Church*, in "The International Theological Library." He attributed a positive value to language study and thought the drill involved the best possible preparation for being able to express yourself adequately in your own language.

But of course literature was the great thing. Gladden was a slave to print from his youth, and he tried his hand at both fiction and verse.[17] The publication of his first book gave him as great a thrill as if he had had no interest except writing, and at one time he was considered the most valuable contributor to the *Century*. He was not a "literary preacher" if by that you mean to imply that he neglected either evangelicalism or social concerns, but he did give many sermons based on history, literature, and biography, and he handled his biographical subjects very much in the spirit and manner of his William Belden Noble lectures in *Witnesses of the Light*. There are times when he seems to prefer biography even to poetry; in *The Christian Pastor* he calls biographies the "best of all books for the pastor," and in his memorial discourse on President Hayes[18] he declares that "in no other form does Truth present herself with so much quickening of the intellect, with so much invigoration of the will. For this reason chiefly was the Word made flesh." Yet he read literature both early and late, with a heavy reliance upon the English poets, among whom Wordsworth, Tennyson, and Browning would seem to have been the favorites. In college days he and his classmates attached "a nonsense refrain of a very flippant sort" to "A Psalm of Life," but he was later ashamed of this, and Longfellow's poem furnished him with a text in *Live and Learn*. He was sufficiently up-to-date in American literature to speak of Mr. Dooley as "a philosopher, with a vision as clear as any of his guild," and he quoted Orestes A. Brownson ("property is communion with God through the material world") long before his modern revival. Among English prose writers, Ruskin clearly meant most to him. "Of all the men who have used the English language John Ruskin has given us the noblest prose." He could "say things more pithily, more keenly, more vividly, more luminously, more beautifully, more magnificently than any one [else] who ever wrote the English language." [19] Gladden always regretted that he had not encountered Scott and Cooper earlier in life than he did, and I think he always retained vestiges of the old-fashioned idea that the novel was somehow inferior to the older types of literature, but he left an unpublished sermon on "Dickens the Preacher." He praised *Vanity Fair*, *Romola*, and *A Modern Instance*, but unfortunately permitted "Professor Richardson of Dartmouth College" to mislead him into finding "moral indifferentism" in Henry James.

Evangelical Christians have generally had less trouble making terms with literature than with either recreation or the other arts. With athletic exercises, Gladden, the country boy, had little difficulty, and though he was sensitive to abuses and misplacement of emphasis in this area (he thought pugilists and acrobats "miserable failures"), he had much less to say about them than about dancing and theater-going. He tells us very little about the country sports of his boyhood (Williams did not do much with games in his time), though we do hear that he later enjoyed driving horses, and once he speaks of learning how to row with a free oar. Billiards and bowling he thought good in themselves and wished to rescue them from the dissolute hands into which they had fallen in his time. When, in 1866, he argued[20] that recreation was a necessity for every human being, not merely innocent but indispensable to both bodily and mental health, and that "the day is not far distant when physical culture will be enjoined as a Christian duty," he shocked a good many of the brethren. Yet even here he was extremely cautious and discriminated carefully in all his allowances and prohibitions.

Gladden attempted to formulate his aesthetic theory in a little book called *The Relations of Art and Morality*,[21] in which he argues that the love of beauty is as much a part of man's nature as the aspiration after righteousness.[22] A successful life involves a reasonable balance between the two elements, but Gladden recognizes that this is not often achieved. "The Greeks after Pericles enthroned beauty and despised righteousness; the Puritans after Cromwell uplifted righteousness, and trampled beauty under foot." Gladden disapproved of both extremes, but he was closer to Puritan than to Greek; art, he thought, became the supreme or exclusive interest only in a decadent society, which cherished but a physical ideal of beauty and showed no recognition, as Michelangelo did, of the struggle going on between the higher and lower nature of man and no aspiration after a higher life. Apparently Gladden was modern rather than classical, especially in his tastes in sculpture; thus the human form, as the Greeks presented it, seemed to him quite satisfying, but the faces were "hard, severe, strong, masterful," reflecting none of the higher graces of character as seen in such modern faces as those of Gladstone, Ruskin, Stanley, Newman, Lowell, Brooks, Curtis, and Lincoln. Gladden could not honestly feel that "the relation between sound ethics and good art has always been as close as Ruskin insists." He granted that some forms of art are non-moral rather than either moral or immoral, and he did not believe that the character of its creator was always to be discerned in a symphony or a sonata, a landscape painting or a design for a building.[23] But, like Matthew Arnold, he believed that at its best art was not decorative nor merely imitative but interpretive, and that true interpretation was not to be looked for from those whose lives were false. Painting, sculpture, and poetry all involved considerations of human character, and figure painting, portrait painting, and historical painting were superior to landscape and still life.

Music Gladden loved. "Rightly ministered," it was "a vehicle of the purest and loftiest emotions,—the only language that can express the aspiration of the soul that thirsts for song, or the rapture of the beatific vision." So we hear of the pastor singing baritone solos or directing his own choir, and C. R. Brown says he played the piano well. He read score with ease, nor did he wholly lose the faculty of musical composition with his college days (he composed the Williams College song, "The Mountains," and other pieces), for he was not young when he recorded that original tunes still sometimes floated through his head. He mentions Beethoven's symphonies, and he was a great Wagnerite, characteristically placing the emphasis upon the spiritual ideas back of the music dramas ("It is the Christ-idea with which his thought is saturated. If woman . . . is the representative of this idea, it is because he thinks that she most perfectly represents it"). Gladden speaks of Hofmann and of Paderewski, and he places "the great singers" with great builders and painters (I wonder why he trusted them so much more than their brother and sister actors of the legitimate drama). In a church service, he insisted, music must be worship, not performance, and anything else was blasphemy. The best church music was choral music and could not be rendered adequately by a paid quartette, though such a quartette, if worshipfully minded, might usefully *lead* in such rendering and in congregational singing as well. Only when music was associated with dancing does he seem to have mistrusted it;

though he did not condemn dancing per se, he thought both waltzes and polkas "a moral abomination."

The principal count in Gladden's indictment of the theater seems to have been his notion that actors in general were morally degraded people. He recognized the moral dangers involved in setting up an inquisition into other people's lives and demanding that they be cleared before you agreed to do business with them,[24] yet he seems to have felt that the odor of contamination somehow leaped the barrier of the footlights, specially when the actor himself became an object of adulation. Worse yet, he thought that the general tone of the plays presented in the commercial theater of his time tended toward degradation. Here again, as with dancing, however, he insisted that the basic impulse was not evil. Intellectually he was convinced that the theater was here to stay and that Christians had an interest in improving it, "even though we may have nothing to do with it ourselves," which would be a pretty difficult combination; as late as *Present Day Theology* he was capable of referring to "a man who never drinks nor smokes nor dances nor plays cards nor goes to the theater."

Opposition to the theater is often strongly associated with sexual puritanism. Like most of the men of his generation, Gladden seems squeamish to us in sexual matters, but it would not be fair to call him a prude. As a young man he seems to have had at least a normal interest in girls. "It must not be inferred, to begin with," he says, "that there is anything evil in the gratification of the senses." He defends the girl who spends her money on beautiful clothes, though he did not want them to be either extravagant or indecent. He thought of "the bodily appetites" as "elements of wholesome life," and the worst sins were not those of the flesh but of the spirit. "To say that that which is necessary to my life is hurtful to my soul is to make a grave accusation against the Author of the universe." He was speaking of property when he said this, but I think he would grant that it applies to sex also. In *Seven Puzzling Bible Books* he does not appear quite comfortable with The Song of Songs, but he understood its erotic character and was not hysterical about it. He did not reject the doctrine of the Virgin Birth, but he did dislike it as placing a barrier between Christ and humanity and throwing "some discredit upon the sacredness of marriage." There are love songs in *Ultima Veritas*, and one poem, "At the Foundling Hospital," is the sympathetic soliloquy of an unwed mother who cannot bear to give up her baby. Gladden understood the economic factors which affect the "vast social ulcer" of prostitution. Yet he condemned marrying without love, for the sake of a home, and urged girls not to be ashamed to earn their own living. He does not seem to have been sure that Dr. Parkhurst's crusade against vice in New York had accomplished anything more than to spread and scatter, and he sometimes gives the impression of regarding the problem as insoluble. So far as specific suggestions are concerned, he does not get far beyond forbidding open solicitation and establishing centers of refuge for girls who wish to break away.

Only when it comes to "the sophistry and wickedness of this doctrine of easy divorce" does Gladden seem unrealistic and even inhuman in sexual matters; apparently he was so frightened by the rising tide of divorce that he forgot all other considerations. "Marriage is not for all of you," he told the girls in *Myrrh and Cassia*, "and it is not of great importance that any of you should know whether it will be your portion or not. . . . No woman is fit to marry who is not fitted to live a happy, noble, serviceable life out of wedlock." Is it possible that such advice was listened to with patience in 1883? Worse still, in *The Christian Pastor*, Gladden gives this as a sample of what a pastor might say, "with all the authority and solemnity of the everlasting truth in his utterance," to a couple whose marriage seemed in danger of foundering:

"You two must live together. You have covenanted to do so before the eternal God, and you must keep your covenant. Separation is not to be thought of. You took each other for better or worse, and you must not desert each other now. The problem for each of you is to win and compel the respect, the affection of the other. You can do it if you try. You had better die than fail. Go home and begin to-day."

One may not doubt that there are many cases in which this would be excellent advice. But there are others in which it quite fails to make either Law or Gospel. And to decide the case beforehand ("Separation is not to be thought of." "You had better die than fail."), this surely is the voice of an inhuman fanaticism which it is hard to associate with Washington Gladden.

V

Gladden wrote his sermons, of which more than 1500 have survived, and delivered them from his own handwritten manuscripts. He had no objection to repeating a sermon, with or without variation, sometimes over a period of years. This does not mean, however, that he was creative only in his study and turned into a phonograph record in his pulpit. Though he attempted no oratorical flourishes, Gladden achieved a close rapport with his audience. He liked to spend the last hour before the service in reading "some stirring book of devotion" or "some presentation of truth that shall awaken the mind and quicken the pulses of the heart." He could not control the minds of his listeners as he did his own, but he could and did see to it that their surroundings were right, not wrong, for the reception of his message. He would not, for example, allow a small prayer meeting group to be scattered over a large room; if those present would not sit together near the front, he would cut off part of the room with ropes or screens, or even, if necessary, take up his own position between the pews.

His Sunday morning sermons were nearly always devoted to personal religion, the discussion of social, economic, and political problems and questions of Biblical scholarship and of literary or historical interest were assigned to the evening. His sermons were both devotional and closely-reasoned, and they were definitely evangelical.[25] Gladden was always able to control his enthusiasm for revival meetings, even when they were not conducted by his special *bête noire*, Billy Sunday,[26] and he had no illusions as to the sudden and magical transformation of sinner into saint through "hitting the sawdust trail," but he did believe in the importance of a definite decision for Christ and the Christian way. "The evangelist who does not care to teach," he wrote, "is apt to become a bad kind of sentimentalist; and the teacher who has no evangelistic fervor is apt to degenerate into a critic or an essayist." At the same time, he tended to feel that a preacher should concern himself with general principles rather than specific rules for conduct, for he disliked prying and scandal-mongering. "The relation between pastor and people," he says, "is one of great delicacy; the happiness of both parties depends on considerateness and justice—not to say kindness—in many matters with respect to which the pastor's lips are sealed."

He preached the Gospel and he preached the Bible. In family worship, in public worship, and in his own study, he was steeped in the Bible from childhood; he had read it through several times before he was thirty. But he preached the Bible as it is, rejecting all the superstitions that had attached themselves to it, refusing to make any claims for it that it did not make for itself, guarding against the possibility that intelligent readers might reject it altogether because of the lies that had been told in its behalf. He had, and he claimed to have, no more independent scholarship in Biblical studies than in science, but he consulted the best authorities in both fields, judging their findings by his own common sense and their relevance to his needs. When he erred, it was on the conservative side. *Who Wrote the Bible?* gave Saint Paul more than is now assigned to him, and both the Fourth Gospel and the Revelation were given to John the Apostle. One may even see the ghost of many a Fundamentalist fulminator hovering in the background of such an ill-advised statement as that the Gospel "is either the work of John, or it is a cunning and conscienceless fraud." [27] Gladden was always "ready to affirm that other than natural forces have been employed in producing" the Bible. "But," he insisted, "the Bible has a natural history also," and since we are men, it cannot meet our needs unless we acknowledge this. Of course present-day standards and beliefs in this field cannot fairly be applied as touchstones to what Gladden said and wrote so long ago. In his time he was quite courageous enough, and even sympathetic listeners may well have been shocked by his reference to "the revelation given by God to half savage men." What did they think, I wonder, when he told them that a familiar verse in the Bible was an interpolation? or disposed of Esther with "Is this history? There is every reason to hope that it is not"? And he adds, "If one wishes to see the perfect antithesis of the precepts and the spirit of the gospel of Christ, let him read the Book of Esther."

Gladden never toned down nor emasculated the Christian claim, and no Fundamentalist ever insisted on a complete surrender of the whole personality to Christ more emphatically than he did, but the theology he preached was sensible and humane. In his eyes, the basic cause of the modern revolt against the old views was the modern insistence that theology must be moral, and that nothing that would be reprehensible in man can be attributed to God.[28] Though he was not prepared to assert that none ever came to the Father except through Christ ("Jesus did not claim to be the Founder of a new religion; he claimed only to bring a better understanding of the religion of his people"), he certainly believed that for us, in our civilization, Christ was the Door of Doors, and that he who did not find God through him was not very likely to find God elsewhere.[29] In reading Dante, he missed the sense of communion and personal friendship with Christ on the part of his penitents. "He is not here. . . . He has done his work once and for all; He has made his sacrifice for them, and they have availed themselves of it sacramentally." Increasingly, as he grew older, Gladden came to feel that "religion is summed up in the word Friendship—that it is just being friends with the Father above and the brother by our side." Like Lowell, in "The Cathedral," on the other hand, he knew that incompleteness, suggestiveness, is the hallmark of modern religious experience, and that even Herbert Spencer's conviction of the unknowability of God was a lesser evil than "that assumption of perfect intimacy with the secret counsels of the infinite Mind which is habitual with some theologians."

Since he believed that God is our Father, Gladden made comparatively little of punishment.[30] He was influenced by F. W. Robertson, Benjamin Kidd, and Henry Ward Beecher,[31] but above all by Horace Bushnell, whom he drafted to preach his installation sermon at North Adams, though Bushnell warned him that the act might cost him dear among conservative Christians. Like Bushnell, he thought of the Atonement as changing man, not God. When we see Jesus suffering and grieving for our sins, we know that God shares this suffering and benevolence, and this "redeems us from our sin . . . by getting us to see our sin as God sees it, and to hate it as God hates it."

Gladden rejected miracles interpreted as interferences by God with the order He himself had established, but refused to believe that the Creator was imprisoned in his own creation. "The proposition that a free, omnipotent Will can act in no other way than in the way it does act, is self-contradictory."[32] He tended to interpret much Biblical supernaturalism in terms of "mental impressions," believing "that Abraham was led, just as you and I are led, by his reason and his love, into the ways of obedience." Nowhere was the deliverance which the New Theology achieved for him more appreciated than in the way it rescued him from the eschatological terrors to which he had been exposed by his youth in the days of Millerites.[33] Immortality of course he retained, but though he did not minimize nor reject extension, quality interested him more. "There is a kind of life that in its very nature is deathless; it goes on by its own momentum. . . . They who share . . . [Christ's] life have the witness in themselves; for them there is no death." He could find no Scriptural warrant for the popular belief that probation ends with bodily death, though he admitted that in many cases the issue must be practically decided by that time, and he was involved, always on the liberal side, in famous ecclesiastical controversies involving both future probation and the salvation of the "heathen." [34] Spiritistic phenomena did not interest him because he knew "that the senses can be deceived and hoodwinked," and when it came to immortality, he was interested only in that which appealed to his "spiritual nature" or satisfied his "moral intuitions." In *The Church and Modern Life* he oddly names Spiritualists among the non-Christian religious groups in the United States! [35]

As is shown by the amount of writing he did on ecclesiastical matters, Gladden was much more of a churchman than was Lyman Abbott. And, though in *The Christian League of Connecticut*, he calls "the distinctive principles of religious denomination" about as important as ribbons and laces, he was always a loyal Congregationalist. At his twenty-fifth anniversary in Columbus, he recalled having made up his mind in boyhood, "when none of my kinsfolk were in that communion, that if I ever joined any church it would be a Congregational church." [36] I am bound to say I do not think Gladden wholly escaped the taint of professionalism in this matter. "The man who professes to be a servant of Christ, and yet neglects to join the church is . . . just as foolish and just as disobedient, as the man who professes to be a disciple of Christ, and yet neglects to study the Bible." Even if this were true, it would come better from a layman than from a clergyman.

> Not seldom service [in the church] is refused on the plea of incompetency. It is a plea that a soldier never thinks of making, and that a Christian ought to be ashamed to make. If you cannot stand at the post assigned to you, you can fall there.

This is as inhuman as what he says about marriage, and considerably more intolerant. Serving on a church committee or ushering at the Sunday morning service might, I should think, be a very poor cause in which to agree to "fall."

In theory, however, Gladden was always clear that, like the Bible itself, the church was a means towards an end, not an end in itself. The end was the Kingdom. He knew that the church had been both enriched and corrupted by her contacts with the world ever since the first century, and he objected that she had accepted the Nicene Creed but not the Sermon on the Mount. Actually she ceased to be Christian when she began to preach theology about Jesus in place of the religion which he himself preached. As he looked back over his own life, Gladden was firmly convinced that the clerical profession was the only one that could have contented him, but when he was in the thick of the fight, this was not always so. Not only was he reluctant to return to the parish ministry after his work on *The Independent*, but he considered giving up the ministry as late as 1882, just before he was called to Columbus.

VI

If the church as a whole did not commit herself to the Sermon on the Mount, Gladden certainly did, and it was this that made him the great herald of the Social Gospel. With him as with Jane Addams the element of social consciousness went back to the very dawn of religious feelings. "It was not an individualistic pietism that appealed to me; it was a religion that laid hold upon life with both hands, and proposed, first and foremost, to realize the Kingdom of God in this world."

But it must not be assumed that he saw all the issues involved quite clearly from the beginning; there is, for example, nothing that could offend any capitalist in what he writes in *From the Hub to the Hudson* of the industrial establishments he encountered between Boston and Troy. It is astonishing to find him writing, as late as *Applied Christianity*, that the "greatest defect" of the poor is "a defect of character," and even in *The Church and Modern Life* there is more than a touch of condescension in his statement that "it cannot be proved that poverty is wholly the fault of the poor." Once he even wants the poor to help themselves in their poverty by staying away from "circuses and nigger-minstrel shows"!

Gladden's first important confrontation with the labor problem came with a shoe strike at North Adams.[37] Later he saw the Hocking Valley coal-mining strike at close range and was involved in a streetcar strike in Columbus. Long before this he had made up his mind that it was as important for a clergyman to understand economics as theology. *Tools and the Man,* his first important book on industrial problems, was published in 1894. Though he did not accept Socialism, he insisted, as many of his contemporaries did not, on separating it sharply from anarchism and other violent forms of revolutionary activity, and subjecting its proposals to the fair test of reason. He certainly believed in a great deal—public ownership of all monopolies, etc.—which most of his contemporaries called socialistic.

He gave careful consideration to profit sharing and cooperatives. If Christianity is to tolerate the wage system, he believed, it must be in much the same spirit that she once tolerated slavery. "A man may be a Christian who is an aristocrat or a plebeian, but the logic of Christianity is democracy. A man may be a Christian who is a capitalist or a wage-laborer, but the logic of Christianity is cooperation." He not only defended the right of workers to organize as long as the wage system endured; he urged upon every worker the duty of joining a union; but at the same time he insisted that the worker who exercised his undoubted right by remaining outside must not be molested. Churches for "upper classes" and "lower classes" ought to be "blotted from existence." ("The conceit of culture is often about as virulent and anti-social as the pride of wealth.") He was particularly grieved that the Congregational church was so emphatically not the church of the common people, and he opposed taking Rockefeller's money not only because he thought it wrong in itself but also because he saw its acceptance driving another wedge between the common man and the church. His attitude was understood and appreciated in Columbus, where both friend and foe recognized him as a friend of labor, but he never brought large numbers of working people into his church, even though the branch churches and schools which First Church established were significant for both settlement and missionary work.[38]

Gladden is often called a pacifist, but this is not quite correct. It is true that many individual utterances support the pacifist point of view. It is certainly true that he hated war and the things that make for war. Thus, in *Tools and the Man:* "I do not think that Christianity contemplates the maintenance of standing armies of any sort." In *The Church and Modern Life* the church must "keep itself free from all suspicion of entanglement with physical force." She "cannot use force in any way, nor . . . enter into any coalition with governments that rest on force." Tell him that the church cannot lead the fight against war because she has other more important work to do, and he will inquire what work. "Was it the saving of souls? But how are souls lost more hopelessly than by filling them with murderous hate of their fellow men? Was it to rescue men from hell? But here were several nations organizing hell and bringing it to earth." In 1916, when the Wilson administration threatened Mexico, Gladden owned to "many doubts as to whether war is ever justifiable." [39] And when Wilson himself went over at last to the "peace through preparedness" people, Gladden published his Church Peace Union essay, *The Forks in the Road*,[40] in which he urged that "preparedness" would convince the nations of Europe that the United States had turned militaristic and thus deprive us of our most valuable asset in aiding in a reasonable settlement after hostilities should cease. Best of all, perhaps, was the fine letter printed in *The New Republic* as "A Pacifist's Apology":

> . . . it may be sweet and beautiful to die for one's country, but to kill for one's country is neither sweet nor beautiful. I could be willing many times over to give my life for my native land, but to kill my brother man—no; that does not invite me. . . . War is the quintessence of unreason; it is the reversal of the nature of things; it is a social solecism. Its motive and mainspring is hate, and hate is not good for men or nations.[41]

Yet the fact remains that, in the last analysis, Gladden supported the Civil War, the Spanish-American War, and, at last, World War I.[42] On many occasions, he holds forth on the evil of war, then decides that it can be the lesser of two evils. He was much impressed by Fichte's flaming German patriotism, and he has many admiring references to the behavior of soldiers. "Surely," he says, "revolutions are sometimes justifiable."

Though he was not quite sure that the Civil War was unavoidable, he wrote many impassioned poems about it, one of which praises those

> Loyal in spite of high taxes and prices;
> Lavishing life, kindred, fortune, all these,
> Rather than sell, in humanity's crisis,
> Liberty's birthright for pottage of peace.

Moreover he reprinted these poems in *Ultima Veritas:* "I am glad that I find in my heart today none of the resentments that resound in these martial lines, but I am not ashamed of the passion and the purpose that called them forth." At the end of the century, a long poem, "Uncle Sam's Christmas," described the old man unselfishly willing to take the burden of subject peoples upon him.[43]

Through the early years of the twentieth century, Gladden, like many other Christian optimists, believed war to be a dying institution. It had become so destructive, they thought, that rulers would no longer dare to employ it, and the demonstration of its horror in the Russo-Japanese conflict must aid the cause of peace. Even when Gladden preached in his old pulpit on August 23, 1914, on "The Futility of Force," he believed that the conflict then raging would be a very short one, since starvation must soon put an end to it. He reiterated that some evils can be worse than war and devoted a good deal of his time to explaining that there are non-physical, non-violent forms of carnal force. If you differ from your Christian neighbors, where one will try to convince you by friendly, logical argument, "at least ten of them will denounce you as a hypocrite and a coward, and will endeavor to convince you that you have forfeited the respect of decent people. I have had large experience in this line and feel qualified to testify." All of which, though profoundly and unhappily true, can have accomplished little toward rousing anti-war sentiment in First Church parish.

Like many of his colleagues among the Social Gospellers, Washington Gladden probably overestimated the rational, benevolent aspects of human nature. Looking back upon his life and thought from more than fifty years after his death, it is easy for us to see his limitations. But the remarkable thing is that he should have seen and done so much and so well. We shall be fortunate indeed if our posterity can find us as clear-sighted and forward-looking as we must in simple justice, find him.

7

LYMAN ABBOTT

The Life of God in the Soul of Man

I

When Lyman Abbott died in 1922, *The Christian Century* declared that "many a minister, in England and in America, hearing the news of his translation, must have felt as the young prophet felt when Elijah was taken away: 'My father, my father, the chariot of Israel, and the horsemen thereof!' " This was no exaggeration. So good a judge as Henry Sloane Coffin called Abbott "the most widely influential teacher of religion in this country" and "one of the half-dozen most potent teachers of Christianity in our national history." And Ira V. Brown, who made the most detailed study we have of his career, wrote of him:

> As minister, lecturer, author, and editor, he regularly reached directly several hundred thousands of people. Many other preachers and writers took their cues from him and thus his teaching radiated in an ever-widening circle. The sales of his books averaged between five and ten thousand each, of the *Outlook* at its height about 125,000 copies.

Lyman Abbott was born in Roxbury, Massachusetts, on December 18, 1835. His father, Jacob Abbott (originally Abbot), who was an important influence upon his ideals, methods, and religious convictions, was the author of the "Rollo Books" and the "Red Histories" for children and of much besides; his was the place of honor in fourteen out of the first forty-four issues of *Harper's Magazine.*[1] Jacob's brother, John S. C. Abbott, was also a popular historian, whose famous, or notorious, life of Napoleon ran through some four years of the same publication.[2] In 1838 the family moved to a ten-acre tract near Farmington, Maine, but when his wife died in childbirth in 1843, Jacob went to New York City, where, with two brothers, he established the Abbott School for Girls.

Lyman attended a school kept by his Uncle Samuel in his old home at Farmington; he also attended Little Blue School nearby. In 1849 he entered New York University, from which he was graduated in 1853, as the fourth man in his class, and, though not yet of age, followed his brothers, Austin and Benjamin Vaughan, into law, reading Kent and Blackstone in their offices and being admitted to the bar as soon as he had turned twenty-one.

During his early New York years, Abbott like his brothers generally lived in hired rooms and took his meals in restaurants, but the temptations of city life made no appeal to him. He had three aunts to whom he could turn for counsel when he needed it, and the mother he had lost so young never ceased to be a potent influence upon him. "I revered her memory as a Roman Catholic reveres the memory of the Virgin. Possibly I idealized her a little, though I do not think so; and for some years I thought a great deal more about what my mother in heaven thought about me than I did about what God thought about me." In 1857 he married a second cousin, Abby Hamlin, a relative of Vice-President Hannibal Hamlin and a niece of the founder of Roberts College, Constantinople, and in 1859 the first of their six children, Lawrence F. Abbott, was born. Like his brother Ernest Hamlin, Lawrence was to be importantly associated with his father on *The Outlook.*

About this same time, Abbott began to attend upon the preaching of Henry Ward Beecher at Plymouth Church and became active in YMCA and other religious work. Though he could not remember a time when he had not passionately desired to be a Christian, he had had his difficulties with the Old Theology. His religious zeal quickened by Beecher's preaching and the Revival of 1858, he soon decided to give up his considerable and growing success as a lawyer and become a clergyman. In the fall of 1858 he went to Farmington with such books as he could afford to buy, planning to spend the winter in independent study at what he called "Fewacres Theological Seminary." After only a few weeks he was asked to supply the pulpit of the church at Wilton. He was licensed at Temple, Maine, in November 1859 and ordained at Farmington the next March. Before the end of the month he had arrived in Terre Haute, Indiana, for his first real pastorate, which he held through the years of the Civil War.

During his years in Terre Haute, he rejected an attractive call from a church in Meriden, Connecticut, because it seemed to him that he could render better religious and patriotic service at Terre Haute. In February 1865 he resigned his pastorate, however, to become secretary of the American Freedmen's Union Commission; his share in the work of Reconstruction turned out to be a considerable disappointment to him. Even more disappointing was his connection with what was finally called the New England Church, on West 41st Street in New York, which he had characteristically chosen in 1866, in preference to a much more attractive call from Portland, Maine; this ended in 1869 in a debacle for which he was in no sense to blame, but which left him, for the time being, with an assured income of only fifty dollars a month for the writing he was doing for Harper and Brothers.[3] To make the situation even worse, his wife was threatening at the same time to collapse into tuberculosis; fortunately the threat passed when the family moved from the New York area to Cornwall-on-Hudson, which remained Lyman Abbott's home for the rest of his life.

Fortunately, too, his literary connections were now producing books as well as serial writing. Harpers published *Jesus of Nazareth* in 1869 and *Old Testament Shadows of New Testament Truths* the next year, and A. S. Barnes issued a series of commentaries on the New Testament. In 1870 Abbott began to supply the pulpit of the Presbyterian Church in Cornwall, where he was to preach for seventeen years, though he rarely had more than seventy-five people in his congregation. That same year he began his work as editor of the American Tract Society's *Illustrated Christian Weekly*, which he continued until 1876, when he became Henry Ward Beecher's second-in-command on *The Christian Union.* ("As the editor-in-chief was always absent, my authority was practically absolute.") In 1893 *The Christian Union* became *The Outlook*, and for the rest of Abbott's life it remained one of the leading American journals devoted to recording and interpreting current events.

After the death of Henry Ward Beecher in March 1887, Abbott was asked to supply the Plymouth pulpit. In October he became "temporary pastor," and the following May he was recognized as Beecher's formal successor. He preached to between 1500 and 2000 persons every Sunday thereafter until 1898, when the strain of combining pastoral with editorial duties became so great that he resigned upon doctor's orders. During his later years, his preaching was done as a guest, mostly upon college campuses.

Lyman Abbott received his first doctorate from New York University in 1877, and this was followed by many honors, scholastic and otherwise, during his later years. He formed a close friendship with Theodore Roosevelt, who served as "Contributing Editor" to *The Outlook* following his Presidency, a circumstance which did not bolster the paper's circulation after the Progressive downfall and during the Wilson era. Abbott died at his apartment in New York City on October 22, 1922, of a respiratory complaint.

II

In his *Christian Union* days, Abbott was "a spare, wiry man, wearing a black beard, and full of nervous energy." [4] But Ernest Hamlin Abbott always thought of his father as frail. Scarlet fever in childhood had left him "feeble, deaf, and subject to severe headaches," and he remembered himself during his school-days as

> pale, meek, mild, never doing anything very wrong, nor anything very right, nor indeed anything at all, punished by the teachers for other boys' escapades, and by the scholars for not getting into the scrapes, a little too big to associate with the little boys and rather too little to associate with the big boys.

In college days he would have a breakdown every spring.

He broke his arm in childhood, and again in 1895.[5] From his insomnia he tried to draw profit by using wakeful hours for prayer and meditation, and he learned how to recruit depleted strength with brief naps. The final break in his health came in 1916, when he acquired the bronchial complaint which finally killed him, and after the summer of 1918 he submitted to a program of sharply curtailed activities.

In law office days, Abbott often worked late into the night (once all night), keeping himself awake with strong coffee and a wet towel around his head. But he soon learned that for him any such regime spelled suicide, and therefore made it a rule to do no work in the evening. He was not far along in his ministry when he learned also that one day of rest in seven was as important for him as for his parishioners; since he believed that rest before work was better than after, he made Saturday his rest day. He got up very early and went to bed early; if there were guests who did not go home by his bedtime, he simply withdrew and left his wife to entertain them. He rested after the midday meal, telling his wife he was not to be disturbed except for fire and then not until the fire had reached the second story, and much of the afternoon he spent out of doors, working or resting or playing with wife and children. He traveled a good deal, both for business and for pleasure, and had considerable experience of cruising on both sides of the Atlantic; for this a yacht would do in a pinch, but he preferred a fishing sloop.[6]

As a country boy, Abbott had learned to swim, skate, climb, and tramp, and was fairly good at wrestling, but was "butter fingers" in a ball game. He loved camping and trout fishing, but he was no good at rough sports. He never boxed or shot and was always hostile to prize fighting. In later years he went swimming and canoeing with his children, and he seems to have ridden a horse sometimes.

Though he speaks of his lack of interest in games as "a defect in my character which I have mildly regretted, but never sufficiently to set myself the task of correcting it," he apparently played both chess and solitaire in his later years. He repeatedly makes the point that Christ, who used the symbol of a great feast to illustrate the Kingdom, "never spoke of dancing with displeasure, and more than once with apparent commendation," [7] but in his novel, *Laicus*, he tells us that the "merry dance" of the skaters on the river is "about the only kind of dance I thoroughly believe in." He could not remember ever having attended more than one ball.

In early life Abbott seems greatly to have enjoyed the theater. He recalled Forrest, Edwin Booth, and Macready with pleasure, as well as Burton, Laura Keene, and the Wallacks, and the pantomimists and acrobats known as the Ravel family were "the delight of my life." He also enjoyed Christy's Minstrels and Banvard's panorama of the Mississippi. But after he joined the church, he rarely went to the theater, and for a time he seemed more or less committed to the anti-theater position of the extreme Puritans. This was soon outgrown, and though he did continue to handle the theater rather gingerly, and more or less to view it as an indulgence, some of his more pious admirers were probably shocked by the friendly prominence he gave Booth and Barnum in *Silhouettes of My Contemporaries* at the very end of his life.[8]

He was apparently a competent performer on both the piano and the organ and during his college years a church organist. In *The Home Builder* he suggests that his wife was more interested in plays, concerts, and art exhibitions than he was, but he also says that she liked simple art best. In any case she saw to it that her children learned to play for the pleasure it could give them. He mentions a number of standard composers,[9] painters, and sculptors,[10] and he was fond of beautiful china. When he heard Jenny Lind sing "Come unto me," it was as if he "could hear the voice of the Master singing down the years,"[11] and when she sang "I *know* that my Redeemer liveth," she seemed "a celestial witness" to the Resurrection. In later life he speaks of both Kreisler and Paderewski. He did not care much for mere imitation in any art ("a man who can simply portray a falling leaf or a silk dress, so that you almost take it for reality, is a skilled artisan and nothing more"), and this led him to downgrade what is sometimes called "program music." "Music is the interpretation of a life which can never be interpreted in any other way. If the printed program tells you what the music means, . . . you have second-class music." Because music as we know it developed during the Christian era, he calls it, with perhaps pardonable exaggeration for a clergyman, "a gift of Christianity to mankind."

When Lawrence Abbott tells us[12] that, in all his experience of his father, he never heard his voice falter or saw a tear in his eye, we may be inclined to wonder whether the man was really human. This, I am sure, is unfair to him. His was "a naturally dependent and clinging nature," with a tendency toward scepticism. He preferred the middle of the road and was never "a good subject" for hypnotism or mass phenomena. But the native Abbott temperament was nervous, perhaps even neurotic. Lyman Abbott had a slow start, and he tells us that he was greatly discouraged as late as the time he left Plymouth Church, fearing that his health would give way altogether, so that he might be obliged to give up *The Outlook* also. He had great moral courage, and he never shrank from taking a stand upon controversial issues, but he could never thrust himself into a situation in which he felt he might not be welcome, and the calmness of spirit he finally achieved was a conquest, not an inheritance.

In his early days, he was much given to a niggling and unprofitable soul-searching, which stands in striking contrast to his later, more rational attitude, when, having accepted the prophet's word that God buries forgiven sins in the depths of the sea, he sensibly showed no inclination to fish them up again.[13] He knew youthful enthusiasm and was always inclined toward an optimistic outlook. Later he tended to think pessimists cynics and egotists and "formed the habit of remembering the pleasant and forgetting the unpleasant, things of the past." [14] He was ambitious too, "and glad of it, for I regarded ambition as a virtue, not a vice." When he was trying to make up his mind about leaving the law for the ministry, he could not pass a church being erected near his home in Brooklyn without imagining himself its pastor and its pulpit his platform.

It must be obvious, of course, that no man could have responded as Abbott did to the robust, passionate enthusiasm of both Henry Ward Beecher and Theodore Roosevelt without having a good deal of ginger in him. Moreover he praised Beecher for appealing to the heart, not merely the intellect, and he knew that strength of character comes not from taking thought but from motive power. Even his basic conception of the fine artist seems to have been that of one who responds to his art with emotional fervor. Conviction, fidelity, and love were far more important than understanding in Abbott's thought of religion. "To me," he says, "Christ is less an object of knowledge than of simple reverence and love."

Moreover, Abbott's emotions were matched by a strong will. Though he says he would not have gone into the ministry if his wife had objected, it is hard to believe that this would have worked for long. He regarded himself as Christ's servant, with his life devoted to Christ's work, but he understood his own nature and capacities and limitations thoroughly, so that he always put himself into the way of doing what he wished to do and was able to do well. He believed that a good editor "must be something of an autocrat," and though nobody has ever suggested that he was difficult to work with, it is clear that it was he who called the shots; he was never servile, even when Beecher was his superior. In a sermon preached at Plymouth the first Sunday after having been installed, he declared himself "a follower of Henry Ward Beecher as Henry Ward Beecher followed Christ." "Not that I agree in all that he said; not that I think just as he thought; certainly not that I recognize in him any intellectual or spiritual authority or mastership over me." Nor was he in any sense dominated by the enormous prestige of Theodore Roosevelt when the latter served under him as the *Outlook* contributing editor. He left the business side of *The Outlook* entirely to others, but that was simply because it did not interest him very much, though he had once told his wife that he was willing to trust in the Lord for everything except money!

Lyman Abbott's interest in women was virtually synonymous with his interest in his wife; except for Alice Freeman Palmer, who "fascinated" him, he has practically nothing to say about any other woman as an individual, though I think it interesting that he should have been more attracted by David Copperfield's Dora than by Agnes. In *The Temple*, which deals with the human body as the habitat of the spirit, he passes over "The Passions" so quickly as to suggest embarrassment; certainly none of the fundamental sexual problems are discussed. His attitude toward divorce, in *Christianity and Social Problems* and elsewhere, is less liberal or progressive than he is upon most other social issues, and though he admits that Christ's reported teaching on the subject, uttered when a Jewish husband had only to give an unwanted wife a bill of divorcement and send her away, does not necessarily hold without qualification under the conditions which now prevail, he comes closer to Biblical literalism at this point than he often does elsewhere. Milton's discussion of divorce he considers "a marvel of theological special pleading," but it is certainly less so than Abbott's own discussion of Christ's teachings about war. And what is one to say in the face of such statements as:

> Marriage is not a union of souls; it is the mating of two persons in one flesh. Two souls may be joined, and yet there be no marriage; marriage there may be, and yet no union of souls. Marriage is the creation of a new earthly relation. . . . Hence, too, marriage is not dissoluble because love is dead.

Surely the only excuse for such teachings must be that they come from a man who is too innocent, or whose experience of life has been too fortunate, to enable him to know whereof he speaks. Yet Abbott carefully disclaims all prudery and self-righteousness: "I see this battle between goodness and vice, truth and falsehood, sensuality and purity, not only in the world without, but in the world within. I am in the seventh of Romans, not yet graduated." [15]

It is clear that his own marriage was a very happy one, and it is easy to understand why he believed that "home and marriage are the nearest approximations we have to heaven." [16] He taught that it was not possible to love too much and that husbands and wives should express their love for each other: God was not jealous of human affection. Yet he tells us that when he was first married, he was so much in love with his wife that he wished to be with her all the time and was willing to neglect his work to do so, and that he almost dreaded the birth of his first child, lest he should have to divide his wife with the baby.

It is clear too that Mrs. Abbott managed all the practical affairs of the household without so much as consulting her husband about them, thus setting him free almost entirely for the work he wished to do. "Society" did not interest her; neither was she "a great churchwoman," though she was certainly very religious. I think about the only thing we know to her discredit is that at the time of the Spanish-American War she wanted a sofa pillow with an American flag on it and the figures "1898." Perhaps her wisdom shows best in her reply to the person who wished to know how it felt to marry a lawyer and find yourself married to a minister instead. "I did not marry a lawyer," was the quiet reply. "I married Lyman Abbott."

Jennie, wife of Laicus, surely reflects the personality of Mrs. Abbott, but perhaps the most beautiful thing her husband ever wrote was his tribute to her in the little book called *The Home Builder*, published in 1908, the year after her death. Her name is never mentioned in it, and the general outline conforms to the idea of presenting the ideal wife and mother in her various manifestations, but so much of the material can be identified with what is specifically related to her elsewhere that there can be no doubt he had her image before him throughout its writing.

Mrs. Abbott wanted the word "obey" in her marriage vows, and though her husband did not, he seems to account it unto her for righteousness that she did. "She looks now with amusement, now with pity, on those who do not know how blessed it is to be love's subject." But she also "preserves her independence of thought more jealously, that she may be a wise counselor." Abbott did not believe in the superiority or inferiority of either men or women; for him the two were complementary; as for her, "she can realize that there may be three Persons in One God, since in her own experience there are two persons in one life." She converted her husband away from his early belief in woman suffrage, thinking that women in general did not desire it and were not ready for it, and cherishing woman's traditional exemption from the civic duties required of men.[17] When, upon her marriage to George Herbert Palmer, Alice Freeman gave up the presidency of Wellesley College and retired to private life, Abbott cordially approved, much as he admired her work, thinking that she had gone from one dignity to another still higher.

Everything we know about Abbott's relations with his own children and others is charming; as Ernest Hamlin Abbott says, he never insisted on a command being obeyed because he gave it, yet neither Ernest nor his brother ever dreamed of disobeying him; when, in later years, Ernest asked his brother why, the reply was, "We never thought of it." Certainly the fact that two of his sons elected to spend their lives with him on *The Outlook* is the best possible testimony to his fairness and kindness. There are a few loving references to dogs, especially collies, and at least one to "the purring cat that lies in your lap."

III

In later years, Abbott said he would no longer be able to enter the freshman class of the college from which he had graduated with honors.[18] The "science of figures" bored him, though "mathematics as a science of invisible values was fascinating. In arithmetic I was a dunce. In geometry I stood with the leaders of my class." Natural science did not interest him either; when his boys were growing up he tried to cultivate an interest in geology and entomology, but he could not communicate what he did not feel. The history of philosophy interested him only slightly but philosophy as a study of man enthralled him.[19] In his *Reminiscences* he denied that he had "the temperament fitted for accurate historical research" and proved it by quoting the titles of at least five of his own books with some inaccuracy. He always called The University of Chicago "Chicago University." Whether he was preparing an editorial on free silver or a book on the Old Testament, he habitually read the best authorities available, made up his mind in accordance with his own notions of reason and justice, and stated his views as clearly and simply as possible. The notes in *The Life and Literature of the Ancient Hebrews* and *The Life and Letters of Paul the Apostle* cite an impressive range of authorities, but it must always be remembered that Abbott went to his books for what they had in them that he could use, and if they started him thinking along some independent line, that was all to the good.

He had some Latin and Greek, but though he flirted with German, French, Italian, and Spanish, he never really learned to read any modern language except his own. For him Greek was "preeminently the language of the greatest literature of the past," but he admitted that it did "pander to vice" and "promote iniquity," and there was a good deal of it that he would rather were not read in our colleges.

He says that he possessed few books that he had not used and, except for fiction and biography, few that he had read through. "I would no more expect to get all a book has to give me in one reading than all that a friend has to give me in one conversation." Yet he was enough of a bookman to find it hard to part with his books even when they had ceased to be useful to him, and he says this helped him to understand how misers feel about other possessions!

He mentions a large number of writers in several literatures, and if he mentions them largely in connection with their religious implications, this is not surprising when we remember that all his writings deal with religion. Thus he speaks of the "stained sensuality" of Burns, Byron, and Moore, but he enjoyed Dumas. He found no more Christianity in Swift's religion than in Bolingbroke's infidelity, and he thought Carlyle "followed his spiritual instincts but a little way, and then halted."

In college he learned how to read English writers for style, not merely for content, as he had hitherto done. Shakespeare is mentioned with reasonable frequency,[20] Tennyson and Browning often. Tennyson's "Closer is He than breathing" is one of his favorite quotations, and he considered Browning, faults and all, England's greatest dramatic poet since Shakespeare. Some of his judgments are surprising:

> I was not a great reader of poetry; but so far as I read it at all, it was poetry of human life. I was not greatly responsive to the musical rhythm of a Shelley or a Keats, or to the spiritual interpretations of a Dante or a Milton. But I traveled the world with Childe Harold, and joined Wordsworth in his "Excursion" among the hills of Westmorland.[21]

That a distinguished religious leader should be more moved by Byron or even Wordsworth than by Dante and Milton is indeed an interesting testimony to the complications of human nature.

Abbott loved Sir Walter Scott and read his novels again and again,[22] but he has many more references to Dickens. He read him with avidity, in parts, as his novels were published, the characters seeming as real as living creatures, and he never changed his mind, no matter what the critics might tell him.[23] Abbott calls a church which waits idly for "something to turn up" "Saint Micawber's Church," and he enlists Dickens's aid in fighting Puritan Sabbatarianism. In *Laicus* Dickens converts the hero to the desirability of celebrating Christmas, though he must go to the Episcopal church to accomplish it. Abbott quotes from the Preface to *Oliver Twist* in *The Temple* and from *The Old Curiosity Shop* in commenting upon the treatment of Theodore Roosevelt in the New York press in 1912. Once Dickens quite innocently helped an ignortant reporter to misrepresent Abbott: the latter called the Book of Jonah *The Biglow Papers* of the Bible, and the reporter changed "Biglow" to "Pickwick"! But Abbott's most interesting reference to Dickens is in *The Christian Ministry*, where he cites Allan Woodcourt's conversation with the dying Jo in *Bleak House* as exemplifying true Christian preaching.

Among many other books and authors he mentions Montaigne, Amiel, Matthew Arnold, Mrs. Humphry Ward (*Robert Elsmere* and *Marcella*), Lewis Carroll's letters, *The Rubáiyát of Omar Khayyám,* Edwin Arnold's *Siddartha, Lorna Doone, The Way of All Flesh,* and Kipling's *Jungle Books* (though he miscalls them "Jungle Stories"). He has one passing, disapproving reference to Restoration drama, and he dismisses Trollope as a merely "comforting" writer. In one passage he seems to place George Eliot at the head of English fiction; in another, he speaks of her as an atheist. When *God the Invisible King* was published, he was moved by H. G. Wells's moral and social zeal and a bit appalled by his ineptness as a theologian.[24]

The most serious question to be raised about Lyman Abbott's literary judgment comes in connection with his interest in the novels of his Cornwall neighbor, E. P. Roe, but though he edited a volume of *Birthday Mottoes* (1882) from Roe's work, he hardly ever speaks of him, and this may have been not much more than a neighborly act. In his old age he loved the novels of Grace S. Richmond. "I like such stories because I like the people to whom they introduce me." So he read Tolstoy, Turgenev, and Gorky for instruction and Miss Richmond for enjoyment.[25]

Laicus is the only sustained work of fiction Abbott ever wrote alone, since both *Cone Cut Corners* (1855) and *Matthew Caraby* (1858) were written in collaboration with Austin and Benjamin Vaughan Abbott and published under the pseudonym "Benauly." If one can hardly call him a novelist, he did have a good narrative style, and he knew how to keep a story moving. His literary theory tends to overemphasize form in literature to mark it off from the sermon, whose essential quality lies in its "life-giving power." But this is important for literature too, which strives for truth as well as beauty, and Abbott admits as much when he calls great writers "the interpreters of life" and says that they furnish the best "material for the study of human nature." In one passage, he finds no aesthetic or rhetorical appeal in the sermons of Jesus as recorded, including, one must assume, the parables, but elsewhere he calls him "a master in the creation of imaginative literature."

The Revised Version of the Bible came out during the years of Abbott's activity, and he took to it at once, always quoting from it in his books. This is certainly not indefensible for a religious teacher, who seeks the most accurate translation possible, yet I find it difficult to understand how any really aesthetically sensitive person can voluntarily relinquish the stylistic glories of King James.

Since Lyman Abbott preached a social as well as a personal Gospel, his politics, his sociology, his economics were as important for his preaching and writing as his literary culture. His basic theory of government was thoroughly pragmatic. He juxtaposed what he considered the Hebraic or Puritan conception against the Latin or French. Rejecting the Social Compact theory and the infallibility of the majority, he regarded universal or limited suffrage as merely matters of expediency. Except during the Civil War, he avoided party labels and believed that the pulpit should endorse principles, not candidates. To his way of thinking, the safety of the country depended upon the independent voter, who held the balance of power and kept both parties on their toes. When he found a flag flying from Plymouth Church the Sunday after McKinley's election, he ordered it taken down. In general, however, his outlook was far more Republican than Democratic, and, as Brown points out, Cleveland, Wilson, and Bryan, though contemporaries, are all missing from his *Silhouettes*.[26] *The Outlook* was generally friendly to Taft until early in 1912, and, though supporting Roosevelt's candidacy, tried to avoid complete identification with the Progressive Party.[27]

For Abbott *laissez faire* was as dead in government as in economics. He rejected the basic idea of the Alabama State Constitution that the only function of government is to preserve order and that whatever goes beyond this is "usurpation and oppression." That which can be done by private enterprise should be left to private enterprise, but whenever necessary the Commonwealth "should assume the administration of those industries, the organization and uniform direction of which are important, if not essential, to its welfare."

Today we ask, not, What is constitutional? but, What is right? If a policy is right, we seek by a liberal construction of the Constitution to find a way to secure it; and if that is impossible, we begin to question, What amendment to the Constitution is required and practical?

Ira V. Brown says that Abbott's "standards of justice and morality tended to reflect the dominant economic concerns of his social class," and there is evidence to support this judgment. In one of his Plymouth sermons he assumes that he is addressing those who close their houses for the summer and go to the country; he alo assumes that his auditors have been to Europe. He opposed the Pullman strikers[28] and failed to speak out with William Dean Howells and others when the Chicago anarchists were hanged for a crime they were not even accused of having committed.[29] Nor did *The Outlook* support its friend Washington Gladden in the Standard Oil "tainted money" controversy.

Yet Abbott advocated many reforms which shocked good Republicans in his time and still shock some of them today. Though he was not keen on muckraking, he admitted that Thomas Lawson had told "some truth" in *Frenzied Finance* and Ida M. Tarbell "the substantial truth" in her study of Standard Oil. His criminology rejected the idea of punishment, seeing the protection of society and the redemption of the criminal as the only legitimate ends to be sought.[30] At least one passage in *The Rights of Man* (1901)[31] leaves the impression that he was a Single Taxer, but I find no commitment to this elsewhere. He did advocate the direct primary, tariff reduction, civil service reform, government ownership or control of public utilities, the establishment of a national board of arbitration, and other reforms. Like Theodore Roosevelt, he wished to regulate, not destroy, big business.[32] He proposed taxing income, not expenditure, and he believed that income from investments should be taxed at a higher rate than wages, because "government does more for the man who has large investments." [33]

But it was in his advocacy of what he called "industrial democracy" that Abbott departed most radically from Bourbon Republicanism.[34]

Does not the capitalist take the laborer's product, give him what the capitalist thinks, or appears to think, is a just return for his labor, and keep the rest of the product for himself? Yes! And that is the reason why I object to capitalism.

The most obvious remedy for the evil would have been Socialism, but Abbott could not accept this because he rejected the romantic view of man involved in the assumption that all evil results from evil conditions. He realized that social forces can be determinative even in matters of morals, and once at least he not only called sin a disease but attributed this view to Christ. Nevertheless a change in conditions alone, however desirable, would not be enough without a corresponding change in man, for some of the difficulty was in him. Abbott was repelled too by what he considered the materialistic ideology of the Socialist movement, and he believed that its adoption would destroy such personal freedom as men still possessed and achieve nothing but servitude to new masters, while still leaving society divided between employer and employed. His own proposed remedy was to do away with the wage system by making the "tool users" the "tool owners" also, and ending industrial warfare by combining the warring factions into a single body.

IV

In the Preface to his *Reminiscences*, Abbott names Charles G. Finney, Horace Bushnell, and Henry Ward Beecher as the main influences upon his preaching, but it seems clear that Stephen H. Tyng was also a force. Beecher he thought "the greatest preacher of our age if not of all ages; a man to whom I owe the greatest debt one soul can owe to another—the debt of love for spiritual nurture." But stylistically Finney was probably the most important, for it was from him Abbott learned that the quiet, conversational style which was congenial to his temperament could be as effective in the pulpit as the more flamboyant rhetoric he had admired not only in Beecher but in such orators as Wendell Phillips and John B. Gough.

His methods of preparing a sermon show that his temperament was that of the speaker rather than the writer, to a surprising extent, I think, in a man who wrote so much and so well as he did.[35] He learned to think on his feet, first in the college society of which he was a member during his teens, later in a village debating society at Farmington. Much of his composition he did in his head, often speaking aloud while he did it. His verbal like his visual memory was weak, and he never dared to quote even from the Bible without verifying the quotation. Compared to Henry Ward Beecher's, his sermons were brief.[36] Though he began to practice preaching as a boy, there were seventeen years of his life during which he composed no sermon, and he came to Plymouth Church without a "barrel."

His sermons grew out of his current studies and the needs of his congregation, which he believed the pastor must be sensitive enough to grasp. The real preacher, he thought, concerned himself primarily with spiritual matters and addressed primarily not the intellect but the will; otherwise he was not preaching but merely engaging in literary composition. He sympathized with the objections of Brooks and Beecher to announcing the subject of a sermon in advance, as if it were a lecture, thus encouraging people to shop in the Sunday papers for their morning sermon, regarding the rest of the service as "preliminaries."

On Saturday nights he slept in his study and took his breakfast there, not seeing his family until he encountered them in church. When he preached on college campuses, he would try to arrive a day or two early, confer with members of the faculty and, if possible, with students, in an attempt to learn "what are the conditions of college life . . . that the sermon may be adapted to the present needs." Afterwards he would hold conferences with individual students and sometimes group conferences involving twenty-five to one hundred people in each body.[37] Once he travelled to Saratoga Springs to preach before the National Prison Reform Association without having the slightest idea what he was supposed to say, and one Plymouth sermon of 1888 treated only the first phase of what he had intended to say, the rest being postponed perforce until the following Sunday.[38]

"A sermon should never be a lake, it should be a river; it should have movement; a *terminus a quo* and a *terminus ad quem.*" During his later years at least, he disbelieved in all direct exhortations and appeals at the end. The whole sermon, he thought, should be so infused with religious passion that the appeal would be implied from the start, and the listener could make the application to himself unaided.

He would not "candidate." The church that wanted him must come to him, and he kept to this resolve even when it deprived him of a pulpit for years. In *Laicus* he gives this same determination to Maurice Mapleson, who was evidently intended as his ideal clergyman. But Mapleson's own grounds seem more idealistic, though no less impractical, than those of Abbott, with whom the refusal appears to have been largely a matter of temperament.

He says, again and again, that he cared more for "pastoral work" than for anything else he did, yet it is clear that, after his earliest years, he never did what most clergymen understand by that term. He did not believe much in house-to-house visitation, and he admits that he was often so preoccupied that he failed to recognize people, not only on the street but even in his own house, until his wife called attention to their presence. What he meant by pastoral work was talking seriously about their religious problems with those who were seriously interested and who had sought him out for his advice. This he did extremely well, and he supplemented it by an enormous correspondence with his "unknown friends." Abbott would not have neglected any essential pastoral function—when a member of Plymouth went to Sing Sing, his church followed him there—[39] but one suspects he must have disappointed those of his parishioners who looked to their pastor for small talk.

Lyman Abbott's favorite definition of religion was the title of a book by Henry Scougall, published in 1671—"the life of God in the soul of man"—and he added that theology was "what philosophers have thought about that life." His God was not "a big man sitting up in the center of the universe, running things"; He was inwrought with the stuff of creation itself. "The doctrine of a great first cause gives place to the doctrine of an eternal and perpetual cause; the carpenter conception of the creation to the doctrine of the divine immanence." [40] But Abbott insisted that he was not a pantheist because he believed that

> The Infinite and Eternal Energy, from which all things proceed, is an energy that thinks, that feels, that purposes and does; and is thinking and feeling and purposing and doing as a conscious life, of Which ours is but a poor and broken reflection.

From his youth on, Abbott longed for fellowship with "the Great Companion." Listening to lectures about health was not being well; reading about polar exploration was not arriving at the Pole. By the same token, religion was not something you believed about God but fellowship with him. "Religion is such a perception of God as affects the moral character of man." Historic record and ecclesiastical authority were secondary, and both means toward an end; the thing itself must be apprehended and developed in terms of the individual's own religious experience. Christ was greater than the religion He founded. "Its accretions are corruptions; it might almost be said that its development is degeneracy." When his second-in-command on *The Outlook*, Hamilton Wright Mabie, died, Abbott remarked that "he thought more highly of the institutions of religion than I do and attached more value to its historic creeds." [41] It seemed to him that his own interpretation of these matters was faithful to the ways of the life of the spirit in general. "The artist does not really create; he discovers. Behind all forms of beauty there is an infinite unity, and this unity, this intrinsic and eternal beauty, the artist is seeking to discern and to make others discern." Moses only interpreted the Ten Commandments. "They are not right because Jehovah commanded them; Jehovah commanded them because they are right."

In the last analysis, then, mystical insight is the seed of religion. "The truths of religion and the truths of morality are not demonstrated; they are perceived." But like conscience, like taste, mystical perception is not inerrant; it must be guided, educated. Abbott found his model for this in Saint Paul:

> If to believe that men can directly and immediately take cognizance of realities which the senses cannot perceive is to be a mystic, then Paul is a mystic. . . . If to believe that every such inward testimony . . . is to be brought before the tribunal of reason and then investigated, that no faith is so sound and no tradition so ancient that it may be accepted without question—if this is to be a rationalist, then Paul was a rationalist.[42]

Thus the knowledge gained through religious experience can never be complete:[43]

I deny that a knowledge of religious truth is the great desideratum of life. I deny that there is or can be any complete or comprehensive system of religious truth. I deny that there is or can be any organization which can furnish such a system of religious truth. And, therefore, of course I deny that there can be any right, either in church or state, to punish, by either physical or moral penalty, the man who dissents from the commonly received religious opinion.

Abbott started reading theology at the age of ten, but actually he had very little interest in it as such. As he told the council which installed him at Plymouth Church: "Historical theology I have studied a little; dogmatic theology hardly at all." When a friend told him that he was not an Orthodox Trinitarian but a Modalistic Monarchian, he was more amused than either shocked or impressed, and he had no interest in either denying or accepting the allegation. Actually he disliked the very term "Systematic Theology," for the finite mind, he thought, could embrace no systematic knowledge of God. He himself, before he found his way, had doubted everything in religion except God and immortality. This pragmatic approach had its drawbacks. He never got far with the problem of evil, for example, not nearly so far as John Fiske did in *Through Nature to God* or, more recently, Edgar Sheffield Brightman and the Personalists. "I have no solution of the problem of evil: the why and wherefore of it. A much more important question seems to me to be this: How shall I meet the evil that comes into my world and get good out of it for myself and for others?" Such counsel has its values. But these are not of the philosophical or theolgical variety.

Abbott was not interested in "the old debates about the Person of Christ" and His metaphysical relationship to God. For him, as for Henry van Dyke, Christ manifested "the human life of God." In Him "the veiled, invisible figure, that is always walking through life, always judging, befriending, forgiving, helping men, was for one moment made so clear that human eyes could see him and human hands could handle him," and this to such an extent that one might pray to Him without hesitation.[44]

> To me Christ is less an object of knowledge than of simple reverence and love. . . . To me he is Light of Light and God of God; to me he is the Wonderful, the Counsellor, the Everlasting Father, the Prince of Peace; before him I bow, crying out as I look up to his thorn-crowned brow and spear-pierced side, My Lord and my God! I know of no reverence that goes beyond the reverence I give to him; no love I ever knew goes beyond the love I want to offer him; there is no loyalty I have toward any being, seen or unseen, known or imagined, that transcends the loyalty I wish to pay him. He is my Lord, he is my Master. I am sorry I do not understand him better; I am sorry I do not love him more; I am sorry my capacity for reverence is so slight; I am sorry I follow him so far off; for he is my all in all; I have no thought of God that runs beyond him; no reverence or affection that ever transcends or can transcend what I want to lay at his feet.

But while this well represents Abbott's emotional response to Christ, it gives an incomplete picture of his thinking about Him. He realized that we have no biography of Christ but only memorabilia, no "continuous history of his life, nor . . . any attempt to trace out the development of his doctrine, or his own intellectual or spiritual growth." Nor are His teaching and example to be "blindly followed. Jesus Christ did not teach in order that he might serve as a substitute for thinking, but that he might inspire us to think."[45] For Abbott, Jesus Christ was actually neither God nor a God-substitute; He was "the image of God, the reflection of God, God manifest in the flesh; that is, such a manifestation of God as is possible in a human life." Christ was the Door through which we pass to God. "I never say, I never should say, Jesus Christ is God. . . . Jesus Christ is one of the manifestations of God, but God is more than the sum of all His manifestations."[46]

The doctrine of the Incarnation was therefore very important to Abbott, but he neither believed nor disbelieved in the Virgin Birth. He could find nothing to support the idea of the Fall in the Bible except "a parable in the Old Testament and a parenthesis in the New." [47] And since Christ was God's revelation to men of His own character, there was obviously no sense in the notion that God was justice and Christ mercy. Brought up on the Governmental Theory of the Atonement, Abbott discarded it completely because the New Testament nowhere says that God needs to be propitiated. Justice cannot be satisfied by punishment, above all by the death of an innocent person. The death of God's Son, as the supreme expression of God's love, changed man, not God. And since Christ came to save men from sin, not merely from punishment for sin, those whom he "saves" are those who identify themselves with His spirit. To debate the salvation or damnation of the "heathen" is barbarous nonsense and beating the air. Names do not matter; life counts, not professions. As Saint Augustine perceived, there were Christians before Christ, and when the Christ spirit appears in an agnostic, a Mohammedan, or a Jew, there God's salvation is made manifest.[48]

Toward this end both church and Bible were means, not ends in themselves. Lyman Abbott's brother Edward, a High Church Episcopal clergyman in Cambridge, Massachusetts, who disapproved of his brother's ideas, once said to him, "There is nothing so glorious as preaching the Gospel except administering the sacraments." To Lyman this was an inconceivable point of view, yet I know no characters in literature who feel the Real Presence of Christ at the Communion table more strongly than Laicus and his wife, and as late as *The Christian Ministry* Abbott wrote that "the one thing we can do for Christ that is not the service of some one else is our participation in the Lord's Supper." And he added "It is an occasion wherein we may especially feel, if we will, the companionship of our Lord."

Abbott's original view of the Bible, as expressed in his first books, was what we would now call Fundamentalistic, and though he later threw this off completely, it is clear that the Book always retained for him a peculiar authority. "Scripture doctrine need not always be stated in Scripture phraseology," he says, "but a doctrine which for its statement *must* use words not to be found in the Scripture may safely be looked upon with suspicion." He accepts the destruction of the Cities of the Plain, claims an early date for Job, clings to the Johannine authorship of the Fourth Gospel, and gives David an absurdly high place among Old Testament worthies. He believed in angels and did not consider demoniac possession impossible. He finally emancipated himself completely from the materialistic doctrine of the Second Coming of Christ, but he was rather slow in achieving this.[49] "The Word of God includes all the languages in which God has ever spoken,—to all races, in all ages, under all circumstances. The Bible is one of his many words, spoken through prophets." We do not accept the Bible when it "contradicts our spiritual consciousness," and "when it contradicts our reason, we seek to find some other interpretation." Actually Bible is even a less satisfactory external authority than church because it is less flexible, less capable of adjusting to the needs of life. "God is not an embalmed God, in a dead book," he cried in an 1887 sermon at Plymouth, and in *Laicus* the man who reads the Bible through, three chapters a night, is compared to him who ate his way down the menu, consuming all the soups before starting in on the fish, and who, when sick, took, in order, all the drugs in the apothecary's shop until he was cured or killed.[50]

As for supernaturalism in the Bible, Abbott was disposed to consider each miracle recorded upon its own merits. He was not a "rationalist," for though he considered God's regular manifestations of Himself in nature as no less wonderful than His extraordinary manifestations in what are called miracles, he did not think extraordinary manifestations impossible. Like Paul Sabatier, he could not accept miracles as violations of the laws of nature, but he could believe in many of them as operating through laws which as yet we understand very imperfectly.

> It is a matter of small account whether a man thinks this or that or the other miracle was wrought [even the raising of Lazarus was a more or less indifferent matter], but it is a matter of very great account whether he believes there is any hand stretched down from heaven to help man in his impotence, or any light streaming down from heaven to guide man in his darkness.

The only New Testament miracle that was very important to Abbott was Christ's Resurrection, which he accepted, without attempting to define his terms exactly, as one of the best attested facts in ancient history, because it occurred against the expectations of the disciples and because the existence of the church was built upon it, but even the Resurrection was significant mainly as "an extraordinary evidence of an ordinary event," for "every death is a resurrection."

It will be remembered that except for the existence of God, immortality was the one article of faith Abbott never doubted.[51] It is not surprising that *The Other Room* was by all means the most popular of his books. Rejecting both the resurrection of the body and all forms of soul sleeping, Abbott insisted that, since the essence of immortality inhered in the quality of the life possessed the Christian was immortal here and now. He insisted too that God "elects" all and that His mercy endures forever, without any arbitrary limits in this world or another, but he refused to call himself a Universalist because he could not be sure that all would ratify their election. For those, if any, who did not, he could more easily accommodate the idea of annihilation than eternal punishment. "I could endure the thought of endless suffering, but not of sin growing ever deeper, darker, more awful. It has grown to me unthinkable; I believe it is unscriptural."

It must not be supposed that Abbott was ever in danger of

permitting Christianity to evaporate in an atmosphere of vague general religiosity.

We may use other spiritual thinkers to interpret this our religion; but we may not amalgamate this with other religions, or think we have yet to search the world for a universal religion because we think that the one we now have is provincial.

He may insist that he believes not in toleration but in catholicity, but he was never in danger of bolting his food. "The Oriental God is absorbing into himself. The Christian God and the Hebrew God is putting out from himself." His own preference is unmistakably clear. He may seem generous when he declares that Judaism and Christianity are one, but condescension enters when he adds that "Christianity is the Hebrew religion in flower; the Hebrew religion is Christianity in the bud." There are also references to Catholics, Mormons, Christian Scientists, and others which today do not seem notably ecumenical.[52]

V

Lyman Abbott's critics have made much of the fact that he was no scholar. This is quite true; it is also quite irrelevant. It is not necessary for a religious leader to be a scholar; religion was no more meant for scholars alone than music is composed for other composers. Abbott was, in the best sense of the term, a popularizer, familiar with the best of current scholarship in his field and making, on the whole, intelligent use of it.

He has been reproached for making his own temperament the criterion of his beliefs. Of traditional Christian theology, he believed what he wished to believe, we are told, and junked the rest. But looked at from another point of view, this is a testimonial to his unerring instinct for finding what he could use in religion, thus making his beliefs a life force, not simply a set of intellectual propositions. There were times, however, when his optimistic nature caused him to make an uncritical application of the evolutionary hypothesis, and when he quotes Hegel ("God governs the world; the actual working of his government—the carrying out of his plan—is the history of the world"), he is lucky if he gets off with nothing worse than derision from those who live in our time. The idea of history as guided by God was behind the whole "Outlook" idea when that title was first used to indicate a department in *The Illustrated Christian Weekly* and *The Christian Union.* Later, for Abbott as for others, this notion bolstered the "manifest destiny" heresy—"a Providence that directs us in ways we know not of"—and at its worst it made God the commander-in-chief in World War I. Nor was his shallow philosophy of evil much more useful in dealing with those of his correspondents whose faith had foundered on the rock of personal difficulties; I doubt that the "Knoll Paper" called "To a Discouraged Friend" was very helpful to a prospective suicide.

In this connection, too, Abbott's treatment of nature is most unsatisfactory. The inaptitude for country life which in the novel he attributes to Laicus before his removal to Wheathedge may not apply to Abbott literally, but one gathers that it does not wholly misrepresent him, for he tells us elsewhere that his hand was never trained to do anything but hold a book. Yet he writes, "God is in nature, filling it with himself . . . so that all nature forces are but expressions of the divine will, and all nature laws but habits of divine action." As if this were not audacious enough in what Melville calls a world of snakes and lightning, he adds that "what we call the forces of nature are only the will of God; what we call the laws of nature are only the habits of God"; once, in a sermon, he even asks, "For what is the difference between nature and God?" Despite the implication that there is none, he elsewhere spells out the differences for us: nature is material, mechanical, unmoral, blindly subject to invisible forces; man is spiritual, intellectual, self-governing, and morally accountable. When Mr. Gear's son is drowned, Laicus admits that if he had only life's book to read, he could not believe in a God of Love, and Abbott himself says, "Nature is not a manifestation of God. . . . Man is the manifestation of God." Some of these contradictory utterances, representing a direct conflict of first principles, occur in a single book, *Letters to Unknown Friends*.[53]

The one social issue upon which Abbott lagged far behind many of the other religious liberals of his time was that of war. Since he was not a fool, he knew that war and Christianity were "absolutely inconsistent," that war put nothing in the place of what it destroyed, and that it ranked with poverty, pestilence, and famine among the scourges of mankind. "The American who attempts to beat the ploughshare into a sword, and the pruning-hook into a spear, is the enemy of his country." Yet the American Peace Society dropped him from membership in 1913 on the unassailable ground that he also belonged to the Army and Navy League and had supported all the wars of his time.

Abbott afterwards believed that he had learned during the pre-Civil War agitation that justice is better than peace and that no political principle has much utility "unless it is worth fighting and suffering for." Certainly he accepted the Civil War long before it came, believing "that the anti-slavery conflict was one which could not be settled by compromise," pondering the possibility of himself going to Kansas "if I was robust enough and knew how to use a pistol or rifle," and fearing "that it may be over before I am old enough to carry arms." That much we have heard in many a crisis from many a sedentary young man, and we need not, I think, fear that he was in great danger, but there can be no question how he felt.[54] Once the Civil War was over, however, he was very conciliatory toward the South, and from then on through the early stages of the Spanish War crisis, his record is clear enough. He stood for conciliation during the Chilean and Venezuelan affairs and supported the movement toward permanent arbitration. Nor did he come out for intervention in Cuba until March 13, 1898, after which William Randolph Hearst hailed him as an ally of the New York *Journal* in urging the country to go to war! Unlike Mark Twain and many others, he did not retreat when the war shifted to the Philippines. "I cannot believe that all war is wrong," he told the Lake Mohonk Arbitration Conference in 1899. "I cannot think that the universal instinct of mankind plays false." American isolationism had reached a dead end, and the country should now enter the international arena as the servant of mankind, holding the Filipinos as its wards until they were ready for freedom.[55]

Between the Spanish War and World War I he straddled his two previous positions. It was not that he himself ever admitted any inconsistency. He still wanted a world court to abolish war between nations as our own American courts had destroyed it between the states, and favored the arbitrament even of questions involving "national honor." In *The Rights of Man* he condemned British imperialism in Ireland and in India, and connected Germany with liberty as he connected philosophy with Greece, art with Italy, and democracy with the United States (poor England had to make do with commerce). Glancing back to the Spanish War, he was still sure that the Spaniards had blown up the *Maine*, but he now thought that we might have gone to war "too precipitately," and when he reviewed Senator Hoar's autobiography,[56] he was willing to grant that whether Hoar or McKinley had been right must be left to the future to decide. He rejoiced in Theodore Roosevelt's victory in the Russo-Japanese War negotiations, had an important influence in bringing about the return of the Boxer indemnity, and granted that China had much more reason to fear a White Peril than we a Yellow one.[57] But he was for "preparedness" and saw a coming struggle between "Slav civilization" and "the Hebrew liberty," which he oddly identified with America. At the time of the Japanese crisis of 1907, he decried war talk but justified exclusion. Later, *The Outlook* did not approve of many of the things Wilson did, but it was with him heart and soul on his senseless expedition into Mexico, even suggesting that we occupy the country and "maintain an orderly and just government, while, during a period which would at least last two or three generations, we are educating the people for self-government." It must have been wonderful to find a "backward" people on your very doorstep, whom you could hasten unselfishly to take under your wing.[58]

In World War I, Abbott was a partisan and an interventionist from an early stage. In his 1894 *Life of Christ* he had admitted that the cleansing of the Temple was made with "a quite harmless whip," but in 1911 he had made the wild suggestion that the figure in Revelation of one with eyes "as a flame of fire" and "feet like unto burnished brass" may have been suggested to Saint John by his memory of Christ driving out the money-changers.[59] Now the whip of small cords almost threatened to become the essence of the Gospel. In 1915 *The Outlook* editorially lauded the notorious film, *The Battle Cry of Peace* (produced by Theodore Roosevelt's Oyster Bay neighbor, J. Stuart Blackton), making a special point of the fact that it had been endorsed by those eminent motion picture authorities, the Navy League, the National Security League, the American Red Cross (which seems to have been getting into odd company), and the American Legion![60] The paper did not think it necessary to mention the fact that Lyman Abbott himself appeared in it, which was more than Roosevelt had been willing to do. No matter now that Christ commands us to put up the sword and turn the other cheek; Tolstoy was "the only consistent literalist." It is true that, as late as March 29, 1916, Abbott writes: "We do not wish that America should enter the war, because we do not believe that this would be the best thing she could do to promote the cause of liberty and justice which we have at heart." [61] But he admits he has been trying to "rouse" America, and if the *Outlook* editorials for some time had not been devoted to fostering a war spirit, it is difficult to understand why they were written.

Once the United States had entered the war, it was "as truly a religious war as the war between Philip II and William of Orange." [62] Christ himself now "calls his followers to the colors and . . . their response to the call constitutes a triumph of Christianity such as the world has never known before." The basic distinction was that love might use force, where self-aggrandizement could not, and since our enemies were fully aware of their sins, they could not claim to be covered by Christ's prayer for those who know not what they do.[63] We could not even be sure that he would not have led an armed revolution in Palestine if there had been any reasonable chance of success.[64] As a matter of fact, World War I was not a war at all but "an international *posse comitatus*, representing more than twenty civilized nations, summoned to preserve the peace and protect the peaceable nations of Europe from the worst, most highly organized and most efficient band of brigands the world has ever known." Beginning with this assumption, it was not unreasonable to ban German music in America, suppress *The Masses*, deny pacifists the right of assembly, and support the notorious Espionage and Sedition Acts. Only on the League of Nations issue could wavering be permitted. *The Outlook* began by supporting it against Lodge and the Senate irreconcilables but finally shifted from the idea of a League to Enforce Peace to a World Court.

Our interest here, of course, is not primarily in whether Abbott was right or wrong in supporting World War I, but rather in what his support of it shows about him. His logic is so weak as to suggest that he believed what he wished to believe, and one therefore begins to wonder uncomfortably whether he may not have done the same thing in other areas. Surely he would have granted that being a Christian involves not only seeking righteous *ends* but employing righteous *means* toward achieving them.[65] But he never even raises this question in connection with any war. The cause is God's cause, and the means is of the devil.

Making all due allowance for whatever Abbott's failures of depth and insight may have been, it is, nevertheless, impossible not to be impressed by his service as a whole. Nobody will ever know how many Americans he helped to retain their faith in the crises posed by the new science and the new Biblical criticism. He accepted John Fiske's idea that evolution was "God's way of doing things," and since religion dealt with values and evolution with processes, he could find no occasion for a conflict between the two. In the eighties he became a convinced evolutionist, and he devoted a good share of the nineties to propagating the new evolutionary conceptions of religion. Without him and those like him, Christianity must have been abandoned by intelligent men, surviving today only in the mental and social backwaters where the Fundamentalists are stranded. No single voice was more important than Abbott's in this area of service, and few spoke so clearly or were heard and heeded by so many.

This, however, is not the final claim for Lyman Abbott as a religious leader. Despite all the vocal vitriol that his detractors spewed in his direction, he was emphatically an Evangelical preacher. He junked every bit of excess baggage which, as he saw it, had attached itself to the Christian Gospel, but he owned himself "suspicious of all philosophies which seem to eliminate the supernatural from the world" and consequently clung to Inspiration, Incarnation, Atonement, and Regeneration. He rejected Unitarianism because he saw it inclining toward naturalism, as the New Theology inclined toward Divine Immanence. "Naturalism regards all religion as simply a growth. Christian faith regards it as primarily and in its conception a gift." His mysticism may have been of a mild variety but it was all his contemporaries could understand, and it helped transplant "the life of God" into "the soul of man." "The Christian religion consists in such a perception of the Infinite as manifested in the life and character of Jesus Christ, that the perception is able to promote in man Christlikeness of character."

APPENDIX

A Postscript on the Beecher-Tilton Scandal

Aside from a few passing references, I have said nothing in my text of Theodore Tilton's charge that Henry Ward Beecher committed adultery with Mrs. Tilton. The controversy which this charge precipitated and the investigations involved were so complicated that any adequate consideration of the matter would require a book at least as long as this one. To treat it even cursorily in my text would have thrown Henry Ward's portrait hopelessly out of balance, but since I do not wish to be evasive, I am stating my conclusions, tentative though they are, in this Postscript.

Gamaliel Bradford once told me that he had started to do a psychograph of Beecher but that after reading the trial records he had given it up. He could not, he said, pronounce Beecher guilty, but he did not feel that he could pronounce him innocent with sufficient emphasis to satisfy his friends. Somewhat similarly, I should have to say that at this juncture I do not believe Beecher's guilt or innocence can be either *proved* or *disproved*. The evidence is so ambiguous and contradictory that the only safe *legal* verdict is the old Scottish "not proven." You can read the testimony, if you like, as Lyman Abbott read it or you can read it as Paxton Hibben read it. E. C. Stedman was right when he said the case might well be written up in the manner of *The Ring and the Book*, and Beecher himself said that he expected to live the rest of his life in its shadow and was resigned to doing so. He never made an attempt to continue social relations with any of his friends after the scandal until they had shown him that they wished to continue such a relationship.

Beyond this I can only say that I *believe* in Beecher's innocence, but this is faith, no knowledge. When it comes to a choice between taking Beecher's word and taking that of the brilliant, unstable, and (I fear) essentially devious Tilton and his allies, I have no choice but to choose Beecher, though I admit that I see both Henry C. Bowen and Francis Moulton, the go-between in the interminable negotiations between Beecher and Tilton, much less clearly than I see Tilton himself. Bowen, one of the pillars and founders of Plymouth Church and Tilton's employer on *The Independent* and elsewhere, supported Tilton by charging that Beecher had also committed adultery with his dead wife, but his behavior in the whole affair is ambiguous on any hypothesis, and both he and Tilton had abundant motivation for attacking Beecher in the business rivalries and relationships of religious journalism in which all three men were engaged. Tilton himself more than once expressed naked malice against Beecher ("my object was to strike him right to the heart, Sir"), and he also said that

> the more I quarreled with Mr. Beecher, the better Mr. Bowen liked it; if as a result of the controversy, Mr. Beecher should be dead, Mr. Bowen would not be one of the mourners, but one that would uplift the horn of gladness; he never wanted peace with Mr. Beecher; he is an enemy of Mr. Beecher, would rejoice in his downfall.

Yet Tilton did not actually accuse Beecher of adultery before the summer of 1874; until then, though Beecher was a villain, Mrs. Tilton was pure as the driven snow; later, when he was asked about this, he said he had "always had a strange technical use of words," and that he had not actually said what he was understood to have meant! As to Moulton, I simply cannot reconcile his assurance to Beecher—"*You* can stand if the *whole* case were published tomorrow—with either his conduct or his testimony. As to Victoria Woodhull, who brought the scandal into the open by "breaking" the hitherto whispered story in *Woodhull and Claflin's Weekly,* how can any question of responsibility or reliability even be raised? Mrs. Woodhull, moreover, had no first-hand knowledge and only knew what others had told her, for her claims of intimacy with Beecher are so fantastic that they have never been taken seriously by anybody; even if the great preacher had been a heretic on the subject of sexual ethics, he certainly could not have been fool enough to make a confidante of so notorious a woman as this, especially when he knew she was pulling every string at her command to attach him to her cause as a social "reformer." Actually, Mrs. Woodhull can be trusted in nothing. She both asserted and denied that Tilton himself had been her lover, and many years later, in England, where she wooed respectability, she also denied that she had ever accused Beecher and sued the British Museum for having on its shelves material derogatory to her!

Mrs. Tilton is, to me at least, a considerably more sympathetic figure than her husband, but Mrs. Tilton both affirmed and denied Beecher's guilt (and her own) on so many occasions that it is impossible to decide what she believed or whether she knew. Moreover, many of her statements do not reach us directly but only through her husband, Beecher's accuser. It is possible that she may not have been entirely responsible for her actions; there were those who doubted the responsibility of her mother, Mrs. Morse. The sanity of Isabella Beecher Hooker, the only one of Henry's sisters who took a stand against him, has also been questioned. This certainly could not be said of Thomas K. Beecher, but we do not know just what Tom meant when he wrote Isabella that "Mrs. Woodhull only carries out Henry's philosophy, against which I recorded my protest twenty years ago," and we must not forget that in the same letter he warned her that she had as yet no proof of Henry's wrongdoing. Statements from Susan B. Anthony and Elizabeth Cady Stanton also complicate the matter, but here again specific information is lacking, and Mrs. Stanton especially shows up unfavorably in an undignified, tattle-tale light.

Beecher is generally regarded as having behaved himself very ineptly during his ordeal; he himself said there was never a greater ass nor a deeper pit. But the accusations were not definite nor made by a responsible party until 1874; at this point he did challenge his adversary, nor did he ever thereafter waver in maintaining his innocence. Up to this point, both he and his advisers might well be pardoned for feeling that he was under no obligation "to run after every rat in creation . . . every leech, and worm, and every venomous insect." Some have found his answers during the civil suit evasive or contradictory, but his performance was good enough so that Tilton's chief counsel, William A. Beach, was converted to a belief in his innocence—"I felt, and feel now, that we were a pack of hounds trying to drag down a noble lion"—[1] and the presiding judge, Joseph

Neilson, occupied the chair at the testimonial dinner offered Beecher upon his seventieth birthday. Obviously he made a serious mistake in using Moulton, but he had never been rated a good judge of men's motives, and he may well have found the whole situation so disgusting that he childishly seized the opportunity to dismiss it from his mind by dropping it into the lap of the first person who promised to take care of it for him. Somehow or other, the words he spoke to the investigating council of churches which Plymouth called after the civil trial was over ring true:

I do not care—so long as God knows and my mother—how it is. I have come to about the state of mind that I do not care for you or anybody else. . . . I am tired of you, and I am tired of the world; I am tired of a community that has not a particle of moral reaction; I am tired of men that make newspapers and men that read them. I am tired of an age that will permit the newspapers to be flooded and to make themselves a common sewer of filth and scandal.

He was convincing too, and courageous beyond all his adversaries, when in 1884 he defended Cleveland's good name, despite warnings that such action would revive his own miserable scandal:

When in the gloomy night of my own suffering, I sounded every depth of sorrow, I vowed that if God would bring the day star of hope, I would never suffer brother, friend or neighbor to go unfriended should a like serpent seek to crush him. That oath I will regard now. Because I know the bitterness of venomous lies, I will stand against infamous lies that seek to sting to death an upright man and magistrate. Men counsel me to prudence, lest I stir again my own griefs. No, I will not be prudent. If I refuse to interpose a shield of well-placed confidence between Governor Cleveland and the swarm of liars that nuzzle in the mud or sling arrows from ambush, may my tongue cleave to the roof of my mouth and my right hand forget its cunning.

The charges of habitual and promiscuous unchastity which both Bowen and Tilton were led to prefer against Beecher as time went on give the impression of desperation: if a well-aimed bullet will not bring the stag down, do let us try birdshot! It is simply not conceivable that Beecher had "been guilty of adulteries with numerous members of [his] congregation ever since [his] Indianapolis pastorate, all down through these twenty-five years" and was "not a safe man to dwell in a Christian community." Had this been the case, the thing could not possibly have been kept under cover until the seventies. (We do indeed know of girls and women who entertained warm feelings toward Beecher, but there is no charge against him which has been made to stick.)

I do not doubt, however, that Elizabeth Tilton was strongly attracted to Beecher, nor do I pretend that I think him wise in handling the situation which developed. He admitted kissing her "as I would my own family," sometimes in her husband's presence and sometimes alone. "I kissed him [Tilton], and he kissed me, and I kissed his wife and she kissed me, and I believe they kissed each other." Sloppy as this is, some will no doubt read it as evidence of Beecher's guilt, but it seems to me just the opposite; if he had been guilty of adultery, I do not see why he should not have denied the kissing too. We must not forget that even Mrs. Moulton testified that one day when Henry was greatly upset, she "leaned over and kissed him on the forehead." He regarded this as a "kiss of inspiration" and "a holy kiss, as I sometimes have seen it in poetry," but he did not return it, because "it was not best, under the circumstances, that she and I should kiss." It all sounds as though kisses were as cheap at Plymouth Church as they are backstage today, and perhaps it should help us to understand the hyper-emotional atmosphere in which all these people lived and in which they wrote endless letters to each other. Beecher always insisted that he apologized to Tilton not for having wronged his bed but for having believed slander about him and given advice which led to his professional downfall. He also berated himself for not having had the wit to see the dangers involved in Mrs. Tilton's affection for him (she said he respected her and encouraged her to develop her highest capacities as a woman, where her husband only belittled her) in time to check them, as an older and presumably wiser man ought to have done. This may, of course, not be true, but it suits the existent circumstances as well as any rival hypothesis.

In the last analysis, however, the argument for Beecher's chastity must rest less upon his character than upon his temperament. He was a frank, open man, who could not keep a secret, and who blurted out everything he believed and sometimes even that which he had not sufficiently pondered to be sure whether he believed it or not. Guilty or innocent, the burden which he carried during his years under accusation was terrible, yet he continued his ministry throughout the ordeal, preaching great sermons and taking his stand upon every public question which called for a commitment, and those closest to him felt that the religious life of Plymouth Church had never been richer than during this period. He told his people, "I have not preached to you a doctrine that I have not practised," and he said that there was "nothing more disastrous to the moral sense" than "to hold one view secretly and preach another publicly." For though he admitted man's right to privacy—"the soul has no more business to go stark naked down the street than a man has to go stark naked as regards his body" —he also believed that while "it is not necessary that a man should always tell everything," yet "whatever he tells" must "always be truth." Could he have accomplished what he did, being the kind of man he was, if he had been living a lie? Perhaps. But if so, he was one of the most phenomenal characters on record.[2]

BIBLIOGRAPHIES AND NOTES

The following abbreviations are employed in this section:

AHS — A. H. Smythe
AL — *American Literature*
AM — *American Mercury*
AUA — American Unitarian Association
BA — Bookman Associates
BP — Beacon Press
C — Thomas Y. Crowell Company
Ce — Century Company
Ce — *Century Magazine*
D — Doubleday & Company, Inc.
DM — Dodd, Mead & Co.
Do — George H. Doran Co.
Du — E. P. Dutton & Co.
FW — Funk & Wagnalls
H — Harper & Brothers
HB — Harcourt, Brace and Company
HM — Houghton Mifflin Co.
HUP — Harvard University Press
I — *The Independent*
K — Alfred A. Knopf
LB — Little, Brown & Company
LG — Longmans, Green & Co.
LHJ — *Ladies' Home Journal*
M — The Macmillan Company
McC — McClelland & Co.
MP — Moody Press
NAR — *North American Review*
NEQ — *New England Quarterly*
NR — *The New Republic*
O — *The Outlook*
P — G. P. Putnam's Sons
PP — Pilgrim Press
R — Fleming H. Revell Co.
Ro — Roberts Brothers
S — Charles Scribner's Sons
TF — Ticknor and Fields
UCP — University of Chicago Press

1. *Lyman Beecher: Great by His Religion*

Three volumes of Lyman Beecher's *Works* were published; the edition I used bore the imprint of John P. Jewett & Company, Boston, 1852 (Vols. I, II) and 1853 (Vol. III). The principal source of information about Beecher is *The Autobiography of Lyman Beecher*, of which the most useful edition is now that edited by Barbara M. Cross in "The John Harvard Library," 2 volumes (HUP, 1961). There is no detailed biographical study, but I have profited by reading John Elmer Frazee's Ph.D. dissertation, "Lyman Beecher: Theologian and Social Reformer" (University of Edinburgh, 1936), of which there is a copy in the Congregational Library, Boston. This work contains an extensive bibliography. See also a brief study by Edward F. Hayward, *Lyman Beecher* (PP, 1904).

Lyman, Henry Ward, and Harriet Beecher Stowe are all treated briefly in Constance Rourke's *Trumpets of Jubilee* (HB, 1927). See also David W. Bartlett, *Modern Agitators: or Pen Portraits of American Reformers* (C. M. Saxton, 1859); John Ross Dix, *Pen Portraits, or Pen Pictures of Distinguished American Divines* (Tappan and Whittemore, 1854); Arthur S. Hoyt, *The Pulpit and American Life* (M, 1921); Joseph F. Tuttle, "Lyman Beecher," *American Presbyterian and Theological Review*, N.S. I (1863), 291–307.

1 Though the other figures in this volume are customarily referred to in my text by their last names, I generally call Lyman Beecher "Lyman" and his son "Henry Ward." This is not because I wish to assume an undue familiarity with either but simply because to speak of two different persons as "Beecher" might well be confusing, especially since there are a number of other Beechers who must be referred to incidentally.

2 Kenneth R. Andrews, *Nook Farm: Mark Twain's Hartford Circle* (HUP, 1950), p. 56.

3 Lyman Beecher Stowe, *Saints, Sinners, and Beechers* (Bobbs-Merrill, 1934), is useful for a general view of the family. It is also very entertaining. Edward has only recently had justice done to him by Robert Merideth in *The Politics of the Universe: Edward Beecher, Abolition, and Orthdoxy* (Vanderbilt University Press, 1968). Max Eastman, who was brought up in his church, wrote charmingly of

Thomas K. Beecher in *Heroes I Have Known* (Simon and Schuster, 1942). For Catharine, see Mae Elizabeth Harveson, *Catharine Esther Beecher, Pioneer Educator* (Philadelphia: n. p., 1922), for Harriet, my *Harriet Beecher Stowe: The Known and the Unknown* (Oxford University Press, 1965).

4 Stowe's "Sketches and Recollections of Dr. Lyman Beecher," *Congregational Quarterly*, VI (1864), 221–35, is the most valuable article that has been published about him.

5 William L. Adam, "Litchfield, Connecticut," *New England Magazine*, N.S. XV (1896–97), 705–19.

6 In 1839 Lyman writes: "My intellect is invigorated by heaven and by use, and my heart rejoices, and my health rises, while I preach every night, and thrice on the Sabbath, attend morning prayer-meeting at five and talk, and four o'clock prayer-meeting and talk, and inquiry meeting after preaching every night, and converse with forty or more, and talk with young men from eight till twelve A.M. besides."

7 *Autobiography*, II, 267–68.

8 Lyman's writing methods were all his own also. As soon as he had written a sentence he liked, he would leave his study to rush off and read it to some member of the household, who must then stop whatever she was doing to listen to him. "One of his daughters said that there were three negative rules by which she could always read her father's writing, to wit: 1. If there is a letter crossed, it isn't a *t*. 2. If there is a letter dotted, it isn't an *i*. 3. If there is a capital letter, it isn't at the beginning of a word."

9 He had one health advantage in being "a glorious sleeper" (Calvin Stowe). He could command sleep at any time, and he slept as soon as his head touched the pillow. This was a considerable achievement for so nervous a man.

10 See *Autobiography*, Vol. II, Ch. XVII, especially, in the Harvard edition, pp. 111–12, 114.

11 By Roxana Foote: Catharine (1800–78); William Henry (1802–89); Edward (1803–95); Mary Foote, Mrs. Thomas C. Perkins (1805–1900); George (1809–43); Harriet, Mrs. Calvin E. Stowe (1811–96); Henry Ward (1813–87); Charles (1815–1900). By Harriet Porter: Isabella, Mrs. John Hooker (1822–1907); Thomas K. (1824–1900);

James (1828–86). In addition one child by each wife died—the first Harriet and Frederick.

12 See the beginning of *Autobiography*, Vol. I, Ch. XXXI.

13 " 'But is it my duty to be willing to be damned?' It is your duty to love the Lord your God with all your heart, and soul, and mind, and strength, and to confide in his government, and to be willing that he should dispose of you, forever, just as he pleases. Do you think such submission synonymous with willingness to be damned? It is as different as heaven is from hell. It is the temper of heaven, and your present rebellious temper is the temper of those who are lost.—'But is it my duty to be willing to be a sinner, and go to hell, and be sinful and miserable to all eternity?' No, it is your willingness to be a sinner which is now preparing you for hell, and leading you, step by step, to destruction. And should you ever enter the abodes of darkness, it will be your voluntary wickedness which will perpetuate your misery."

14 For further comment on Harriet Porter and her relations with the Beechers, see my *Harriet Beecher Stowe: The Known and the Unknown*, pp. 24–7.

15 See *Autobiography*, Vol. I, Ch. LXIX. Harriet included partial portraits of her father in both *Poganus People* and *Oldtown Folks.* See Charles H. Foster, *The Rungless Ladder: Harriet Beecher Stowe and New England Puritanism* (Duke University Press, 1954), especially pp. 233 ff.

16 Cf. *Autobiography*, Vol. I, Ch. VIII.

17 Foster, *The Rungless Ladder*, pp. 93–94, 256–57.

18 See *Autobiography*, Vol. II, Ch. XVI.

19 I have found only one suggestion of paranormal experience in Beecher's life, and this is far from being a clear case. On the way home from England, his ship ran into a hurricane. It was considered in danger, and the passengers were badly frightened. After conducting services in the saloon Sunday noon, Beecher declared, "I have seen Christ, and have the assurance that not one of us will be lost. Be of good cheer." I may add that his worst examples of special pleading occur in his "Objections to the Inspiration of the Bible," where he attempts to clear the Book of all moral charges which have been brought against it. Here he argues, for example, that God hardened

Pharaoh's heart only by causing reasonable demands to be made of him, which Pharaoh himself rejected. His heart was hardened as the result of his own intransigence, and God was not responsible for it. The hearts of all sinners are hardened by resistance to God. Was the extermination of the Canaanites unworthy? As the result of the Fall, 800 million people die every thirty years. On this particular occasion, "God . . . selected one nation to exterminate other nations, for the violation of the natural and moral laws of his government. He might have chosen earthquake, fire, or pestilence. But he chose other agents; and they, with miraculous evidence of his aid, fulfilled their vocation."

20 Lyman Beecher lost his fight against "Popery" in Boston, which became a Catholic city, though not to the destruction of the old Puritan element in it. Yet the country at large has never ceased to think of it as a Puritan stronghold, for the Irish who came in were, if possible, more puritanical, especially in sexual matters, than the Puritans themselves had been.

21 "The Remedy for Duelling" was simply to refuse to elect any duelist to public office.

22 He lived into the Civil War years, but since he was by this time in no condition mentally to consider the problems involved, his devotion to peace was not tested by this crisis.

2. *William Ellery Channing: Messages from the Spirit*

Channing's *Works* runs to six volumes. I used the set in the Mugar Library at Boston University, but the imprints differ from volume to volume, and the dates range from 1843 to 1849. William Henry Channing's *Memoir of William Ellery Channing*, 3 volumes (Boston: Wm. Crosby and H. P. Nichols, 1848), is the basic collection of biographical materials. Other indispensable books are *Dr. Channing's Notebook: Passages from the Unpublished Manuscripts of William Ellery Channing*, selected by his granddaughter, Grace Ellery Channing (HM, 1887); Anna Letitia Le Bretton, ed., *Correspondence of William Ellery Channing, D.D. and Lucy Aikin, from 1826 to 1842* (Williams and Norgate, 1874); and Elizabeth P. Peabody, *Reminiscences of Rev. Wm. Ellery Channing, D.D.* (Ro, 1880).

John White Chadwick's *William Ellery Channing, Minister of Religion* (HM, 1903) is by all means the most important early or intermediate biography. As a general study of Channing, it still stands unequalled. See also Henry W. Bellows, *William Ellery Channing, His Opinions, Genius and Character* (P, 1880); Charles T. Brooks, *William Ellery Channing: A Centennial Memory* (Ro, 1880); Paul Revere Frothingham, *William Ellery Channing, His Messages from the Spirit* (HM, 1903); and Thomas S. Matthews, *Channing, A Study* (Marseilles, "Studies" Publications, 1928). Theodore Parker's *An Humble Tribute to the Memory of William Ellery Channing, D.D.* (Boston: Charles C. Little and James Brown, 1842) is of special interest among the memorial tributes. The Channing centenary (1880) called forth much more such material; see Russell N. Bellows, *The Channing Centenary in America, Great Britain, and Ireland* (George H. Ellis, *1881*) and *The Centenary Commemoration of the Birth of Dr. William Ellery Channing . . . Reports of the Meetings in London, Belfast, Aberdeen, Tavistock, Manchester, and Liverpool* (London: British and Foreign Unitarian Association, 1880). See also Mme Robert Holland, *Channing, Sa vie et ses oeuvres* (Didier, 1857) and René Lavollée, *Channing, Sa vie et sa doctrine* . . . (G. Plon & Cie, 1886).

The extraordinary Channing revival of recent years has produced these books: Arthur W. Brown, *Always Young for Liberty: A Biography of William Ellery Channing* (Syracuse University Press, 1956) and *William Ellery Channing* (Twayne, 1961); David P. Edgell, *William Ellery Channing, An Intellectual Portrait* (BP, 1955); Madeleine H. Rice, *Federal Street Pastor: The Life of William Ellery Channing* (BA, 1961); Robert Lee Patterson, *The Philosophy of William Ellery Channing* (BA, 1952); Hester Hastings, *William Ellery Channing and L'Académie des Sciences Morales et Politiques, 1870* . . . (Brown University Press, 1960).

See also Anne Holt's article, "William Ellery Channing (1780–1842)," *Hibbert Journal*, XLI (1942), 42–49, and the following articles: Sydney E. Ahlstrom, "The Interpretation of Channing," *NEQ*, XXX (1957), 99–105; Warner Berthoff, "Renan on William Ellery Channing and American Unitarianism," *NEQ*, XXXV (1962), 71–92; Neal F. Doubleday, "Channing on the Nature of Man," *Journal of Religion*, XXIII (1943), 245–57; L. H. Downs, "Emerson and Dr. Channing: Two Men from Boston," *NEQ*, XX (1947), 516–34; Arthur Ladu, "Channing and Transcendentalism," *AL*, XI (1939–40), 129–40; John E. Reinhardt, "The Evolution of William Ellery Channing's Sociopolitical Ideas," *AL*, XXVI (1954–55), 154–65; Robert E.

Spiller, "A Case for William Ellery Channing," *NEQ*, III (1930), 55–60; Renio Vertanen, "Tocqueville and William Ellery Channing," *AL*, XXII (1950–51), 21–28.

The following books, which differ widely in method and value, all have sections devoted to Channing: George Willis Cooke, ed., *The American Scholar* (AUA, 1907); Charles W. Eliot, *Four American Leaders* (AUA, 1906); Stephen H. Fritchman, *Men of Liberty: Ten Unitarian Pioneers* (BP, 1944); Joseph M. Gray, *Prophets of the Soul* (Abingdon Press, 1936); F. H. Hedge, *Martin Luther and Other Essays* (Ro, 1888); A. B. Muzzey, *Reminiscences and Memorials of Men of the Revolution and their Families* (Estes and Lauriat, 1883); Vernon Louis Parrington, *The Romantic Revolution in America* (HB, 1927); Lyman P. Powell, *Heavenly Heretics* (P, 1909); Wallace P. Rusterholtz, *American Heretics and Saints* (Hawthorn & Burack, 1938); Henry T. Tuckerman, *Characteristics of Literature, Illustrated by the Genius of Distinguished Men* (Lindsay and Blakiston, 1849); George Edward Woodberry, *Studies in Letters and Life* (HM, 1890).

1 Rice, *Federal Street Pastor.*

2 Chadwick, *William Ellery Channing.*

3 Chadwick. Much of what we are told about Channing in this aspect suggests what Hawthorne writes of Dimmesdale in *The Scarlet Letter*, except of course that there was no suggestion of concealed guilt about Channing.

4 Conrad Wright, *The Liberal Christians: Essays on American Unitarian History* (BP, 1970), argues against the tendency to stress the influence of Hopkins upon Channing and balks at calling him a Transcendentalist. Wright especially attacks Herbert W. Schneider, "The Intellectual Background of William Ellery Channing," *Church History*, VII (1938), 3–24, also David P. Edgell's *William Ellery Channing, An Intellectual Portrait.*

5 See his essay on Fénelon in *Works*, Vol. I.

6 See *Memoir*, II, 206–7.

7 "Still, it is not by nature that we first approach God, nor does this constitute our great tie to him. I am not unjust to it, for I live in and by its light. But without a higher revelation than itself, it would be dark and voiceless. We must look for God in our own souls." *Memoir*, II, 429.

8 I have not found many references to Channing's contacts with animals, but it is clear that he was very tender toward them. He was always glad to remember that even as a boy he had never killed a bird, and once he even liberated some rats from a trap because he could not stand the sight of their obvious torment. The story of the slaughtered birds he encountered during his childhood is touching in the extreme. He had been feeding them in their nest until one day he found them cut into quarters. In a nearby tree their parents were mourning, and the last turn of the screw for Channing was his notion that they supposed him to be the murderer.

9 Chadwick.

10 Anna Cora Mowatt Ritchie, *Autobiography of an Actress* (Ticknor, Reed, and Fields, 1854).

11 Channing's father-in-law had at one time owned a distillery, and some of its products were sometimes exchanged for slaves. This caused embarrassment to Channing and presented his enemies with a rich opportunity. He was accused of "living in luxury at the price of blood." See his letter on this charge in Elizabeth Peabody, *Reminiscences*, pp. 360–63.

12 Channing was not, however, consistently liberal about such matters. He thought it unseemly for a woman to publish her memoirs. In his essay on Milton he passed over Milton's divorce views altogether: "On this topic we cannot enlarge."

13 Chadwick.

14 Chadwick.

15 See Chadwick, pp. 362–63. Channing wrote his sermons in his all but illegible hand, and no copies were made for publication until Elizabeth Peabody came along to provide them. His handwriting was very sloppy for a man who was so very precise in all other matters. The small number of sermons preached at Federal Street during Channing's last year were not due to his ill health alone but to the estrangement between his church and himself over anti-slavery agitation; I know of no other distinguished American clergyman whose pastoral relations ended upon so sad a note. After the church had refused Channing the use of the auditorium for a memorial service for Charles Follen, he did not resign his charge in a huff, as many other men would have done, but he did insist upon serving thereafter at his own volition and without salary.

16 James Freeman Clarke, *Memorial and Biographical Sketches* (HM, 1878).

17 Printed with the "Personal Poems" in all collected editions of Whittier.

18 See the long discussion of the Trinity in *Memoir*, I, 406, and cf. "Unitarian Christianity" in *Works*, Vol. III.

19 We have already seen something of the spirit in which Channing approached the Roman Catholic Church through his relations with Bishop Cheverus. Its "doctrinal errors" did not greatly concern him, but he could not stomach the "insolent, intolerant pretension to infallibility." See also the "Letter on Catholicism" in *Works*, Vol. II. But his essay on Fénelon gave him a welcome opportunity to express his admiration for a prominent Catholic writer, and he was no less critical of Protestant churches than he was of the Catholic Church itself. The "spirit of domination" shown in the Methodist Church was intolerable to him. "No sect seems to me more fettered, or to have more the spirit of a sect." But Channing was not willing to be excluded even from what he criticized. "You may exclude me from your Roman Church, your Episcopal Church, and your Calvinistic Church, on account of supposed defects in my creed or my sect, and I am content to be excluded. But I will not be severed from the great body of Christ. Who shall sunder me from such as Fénelon, from Pascal, and Borromeo, from Archbishop Leighton, Jeremy Taylor, and John Howard? Who can rupture the spiritual bond between these men and myself? . . . A pure mind is free of the universe. It belongs to the church, the family of the pure, in all worlds." God must not be shut up in any denomination. "We must think no man the better for belonging to our communion; no man the worse for belonging to another." Mrs. Ritchie says that, just before his death, he took part in certain experiments in what would now be called ESP and did not seem unsympathetic toward it. There is a very amusing article by Abe C. Ravitz, "The Return of William Ellery Channing," *American Quarterly*, XIII (1961), 67–76, in which Channing appears as "communicating" with John Pierpont.

20 See Channing's fuller discussion of this matter in his letter to Peabody, *Reminiscences*, pp. 434 ff.

21 See the "Address on Temperance" (*Works*, II). But there is a curious passage in "Remarks on Associations" (*Works*, I) in which

Channing clearly wishes to make an exception in favor of wine. This seems out of harmony with what he has written elsewhere.

22 *Works,* II.

23 *Works,* II.

24 See, further, various pieces in *Works,* III, IV, and V.

3. *Henry Ward Beecher: God Was in Christ*

Henry Ward Beecher was one of the most famous men of his century, and his bibliography is too extensive to be more than glanced at here. Extensive check-lists, both ill arranged, may be found in Lyman Abbott, *Henry Ward Beecher* (HM, 1903) and Paxton Hibben, *Henry Ward Beecher, An American Portrait* (Do, 1927).

Among the many books published over Beecher's by-line, mention may here be made of *Bible Studies in the Old Testament* (R, 1892); *Evolution and Religion* (PP, n.d.); *Eyes and Ears* (TF, 1863); *Freedom and War* (TF, 1863); *Lecture Room Notes* (J. B. Ford & Co., 1870); *Lectures and Orations,* Newell Dwight Hillis, ed., (R, 1913); *Lectures to Young Men . . . ,* New Edition (Ford, 1873); *The Life of Jesus the Christ, Part I: Earlier Scenes* (Ford, 1872), *Part II: Later Scenes* (Bromfield and Company, 1891); *The Life of Christ Without-Within* (H, 1906); *New Star Papers* (Derby and Jackson, 1859); *Norwood; or Village Life in New England* (S, 1868); *Patriotic Addresses,* John R. Howard, ed. (Fords, Howard & Hulbert, 1887); *Pleasant Talk about Fruits, Flowers, and Farming* (Ford, 1874); *Prayers from Plymouth Pulpit* (S, 1868); *Star Papers . . .* (J. C. Derby, 1885); *Yale Lectures on Preaching, First, Second, and Third Series* (Fords, Howard & Hulbert, 1886). There are a number of Beecher anthologies, containing quotations from extemporaneous discourses as well as selections from his published writings; see *Comforting Thoughts* (Fords, Howard & Hulbert, 1885); *The Crown of Life,* Mary Storrs Haynes, ed. (Lothrop, 1890); *Life Thoughts,* Edna Dean Proctor, ed. (Phillips, Sampson, 1859).

The authorized biography is William C. Beecher and Samuel Scoville, "assisted by Mrs. Henry Ward Beecher," *A Biography of Rev. Henry Ward Beecher* (Charles L. Webster & Company, 1888). Lyman Abbott edited *Henry Ward Beecher: A Sketch of His Career* (FW, 1883), in collaboration with S. B. Halliday, and produced a substantial study of his own, noted above. To this the sketch included in his *Silhouettes of My Contemporaries* (D, 1922) is an important supplement. See also John Henry Barrows, *Henry Ward Beecher: The Shakespeare of the Pulpit* (FW, 1893); Thomas W. Knox, *Life and Work of Henry Ward Beecher* (Park Publishing Co., 1887); and J. B. Pond, *A Summer in England with Henry Ward Beecher . . .* (Fords, Howard & Hulbert, 1887), which is an omnibus volume, containing also many lectures and sermons. Edward Bok edited *Beecher Memorial: Contemporary Tributes to the Memory of Henry Ward Beecher* (Brooklyn: Privately printed, 1887), and there is a later collection, *Henry Ward Beecher as His Friends Saw Him* (PP, 1904).

Lyman Beecher Stowe's *Saints, Sinners and Beechers* has several chapters on Henry Ward. I have spoken of the books by Paxton Hibben, Robert Shaplen, and William G. McLoughlin in my notes. McLoughlin's, which is at this writing the latest book about Beecher, is also one of the few really scholarly studies that have been made of him at any time. Professor Clifford Clark's biography, in preparation as I write, should see print not very long after this book of mine.

There are references to Beecher in hundreds of nineteenth-century memoirs, and he appears in most of the miscellanies devoted to American preachers which I have listed in connection with other chapters, and in others too numerous to mention here. By all means the best brief study is that of Constance Rourke in her *Trumpets of Jubilee.*

1 Lyman Abbott, who worked under Beecher in religious journalism and succeeded him as pastor of Plymouth Church, considered Phillips Brooks the greater preacher, and Beecher the greater orator (*Henry Ward Beecher*, pp. 402–3; see also his "Henry Ward Beecher as an Orator," *O*, LIV [1913], 377–81). But Abbott also says that Beecher, "beyond any minister whom I have ever heard, or any minister whose sermons I have ever read—preached Jesus Christ; not theories about him, not speculations about him, but the story of his life" (*My Four Anchors* [PP, 1911]). Brooks himself called Beecher the greatest preacher in America.

2 It is true that Roosevelt was once, absurdly, called a drunkard, but he immediately filed a libel suit, and the charge was swiftly and decisively squelched.

3 For further discussion of this matter see Appendix.

4 Among the advertising testimonials to which Beecher lent his name there was one for a truss, but I do not know whether or not he had had occasion to test this.

5 Beecher had no fear or suspicion of science, but I do not feel he was greatly interested in it for its own sake. Like many nineteenth-century worthies he was seduced by phrenology, not because the science of bumps interested him particularly, but because he thought that, imperfect as it was, phrenology gave "a formulated analysis of mind" and helped him in his approaches to different types of people. See "Phrenology" in *Eyes and Ears*. Beecher's interest in ventilation was far ahead of that of most of his contemporaries, and he claimed never to have seen a public hall that was properly ventilated. In *Norwood* he permitted Uncle Eb to say: "One of these days men will call things by their right names. Then they won't say: he's of a good disposition; but, he has a good stomach. Half the grace that's going is nothing but food. Paul said the kingdom was not meat and drink. Very likely not hereafter. But it is here."

6 "The Dandelion and I," in *Eyes and Ears*. See also "A Discourse of Flowers," in *Star Papers*.

7 See "Book Stores," in *Star Papers*, and "The Duty of Owning Books," in *Eyes and Ears*.

8 Whether it was all "holiness" or not, such a passage makes one wonder whether Henry Ward really liked sermons. He enjoyed preaching, of course. But did he like to hear others preach when he had the chance? (How many preachers do, I wonder?) Would he rather have been a great painter than a preacher if he had had the gift? Or is all this merely another example of the familiar phenomenon of a man being most impressed by what he himself cannot do?

9 Nicolai Cikovsky, Jr., *George Inness* (Praeger, 1971).

10 Pictures of Christ generally failed to please Beecher, not coming up to his ideal. But at the Bodleian: "I was much affected by a head of Christ. . . . For one blessed moment I was with the Lord. I knew Him. I loved Him. My eyes could not close for tears. My poor tongue kept silence, but my heart spoke, and I loved and adored."

11 See Marvin Felheim's tendenciously entitled and oriented "Two Views of the Stage, or the Theory and Practice of Henry Ward Beecher," *NEQ*, XXV (1952), 314–26. Beecher allowed Augustin Daly to dramatize *Norwood* but did not go to see the result.

12 See Howard, ed., *Patriotic Addresses*, pp. 138–39, for a vivid description.

13 In his oration on Wendell Phillips, however, Beecher himself states that he told two Plymouth trustees he would break with them (whatever that may mean) if they did not give Phillips permission to speak in the church.

14 Matthew Arnold attended Plymouth Church in 1883. Since it was not in his nature to approve without qualification, it is not surprising that he thought the sermon poor though the delivery was wonderful. His impressions of Henry's personality were very favorable, however. "At the end of the service he came down into the area to see me, gave me the notes of his sermon, said that I had taught him much, that he had read my rebukes of him, too, and that they were just, and had done him good. Nothing could be more gracious and in better taste than what he said." Another distinguished English visitor, Charles Dickens, was similarly impressed, finding Beecher's personality attractive and even his competence in the aesthetic field respectworthy.

15 See Harriet's account of her brother in her *Men of Our Times* . . . (Hartford Publishing Co., 1868), and, for further analysis of the relations between the two, my *Harriet Beecher Stowe: The Known and the Unknown.*

16 Even so careful a writer as William G. McLoughlin has said of Eunice Beecher that Henry did not love her (*The Meaning of Henry Ward Beecher* [K, 1970], p. 86) and that, during and after her life in Indiana, she "gradually developed into a hypochondriacal shrew who made his life miserable" (p. 18), but when I asked him for his evidence, he said frankly that these were only general impressions and acknowledged that he might have been too much influenced by Paxton Hibben, whose anti-Beecher bias he recognized. There can be no question about Mrs. Beecher's sufferings in Indiana; she herself wrote in 1846 that she had become a "thin faced, gray haired, toothless old woman." Actually she was only two years older than her husband, but she looked much older than that, and once, when she was ill while travelling, a fellow passenger bade her be grateful to God for having given her such a kind and attentive son. (See my *Harriet Beecher Stowe*, pp. 226–27, for a suggestive letter of Harriet's on Henry's loving care of his wife when she was ill.) Later in life, he did not tell her about his own failing health; neither, apparently, did he confide in

her about the Tilton trouble until he could no longer avoid it, but this may have been merely to spare her pain. During the late Brooklyn years, she and the children spent more time at the farm than Henry could spare away from the city, and if her (or Samuel Scoville, Jr.'s) account of Lincoln's secret visit of 1864 (see n. 23) is accurate, Beecher did not tell her who his visitor had been until after the assassination. There is nothing shrewish in Mrs. Beecher's novel, *From Dawn to Daylight: The Simple Story of a Western Home*, by a Minister's Wife (Derby and Jackson, 1859), which is a thinly disguised record of her early married life, nor yet in her articles, "Mr. Beecher as I Knew Him," which ran through nine numbers of *LHJ*, Vols. VIII–IX, between October 1891 and August 1892. The present writer is indebted to both Professor McLoughlin and Professor Clifford Clark for courtesies extended during the writing of this book.

17 Mary Thacher Higginson, *Letters and Journals of Thomas Wentworth Higginson, 1846–1906* (HM, 1921).

18 Ellen Terry, *The Story of My Life* (D, 1909), pp. 315–18.

19 Edwin Booth, for one, testified to this effect. Beecher's essay on the doorbell ("Back Again," in *Eyes and Ears*) suggests that there were times when his attention was almost as incessantly solicited as was that of Phillips Brooks.

20 McLoughlin's *The Meaning of Henry Ward Beecher* is much the best study of Beecher's social thinking. It is difficult to fault the author on any particular point, yet I feel, perhaps inconsistently, that the general tone of his discussion does not carry complete conviction. Beecher was not an academic logician. He was a public teacher facing practical problems. Were not some of his inconsistencies determined by his comprehensiveness and his attempt to see all sides of the problem? If he was inconsistent, life is much more so, and though his solutions are seldom heroic, they are often sensible.

21 For Beecher and the anti-slavery fight, see McLoughlin, Chs. IX–X; for a considerably more admiring account, cf. Lyman Abbott, *Henry Ward Beecher*, pp. 274–81, which deals especially with the Reconstruction period. Cf. also Louis Filler, "Liberalism, Anti-Slavery, and the Founders of *The Independent*," *NEQ*, XXVII (1954), 291–306.

22 Apparently he believed in capital punishment; at least he was disgusted by attempts to shield notorious murderers from the conse-

quences of their crimes. He justified the killing of house burglars and praised the Old Testament punishment of abortion by death. "It would be well if the humanity of that economy could be made imperative in modern times."

23 See Samuel Scoville, Jr., "When Lincoln and Beecher Met," *I*, CXVI (1926), 180–82. On the authority of his grandmother, Mrs. Henry Ward Beecher, Scoville tells the famous and much controverted story of how Lincoln came incognito, late one night, probably in 1864, to Beecher's residence in Brooklyn for comfort and prayer.

24 The introduction to Augusta Moore, ed., *Notes from Plymouth Pulpit . . .* , New Edition (H, 1865), gives much information about Beecher's appearance and manner in the pulpit and in the lecture room. On Plymouth's informality see Rollo Ogden, *Life and Letters of Edwin Laurence Godkin* (M, 1907), I, 117–18. For detailed analysis of Beecher in standard, traditional rhetorical terms, see Lionel Crocker, *Henry Ward Beecher's Art of Preaching* (UCP, 1934) and *Henry Ward Beecher's Speaking Art* (R, 1937).

25 "If you are preaching to pedants, you may properly enough illustrate by the ancient classics; but if you are preaching to common people you must not confine yourself to that course, although it is allowable, once in a while, to use some illustration drawn from the heroes of ancient history and mythology. But what may be called scholarly illustrations are not generally good for the common people" (*Yale Lectures on Preaching*). Note the unspoken assumption that those who know the classics are pedants: also, the tendency to divide human beings into classes.

26 *Progressive Religious Thought in America* (HM, 1919), p. 33.

27 Lyman Abbott, *Henry Ward Beecher*, pp. 429–49.

28 Beechers, like other men, were not wholly consistent; hence we should not be too much surprised to find Henry telling us that Christ shared the ideas of his time about demoniac possession, and declaring that "there was in the life of the Savior as regular a development, both external and internal, as ever takes place in the life of any man." He sometimes says Christ where he means Jesus. In *Life of Christ*, II, 222, there is a rather impressive consideration of how Christ did his work under what would have seemed the least propitious conditions, and why spiritual progress was better served thus than if he had remained here to spell everything out for us.

29 Since sexual matters were not openly discussed in his time, Beecher says little about the grossness of some parts of the Old Testament; in his Yale lectures, however, he admits that this element must be faced. It is clear that he thought the allegorical reading of The Song of Solomon a pious, euphemistic modern interpretation. The discussion of "The Strange Woman" in *Lectures to Young Men* recognizes "niceness" as a difficulty in the way of a fruitful discussion of such themes. "I solemnly warn you," he says, "against indulging a *morbid imagination*," but some listeners found him doing it in this lecture. See *The Americanization of Edward Bok* (S, 1922), pp. 93–94, on Beecher's prudery concerning women's dress and even, on at least one occasion, harshness toward them.

30 *The Meaning of Henry Ward Beecher*, p. 97.

31 Odell Shepard, ed., *The Journals of Bronson Alcott* (LB, 1938), p. 288.

4. *Phillips Brooks: The Lord Our God Is a Sun*

The authorized biography is Alexander V. G. Allen's monumental and magnificent *Life and Letters of Phillips Brooks*, 2 volumes (Du, 1900). All books in this section of the bibliography not otherwise accredited are published by Du.

There is an excellent modern biography by Raymond W. Albright, *Focus on Infinity* (M, 1961), where see further bibliography.

Brooks's own books include *Eight Lectures on Preaching* (S.P.C.K., 1959, reprinted from the 1879 edition); *Essays and Addresses* (1894); *The Influence of Jesus* (1879); *Letters of Travel* (1894); and *Tolerance* (1893). There are many collections of sermons, some of which appear in more than one collection. The most recent and most comprehensive volume is William Scarlett, ed., *Phillips Brooks: Selected Sermons* (1949).

Among the many other books and pamphlets about Brooks, I have found the following of interest: Edward Abbott, *Phillips Brooks: A Memory of the Bishop, an Impression of the Man, A Study of the Preacher, with a Digest of His Theological Teachings* (Cambridge: Powell & Company, 1900); Arthur Brooks, *Phillips Brooks* (H, 1893); William Henry Brooks, *A Sketch of the Late Rt. Rev. Phillips Brooks, D.D.* (Boston: D. W. Colbath & Co., 1894); George A. Gordon, *Phillips Brooks as the Messenger of God* (Boston: Damrell and Upham, 1893); M. A. DeWolfe Howe, *Phillips Brooks* (Small, Maynard, 1899)—see also his *Causes and Their Champions* (Atlantic-Little, Brown, 1926); William Lawrence, *Phillips Brooks, A Study* (HM, 1903) and *Life of Phillips Brooks* (H, 1930); Leighton Parks, *The Theology of Phillips Brooks* (Damrell & Upham, 1894); Henry G. Spaulding, *The Preaching of Phillips Brooks* (Damrell & Upham, 1893). M. C. Ayres, ed., *Phillips Brooks in Boston: Five Years' Editorial Estimates* (Boston: George H. Ellis, 1893), collects material from Boston newspapers.

Brooks appears in many miscellanies devoted to the great preachers and other worthies of his time. These are too numerous to be listed here, and most of them are not very significant. The following may be noted: Lyman Abbott, *Silhouettes of My Contemporaries;* Lewis O. Brastow, *Representative Modern Preachers* (M, 1904); Albert H. Currier, *Nine Great Preachers* (PP, 1912); Samuel A. Eliot, "Phillips Brooks and the Unity of the Spirit," in *Pioneers of Religious Liberty in America* (AUA, 1903); Charles C. Everett, *Sons of the Puritans* (AUA, 1908); F. W. Farrar, *Men I Have Known* (C, 1897); Arthur S. Hoyt, *The Pulpit and American Life* (M, 1921); Clarence E. MaCartney, *Six Kings of the American Pulpit* (Westminster, 1943); Henry K. Rowe, *Modern Pathfinders of Christianity* (R. 1928); Frederick F. Shannon, *A Moneyless Magnate and Other Essays* (Do, 1923); Charles Franklin Thwing, *Friends of Men* (M, 1933). See also Washington Gladden, "Phillips Brooks: An Estimation," *NAR*, CLXXVI (1903), 257–81.

1 Lawrence, *Memories of a Happy Life* (HM, 1926), p. 76.

2 In his sermons, Brooks is not always consistent in his treatment of pain, nor quite convincing either. In "Prayer" he tells us that he in whom God's word abides cannot vex God "with querulous supplications to be released from suffering" when he should be "delighting God with holy petitions that he may be brave and patient" under his affliction, and "purified and made perfect by it." The passage on the sick man in "The Valley of Baca" is even worse: "Day by day his Maker took some strength out of his life, unstrung some nerve, put some pain in; but the suffering of a decaying body was so far surpassed by the rare joy of feeling his Maker's hands busy on the body and the spirit he had made, and of studying his wondrous ways of working, that his hours of sickness were the happiest that he had ever lived." And in "The Sacredness of Life" Brooks rejected not only

suicide but also euthanasia. The doctor is "arrogant" when he argues that life may be taken when there is nothing but suffering in store for the patient. "As if God were not every day using the body's suffering to cultivate the soul's eternal life. As if just as there was a hard lesson to be learned you ought to kill the scholar."

3 The sermons contain many references to both drunkenness and sexual sin, as in "Higher and Lower Standards": "Here is a community where everybody drinks. You live in it, and you drink too. Why should you not? What call of right have you to set yourself up for an exception? None, if you get your standard wholly from your time; but surely reason enough, if all the world and all the ages speak to you and tell you how the curse of drink is at the root of a large part of human misery, and that the earth would almost burst to blossom if the blight of drunkenness were taken off. Reason enough, if your own conscience speaks to you and tells you that you have no right to degrade your own nature from its best activity, or to put one grain more of temptation in the way of your hindered and burdened fellow-men." And he proceeds to apply the same reasoning to gambling.

4 There is an interesting passage on the differences between the scientific and the poetic views of nature. The former tends toward "hard superficialness" and "spiritual poverty." But the poetic view has its "corrupt tendency" also, "toward superstition,—toward that excessive human self-consciousness which thinks that stars move and winds blow only to bring us messages out of the unseen world."—*The Influence of Jesus*, p. 248.

5 See his paper on Henry Hobson Richardson in *Essays and Addresses*.

6 The quotations are from Allen, *Life*, I, 587; II, 129.

7 "I think there might be a comparison drawn between the Sphinx and the Dresden Madonna, as the highest art expression of the two great religions, the East and the West,—Fatalism and Providence, for that they seem to mean. Both have recognized the feminine nature of the religious instinct, for each is a woman. Both have tried to express a union of humanity with something its superior, but one has joined it only to the superior *strength* of the animal, the other infused it with the superior spirituality of a divine nature. One unites wisdom and power, and claims man's homage for that, the other unites wis-

dom and love, and says, 'Worship this.' The Sphinx has life in her human face written into a riddle, a puzzle, a mocking bewilderment. The Virgin's face is full of mystery we cannot fathom, but it unfolds to us a thousand of the mysteries of life. It does not mock, but bless us. The Egyptian woman is alone amid her sands—to be worshipped, not loved. The Christian woman has her child clasped in her arms, enters into the companies and the sympathies of men, and claims no worship except love."

8 See Allen's lists, *Life*, II, 179–81, 218–19.

9 See Brooks, *Christmas Songs and Easter Carols* (Du, 1894), also the sonnets quoted by Allen.

10 There is a curious passage on "unhealthy" imagination in the essay on "Poetry" (*Essays and Addresses*): "First there is the Baron Munchausen kind, where the land is real and has old familiar names, but the men and things done are wild and visionary and absurd. This is, I grant you, thoroughly unhealthy and untrue. Then there is the Robinson Crusoe kind, where the land is unreal, some fancied island in a fancied sea, but the men are plain homespun brother-men to all of us. This last is a good deal better than the first, but it is not quite right yet. The true thing comes when men of flesh and blood tread flat on solid ground, and then imagination and poetry become the healthiest diet of the soul."

11 See the essay on "Biography" in *Essays and Addresses.*

12 See Eliot's article in the Phillips Brooks memorial number of *The Harvard Monthly*, XV (February 1893).

13 "In all this travelling one is overcome and oppressed with the multiplicity of life. The single point where we stand is so small, yet it is the best and dearest of all. I would not for the world be anything but this, if I must cease being this in order to be that other thing. But I would fain also be these other things,—these College Students, these soldiers in their barracks, these children playing around the old fountain, these actors in their dotage, these merchants in their shops, these peasant women at their toil, these fine ladies with their beauty; I want somehow, somewhere, to *be* them all! and the simplicity, the singleness of my own life, with its appointed place and limits, comes over me oppressively."—Allen, *Life*, II, 360.

14 For Brooks's relations with children, see *Letters of Phillips Brooks to Helen Keller* (Privately printed, 1893); W. Wilberforce Newton,

The Child and the Bishop, Together with Certain Memorabilia of Rt. Rev. Phillips Brooks, by an Old Friend (J. G. Cupples & Co., 1894); Lyman Abbott, *Silhouettes of My Contemporaries;* Allen, *Life*, II, 805–6; Miriam Storrs Washburn, "Phillips Brooks in a Home," *Christian Union*, XLVII (1893), 363.

15 His loathing of illegible handwriting was one of Brooks's most marked idiosyncrasies. "What right has that man to save his time in writing badly and steal mine?"

16 See Albright, *Focus on Infinity*, pp. 181–84. The same book contains a brief discussion of the possible connection between Brooks and Henry Adams's novel *Esther*. Since Brooks's celibacy suggests that of Henry James, it is interesting to remember that Minny Temple, between whom and James there was a kind of attachment, was greatly impressed by Brooks's preaching; see R. C. Le Clair, "Henry James and Minny Temple," *AL*, XXI (1949), 35–48.

17 "Nothing could be more remote from his pulpit method than the statue which represents him with uplifted arm in an attitude of exhortation"—Francis G. Peabody, *Reminiscences of Latter Day Saints* (HM, 1927). Peabody adds that Brooks often made no movement while preaching except to raise his eyes from his manuscript and grasp his gown from time to time. The statue referred to is of course the posthumous Saint-Gaudens work outside Trinity Church, which nobody who knew Brooks ever seems to have liked. For a good statement of the case against it, see Lawrence, *Memories of a Happy Life*, pp. 289–91.

18 "Here he attempted, what he seemed to avoid in the pulpit, the impartation of religious knowledge, the discussion of religious theories and theological opinions."—Allen, II, 508. Such lectures required a great deal of reading in contemporary theological writing.

19 See Allen, *Life*, I, 113 ff. and the specimen there reproduced.

20 Allen divides Brooks's sermons into three periods. "In the first, which included his ministry in Philadelphia, he had written, perhaps, his most beautiful sermons, full of the poetry of life, disclosing the hidden significance of the divine allegory of human history,—a great artist, himself unmoved as he unrolled the panorama of man. In the second period, he had been at war with the forces which were undermining faith, and not without suffering, his own soul being torn with

the conflict; yet in those dark days, always appearing like a tower of strength. That period was over now [1883]. He had felt while abroad that another subtle imponderable change in the atmosphere of human existence was modifying the situation. The tendency was toward theism, not yet, perhaps, distinctly toward Christianity, but there was improvement visible from the highest outlook. The mechanical theory of the world was yielding to the evidences of faith. . . . His preaching changed to correspond to the change within. He addressed himself in his totality as a man to the common humanity, doing greatly whatever he did, and assuming the greatness of those to whom he spoke. . . . Now the idea of rescue became more prominent, but it was the rescue of men from the danger of losing the great opportunity of life,—the chance which was given of making the most of the divine privilege of the children of God."

21 It is interesting to compare this with a statement made by Brooks himself in his lectures on preaching: "I always remember one special afternoon, years ago, when the light faded from the room where I was preaching and the faces melted together into a unit as of one impressive pleading man, and I felt them listening when I could hardly see them; I remember this accidental day as one of the times when the sense of the privilege of having to do with people as their preacher came out almost overpoweringly."

22 He is not quite consistent about this. In his sermon on "The Mystery of Iniquity" he sees evil as an active positive thing. "Vice is a hardy plant. Let it alone and it will grow on of itself. Virtue is a delicate and fragile thing, and needs all the care and petting it can get." In "Literature and Life" (*Essays and Addresses*), on the other hand, he says that "hate is only love turned backward," and he was committed to the thesis that the chessboard of human life is black on white, not white on black. "The great truth of Christianity, the great truth of Christ, is that sin is unnatural and has no business in a human life." In his sermon on "The Temptation of Christ" he does not actually commit himself to believing in the devil, but he does say that the power which tempts "is some power external to the life of men which enters into conspiracy with something in man to bring sin upon the soul." On the other hand, Charles R. Brown heard him tell a Bible class that he believed in many personal devils and had seen them at work, "but that he did not believe in one evil being who was omni-

present (if not omniscient and well-nigh omnipotent) who presided over and carried on pretty much all the wicked business of the world. He felt that such a faith would be like believing in two gods, one good and one bad."

23 "How To Abound" and "How To Be Abased."

24 See also "Address at the Dedication of the Memorial Hall, Andover . . ." in *Essays and Addresses*.

25 Though Brooks was regarded as one of the great champions of toleration in his time, he sometimes permitted himself to speak of other religionists in terms which no tolerant person would employ today. He speaks of the "dead Quaker atmosphere" of Philadelphia, and though he did not reject faith healing out of hand, he had no respect for it as practised by Christian Science. Spiritualism tried "to bring souls together in carnal manifestation" (a difficult undertaking, I should think). He was sure we did not need to know anything more about the dead than the Bible tells us, and he hated the séance room so much that he apparently would have liked to sweep all ghost stories away with it. Even mysticism, though at best "a very high and thorough action of the whole nature in apprehending spiritual truth," was dangerous because it overemphasized feeling and claimed to be religion. The Roman Catholic Church was a "spiritual tyrant" who tried to master the world in a "false fashion," and whose "fundamental tenets" could not be reconciled with "the first ideas of our Republic." Even so, she was better than the Greek Church, which was dead "because the thing it cherishes and worships is not a living thing." "The Greek Church stands for orthodoxy. The Latin Church stands for catholicity. Protestantism stands for truth."

26 Brooks had no interest in the accumulation of riches; he lived simply, gave freely, and left a comparatively small estate; see Albright, pp. 398–99. He could not even live in the rectory which Trinity Church had provided for him without remembering that passers-by might be saying, "A fine sort of Christian teacher he must be to live in a grand house like that." He continues, "But I believe that I have a right to live here, with this beauty and luxury about me. I enjoy it all, and I do my work as a Christian minister better for having these surroundings. A man is no better Christian for wearing overalls than for working in a beautifully furnished study. He can be one in either situation, if only he has the spirit of Christ." When Charles E. Jefferson visited Brooks at the rectory, he thought the place a palace in the

profusion of the art works displayed there.—*I Remember the Days of Old* (Privately printed, 1931).

5. *D. L. Moody: Whosover Will May Come*

The best and most definitive life of Moody is James F. Findlay, Jr., *Dwight L. Moody, American Evangelist, 1837–1899* (UCP, 1969), whose only fault is that there are times when Moody himself seems to disappear into his background. The only other recent books, both of which are of value, are J. C. Pollock, *Moody: A Biographical Portrait of the Pacesetter in Modern Mass Evangelism* (M, 1963) and Richard K. Curtis, *They Called Him Mister Moody* (D, 1962). Janet Mabie's *The Years Beyond: The Story of Northfield, D.L. Moody, and the Schools* (The Northfield Bookstore, 1960) is valuable in its specialized field.

William R. Moody published an authorized *Life of D. L. Moody* (R, 1900), which was hurriedly written, as soon as possible after Moody's death, to forestall unauthorized accounts, and W. R. Moody did not get round to what he wished to have regarded as his mature, considered word about his father until he published *D. L. Moody* (M) in 1930. Paul Moody's *My Father, An Intimate Portrait of Dwight Moody* (LB, 1938) is a briefer but far more personal book by Moody's younger son, who had already collaborated with his brother-in-law, A. P. Fitt, in *The Shorter Life of D. L. Moody* (The Bible Institute Colportage Association, 1900). Fitt also published *Moody Still Lives: Word Pictures of D. L. Moody* (R, 1936); see also John McDowell *et al.*, *What D. L. Moody Means To Me* (The Northfield Schools, 1937).

Unique among studies of Moody is a very sophisticated and highly literate study by Gamaliel Bradford, *D. L. Moody, A Worker in Souls* (Do, 1927), in which the whole Moody phenomenon is seen against an elaborate background of religious and metaphysical speculation and from the point of view of a developed and highly individual temperament. See also Bradford's article, "D. L. Moody the Educator," *Advance*, LII (1930), 675.

In addition to these there are some fifty books about Moody, many of them repetitive and without scholarly or critical value. Some of these, however, contain useful material, drawn from first-hand knowledge. This is true, for example, of W. H. Daniels, *D. L. Moody and His Work* (American Publishing Company, 1875) and of J. Wilbur

Chapman, *The Life and Work of Dwight L. Moody . . .* (Winston, 1900). For fuller bibliographies and bibliographical guidance, see the works by Findlay, Bradford, Pollock, and Curtis listed above. Paul Moody (*My Father*) also has a useful commentary on Moody books. The fullest bibliography is Wilbur M. Smith, *An Annotated Bibliography of D. L. Moody* (MP, 1948), but the evaluations are from the Fundamentalist point of view.

There have been many collections of Moody's sermons, many of them printed from newspaper reports, and most of them highly repetitive. Among the largest and most useful compilations are *Glad Tidings*, the New York *Tribune* reports of the Hippodrome talks, and *Great Joy*, the Chicago *Inter-Ocean* reports on the first Chicago campaign (E. B. Treat, 1876, 1877), and *Fifty Sermons and Evangelistic Reports* (Cleveland: F. M. Barton, 1899).

Important critical studies of Moody's work will be found in Robert B. Huber, "Dwight L. Moody," in Marie Kathryn Hochmuth, ed., *A History and Criticism of American Public Address*, Vol. III (LG, 1955) and in William G. McLoughlin, *Modern Revivalism: Charles Grandison Finney to Billy Graham* (Ronald Press Company, 1959). Lyman Abbott's sketch in *Silhouettes of My Contemporaries* is based on personal knowledge. Robert L. Duffus, "The Hound of Heaven," *AM*, IV (1925), 424–32, is a highly competent paper. Considering how well the author knew Moody, Henry Drummond's "Mr. Moody: Some Impressions and Facts," *McClure's Magazine*, IV (1894–95), 55–69, 188–92, is surprisingly thin.

1 *AM*, XXI (1930), 124.

2 "All but two of his books that were published after 1893 were compiled by me. I came to know his vocabulary and mannerisms of language so well that I could do him justice and reproduce his true flavor."—A. P. Fitt. Paul Moody adds that when another member of the family wrote an article that appeared over Moody's by-line, the honorarium always went to the actual writer.

3 Late in 1867 Chicago got the first fully equipped YMCA building in America. In January 1868 it burned. Moody and his co-workers immediately set to work to replace it, and the replacement was destroyed in the Chicago Fire of October 1871.

4 See Emma Moody Powell, *Heavenly Destiny: The Life Story of Mrs. D. L. Moody* (MP, 1943). The publisher Fleming H. Revell, his

father's namesake, was Mrs. Moody's brother. She bore her husband three children: Emma (later Mrs. A. P. Fitt), William Revell, and Paul D. The death of two of William's children, Dwight and Irene, in the last year of the evangelist's life, was the greatest sorrow he ever experienced. Irene must have been an enchanting child. In the few pictures we have of her, her charm leaps out through the stiff, voluminous clothes in which small children were encased in her time and triumphantly seizes the viewer.

5 Moody never allowed the names "Moody Bible Institute" and "Moody Church" to be used during his lifetime. The establishment of the Institute was marked with difficulties from the beginning; in later years its extreme Fundamentalism has estranged it from large sections of the church. In the twenties, Paul Moody precipitated a bitter controversy by declaring that if his father were alive, he would stand with men like Harry Emerson Fosdick rather than the spokesmen for the Institute. Whether he was right or wrong, there was little of Moody's own irenic spirit in the replies that were made to him. The Northfield schools, on the other hand, have turned toward liberalism, and when Billy Graham visited there, he was not invited to address the students.

6 Here is a specimen of Moody's daily schedule during a London campaign: "Drive three miles to noon meeting; lunch; Bible reading at 3:30 followed by enquiry meeting till at least five; then preaching in the Opera House at 6:30; then very short enquiry meeting; then drive five miles to East End and preach to twelve thousand at 8:30; then enquiry meeting; then drive five or six miles home."

7 Robert Morss Lovett, "Moody and Sankey," *NR*, LIII (1927–28), 94–96, compares Moody to President William Rainey Harper of The University of Chicago "in physical structure, in energy, in persistence." Both relied on publicity, went boldly before worldly men, and got them to back unworldly schemes.

8 *The Pilgrim's Progress* is the only work of English fiction I have found Moody referring to. Once he says it comes closer to the Bible than any other book; I wonder how he knew. "What Christ Is to Us" includes the narration of a dream which greatly resembles the Middle English "Pearl," but Moody surely got it at least second-hand. W. R. Moody does not claim much for his father as a reader of literature, but he does say that he owned a good many historical works and that the markings contained in them show that he read more than he is

often given credit for. Once he asked Frances Wells to read for him, marking passages in books that she thought he might like. He seems to have admired Luther, Wesley, and John Knox; it is hard to believe he could have cared for Knox if he had known very much about him. What he really liked to do was to "pick the brains of those whom he trusted." "When I get hold of a man who is versed in the Word of God, I just pump him."

9 See the fairly detailed account of all this in Paul Moody's *My Father. . . .*

10 He is often said to have dropped co-workers without a word when he no longer found them useful. In Sankey's case there does not seem to have been anything to this charge. Sankey's voice was pretty well gone by the eighties, and the pompous affectations which had always been a little trying were getting worse. Whatever the wishes of the two men, they could not have continued working together much longer than they did. One of Moody's co-workers admits that the evangelist had antipathies but no enmities: "He had no hard feelings. He was simply repelled. He gave men a wide berth if he did not like them."

11 Paul Moody's chapter on "The Schools" makes clear the source of Moody's power over the Northfield boys and girls. But when Robert Morss Lovett as a boy visited Northfield, he "had a wonderful time . . . but heard or saw little of Moody. . . . It was almost as if I had secured an audience with the Pope when I was told that Mr. Moody would receive me." The interview was brief, and he did not ask, "Are you a Christian?"

12 See Findlay, *Dwight L. Moody, American Evangelist*, Ch. IX, for an account of the difficulties between Moody and his Chicago supporters which almost prevented the establishment of the Bible Institute.

13 D. L. Moody, *The Fulness of the Gospel* (R, 1908).

14 Findlay, *Dwight L. Moody*, pp. 232 ff.

15 In *Glad Tidings.*

16 Moody's reasoning in a sermon on "Repentance" (in *Great Joy*) seems odd and out of character for him: "Don't you see on the face of it, if your boy won't repent you cannot forgive him, and how is God going to forgive a sinner if he don't repent? If He was allowing an unrepentant sinner into His Kingdom, there would be war in

heaven in twenty-four hours." Surely the general tenor of Moody's preaching is rather that the unrepentant sinner *is* loved, *is* forgiven, but that his own hardness of heart prevents him from accepting God's grace. As Moody himself says elsewhere, "You may spurn God's remedy and perish; but I tell you God don't want you to perish. He says, 'As I live I have no pleasure in the death of the wicked.' 'Turn ye, turn ye, for why will ye die?' "

17. Asked what he "did with" a difficult Bible passage, Moody replied:

"I don't do anything with it."
"How do you understand it?"
"I don't understand it."
"How do you explain it?"
"I don't explain it."
"What do you do with it?"
"I don't do anything with it."
"You don't believe it, do you?"
"Oh, yes, I believe it."

18. *They Gathered at the River: The Story of the Great Revivalists and Their Impact upon Religion in America* (LB, 1958).

19. Moody is credited with having raised some two and a half million dollars for benevolent purposes, but neither he nor Sankey was on salary; both lived on the voluntary gifts which the local committees made to them at the end of a campaign. What he received has, so far as I know, never been made known. He turned all his property and business affairs over to his wife and lived as completely without money as a man can. When he died, the house at Northfield was still lighted by kerosene lamps; it had had an adequate furnace for only four years. Moody also made provision for a modest income for his widow, and it was found that he held a $500 mortgage, which he had forgotten he had, as covering for a loan. His only extravagance seems to have been that when he needed suspenders, shoes, or neckties, he was likely to order by the gross. Once he bought enough Oriental rugs to start a store, and his tables and chairs were made to order.

6. *Washington Gladden: Where Does the Sky Begin?*

Washington Gladden's *Recollections* (HM, 1909) is an absorbing book, but after it gets through the early years, it is much more concerned with the movements in which Gladden participated than with his personal life. Jacob Henry Dorn, *Washington Gladden, Prophet of the Social Gospel* (Ohio State University Press, 1967) is an admirable biography. Richard D. Knudten, *The Systematic Thought of Washington Gladden* (Humanities Press, 1968) is a useful compilation of Gladden's views. Both these works contain much fuller bibliographies than can be given here.

Gladden was a very prolific writer, and only a few of his multitudinous articles are listed in my notes. The following list includes all his important books:

Applied Christianity (HM, 1886); *Being a Christian: What It Means and How To Begin* (Congregational Publishing Society, 1876); *Burning Questions of the Life That Now Is and of That Which Is To Come* (Ce, 1890); *The Christian Pastor and the Working Church* (S, 1898); *The Christian Way: Whither It Leads and How To Go On* (DM, 1877); *Christianity and Socialism* (Eaton and Mains, 1905); *The Church and Modern Life* (HM, 1908); *Commencement Days* (M, 1916); *From the Hub to the Hudson: With Sketches of Nature, History, and Industry* (New England News Company, 1869); *How Much Is Left of the Old Doctrines?* (HM, 1899); *The Interpreter* (PP, 1918); *The Labor Question* (PP, 1911); *Live and Learn* (M, 1914); *The Lord's Prayer* (HM, 1880); *Myrrh and Cassia* (Columbus: AHS, 1883); *The New Idolatry* (McClure, Phillips, 1905); *Organized Labor and Capital* (PP, 1904); *Parish Problems*, ed. by Gladden (Ce, 1887); *Plain Thoughts on the Art of Living* (TF, 1868); *The Practice of Immortality* (PP, 1908); *Present Day Theology* (Columbus: McC, 1913); *Ruling Ideas of the Present Age* (HM, 1895); *The School of Life* (PP, 1911); *Seven Puzzling Bible Books* (HM, 1897); *Social Facts and Forces* (P, 1897); *Social Salvation* (HM, 1902); *Things New and Old* (AHS, 1883); *Tools and the Man: Property and Industry Under the Christian Law* (HM, 1893); *Where Does the Sky Begin* (HM, 1904); *Who Wrote the Bible?* (HM, 1891); *Witnesses of the Light* (HM, 1903); *Working People and Their Employers* (Boston: Lockwood, Brooks and Company, 1876).

Gaius Glenn Atkins, "Washington Gladden and After," *Religion in Life*, V (1936), 593–604, is a moving personal tribute. There are brief but useful accounts of Gladden's work in Charles R. Brown, *They Were Giants* (M, 1934) and in John Wright Buckham, *Progressive Religious Thought in America* (HM, 1919).

1 See especially the chapter on the Trinity in *How Much Is Left of the Old Doctrines?*

2 "Urbs Beata," in *Ultima Veritas* (PP, 1912).

3 See Max Eastman's exciting account of Thomas K. Beecher, in his *Heroes I Have Known.*

4 This involved the printing of paid advertisements in such fashion that the careless reader might mistake them for expressions of editorial opinion. See Gladden's own account of the matter in *Recollections*, pp. 132–37.

5 For doubts which have been raised concerning the Western Reserve matter, see Richard D. Knudten, *The Systematic Thought of Washington Gladden.*

6 Gladden won the undying gratitude of American Catholics when, in the mid-nineties, he courageously spoke out, with very little support from his fellow ministers, against the idiotic anti-Catholic lies propagated by the American Protective Association, a kind of revival of Know-Nothingism. In addition to the accounts of this matter in his *Recollections*, pp. 358–65, and in Dorn, pp. 116 ff., see Gladden's articles in *Ce*, N.S. XLVII (1894), 789–96, and in *Harper's Weekly*, LXIX (1914), 55–56, 255–56. On Gladden's work for ecumenicalism, see Dorn, pp. 349 ff.

7 Dorn says that though Gladden was "genial, warm, and a lover of children," he nonetheless seemed shy, and that "one did not approach him with trivial matters." In *The Christian Pastor*, Gladden himself remarks that the "sanctity" of the clergyman's character must be preserved.

8 There is more food for thought in the comments which follow: "Yet under present conditions it appears necessary that some should labor under this disability. . . . I suppose everything is done that can be done to keep them supplied with air to breathe, but even that is imperfectly accomplished, and the conditions under which their work must be carried on are at best very deplorable."

9 *The Life Unfailing* (McC, 1916).

10 He perhaps overestimated the power of man's free will and underestimated the forces which condition it. He also tended to assume too cavalierly that once the right course has been laid out before men,

they will be sure to walk in it. For this reason the triumphant progress he ascribes to both the Christian League of Connecticut and the Cosmopolis City Club seems just too easy. Once he suggested that church members go to live in the slums for benevolent purposes. "Of course," he adds, "this would mean that the sanitary conditions of those districts would be sharply looked after, for it would not be right for the well-to-do Christians to take their families into these precincts unless they were made habitable; and thus their very advent would bring saving health to their new neighbors." Once, at least, he says that "the government of nature" is also that of God. On the other hand, he perceived that "poverty and wretchedness, vice and crime are not going to be disposed of in a hurry. They will be with us for a long time yet."

11 See Gladden's article, "Religion and Wealth," *Bibliotheca Sacra*, LII (1895), 153–67.

12 See Dorn, pp. 97, 101–2, 119–22.

13 *I*, XXIII (1871), 4; reprinted in Handy, *The Social Gospel in America*, pp. 33–37.

14 See Gladden's own account of this fight in *Recollections*, Ch. XXVI, and in a number of magazine articles, especially "The Church and the Reward of Iniquity," *I*, LVIII (1905), 867–70, and "Mr. Rockefeller as a Truth Teller," pp. 1290–91. Cf. Dorn's account, pp. 240 ff.

15 See his impressive investigation of a legend in "The Myth of Land-Bill Allen," *Ce*, N.S. XLVII (1891), 609–16.

16 *Who Wrote the Bible?* pp. 132–43.

17 Graham Taylor, *Washington Gladden* (National Council of Congregational Churches, 1919) points out that *The Christian League of Connecticut* (1883) antedated all plans for church federation by about twenty years, and that *The Cosmopolis City Club* (1893) came before the Chicago Municipal Voters' League. Gladden also wrote *Santa Claus on a Lark and Other Christmas Stories for Children* (1893). (All these books are published by Ce.) He also wrote some Christmas stories for adults, of which one, "The Shepherd's Story," has been reprinted in Phebe A. Curtis, ed., *Christmas Stories and Legends* (Meigs Publishing Co., 1916, 1952). Gladden's activities as a poet began in his college days and culminated in the publication of *Ultima Veritas*. In his introduction, Gladden is as modest as possible in his

claims for these poems ("How old-fashioned these verses are; how completely they fail to answer the high demands of modern poetic art, no one knows better than I; it is only to a few old-fashioned folk that they are likely to make appeal"), but though it would be absurd to enter significant claims for them, they are nothing to be ashamed of. In his sermons Gladden quoted a great deal from both prose and verse ("When a thing has been said by others better than I can say it, I feel that those to whom I speak are entitled to hear it"). Much of the verse would, one would think, have been read dramatically, and we know that Gladden sometimes gave poetry recitals in his church. In *Recollections* each chapter is headed with a poetic epigraph, like Sir Walter Scott's novels.

18 *The Great Commoner of Ohio: Discourse in Memory of Rutherford Birchard Hayes, Delivered in the First Congregational Church, Columbus, Ohio, January 22, 1893* (N.d., n.p.).

19 In *Art and Morality* Gladden apostrophized Ruskin as follows: "Dear teacher and master whose face we never saw, but whose living words have been to us so many years a guide and inspiration, we are glad already for what you have shown us; and we pray that the morning light may yet for many a day be visible to you on the green English hills, or ever you open your eyes upon the glories of the land that needs no sun!"

20 *Amusements: Their Uses and Their Abuses* (North Adams, Mass.; James T. Robinson & Co., 1866).

21 Wilbur B. Ketcham, 1897. See also his article, "Christianity and Aestheticism," *Andover Review*, I (1884), 13–24, which was the first article ever printed in that journal, after its opening statement of purpose. "It was by thinking of something greater than art that Phidias and Aeschylus and Sophocles became great artists." Gladden takes a dim view in this article of both Rossetti and Wilde. When Wilde rails against mammon-worship, "it is as if a delicate toadstool should turn and rail at the compost heap on which it grows."

22 In *The Lord's Prayer*, Gladden observes of God that "He no more wills that I should be holy than that this flower should be beautiful," and in one of his Commencement addresses, he told his young hearers that "Beauty, not less than Truth and Love, is a divine attribute; no man knows God, in any adequate sense, whose soul is not keenly responsive to all forms of beauty."

23 The old Puritan idea of art as guilt perhaps lingers on in a measure in Gladden's thinking about church architecture. He wanted God's house to be "noble" and "attractive" whenever possible. "It is not seemly that those who themselves dwell in palaces should offer to the Lord a barn for his sanctuary." But a church should not have "the look of elegance or luxury. It should never be a building whose exterior or interior would make upon any working man the impression that the people worshipping in it were too fine to associate with him." Elsewhere he speaks rather contemptuously of "the splendors of architecture and art, of upholstery and decoration, of ecclesiastical millinery and music, with which we now so often seem to attract men to the house of God." There is a perceptive and sophisticated passage in *Where Does the Sky Begin* in which Gladden argues convincingly that the camera does lie when it presents persons in motion because it captures and immobilizes a split second which we never see as the photograph presents it. "The artists who trust their eyes, and paint for us moving creatures *as they look to them*, will give us a better idea of their movement than we can possibly get from a photograph."

24 It is interesting to note that this was the reason why Lyman Abbott declined to side with Gladden in the "tainted money" controversy. Abbott refused to look beyond the deed; it seemed to him Pharisaical and impractical to refuse to accept either service or money from people who were not quite perfect, and when he was told that he certainly would not accept money from a bartender or a prostitute, he replied emphatically that this was just what he would do, being ready to cooperate with anybody in doing good, just as far as the sinner was ready to go, and regarding all this as the best means available of saving him from himself. The "tainted money" controversy was extremely complicated, and many good people were unable to see their way through it clearly. To begin with, the American Board announcement of the Rockefeller benefaction was disingenuous, for it created the impression that the gift had come unsolicited, and this was not the case. Jane Addams testified long after the event that when she was asked to speak or write on the "tainted money" controversy, she always refused, being unable to see the issues clearly enough to take a definite stand.

25 Gladden rejected merely ethical sermons as inadequate. He comments on Ruskin's childhood sermon ("People, be dood! If you are dood, Dod will love you: if you are not dood, Dod will not love

you. People, be dood!"): "It lacks the elements of sound doctrine. It puts too much stress on 'mere morality.' "

26 See Dorn, Ch. XIII, for an excellent account of the conflict between Gladden and Sunday when the leading pastor of Columbus refused to back the evangelist's campaign in that city.

27 Gladden also suggests that perhaps the question whether the Gospels were written by apostles or disciples "was left somewhat obscure for the very purpose of stimulating study," and again that inaccuracies may have been "suffered to lie upon the face of the narrative that our thoughts may be turned away from these details of the record to the development it reveals to us." On his attitude toward Biblical literalism in general, see his article, "A Dangerous Crusade," *Biblical World*, N.S. XLIV (1914), 3–14.

28 For Gladden's account of his own early difficulties in trying to conform to the conversion patterns insisted upon in his boyhood, see *Recollections*, pp. 34–39. On the matter of Jehovah's relationship to David's census, he says in *Who Wrote the Bible?*: "Let no man open his mouth in this day to declare that the Judge of all the earth instigated David to do a presumptuous deed, and then slew seventy thousand of David's subjects for the sin of their ruler."

29 In the early *Being a Christian* he seems to claim that before one can follow Christ, he must believe in him in a sense in which a Unitarian, for example, could not believe. But he may have changed his mind about this later.

30 Such a sentence as this in *The Lord's Prayer* seems rather out of character for Gladden: "His will is that men shall obey his laws; but that if they do not obey they shall suffer." Generally he makes a clear distinction between salvation from sin and remission of penalty. Moreover, like Bunyan in *Mr. Badman*, Gladden knew that though the wages of sin is death, "spiritual death is often a painless process." Even though God should arbitrarily cancel penalty, he could not thus set the sinner free from his sin without his own cooperation. He is not, I think, absolutely consistent in applying all this to the social order. Once he tells us that "he who does wrong ought to suffer, and society ought to be so organized that he shall suffer." But he also says: "I doubt whether we are called to punish anybody. I doubt whether any of us are wise and good enough to punish evildoers. It may sometimes be necessary for society to confine and restrain those who have

shown that they cannot safely be allowed their liberty; but to punish them—who knows enough to mete out the just retribution?"

31 Apparently, however, Gladden was considerably less impressed by Henry Ward Beecher than Lyman Abbott was, for he writes of Thomas K. Beecher: "I have heard from him more persuasive and convincing speech than I ever heard from his more famous brother."

32 Prayer, Gladden believed, often created the condition which made it possible for a human being to receive God's ever-ready blessing. It is interesting—and typical of his time—that he does not discuss prayers for the dead.

33 "I remember as well as if it were yesterday a blackboard hanging in the pulpit, on which some of these figures in Daniel were added and subtracted by the preacher, showing with the precision of mathematics that the world must come to an end in 1843. That was the date at which we were then living. And I remember well the chilling fear which fell upon the heart of a child at the sight of these ominous figures, a fear which was never lifted till the sun rose bright and clear on New Year's Day, 1844. That blessed morning banished many terrors, and loosened the grip of uncanny superstition. I have heard the ravens croak, ever since, with considerable equanimity."—*Seven Puzzling Bible Books.*

34 See especially *Recollections*, Ch. XVIII.

35 See also Gladden, "Truths and Untruths of Christian Science," *I*, LV (1903), 776–79.

36 For Gladden's denominational activities, see Dorn, Ch. V.

37 Since Chinese strikebreakers were brought into North Adams, Gladden also here took a lesson in race relations. The strikers showed amazing and highly praiseworthy restraint in refraining from all violence, and after the strike was over the Chinese community continued in the town, largely ignored by all the townsfolk except Gladden and some of the members of his church, but quite unmolested. Advocates of the Social Gospel are often accused of being less sensitive to racial discrimination than they were to a number of other social problems, and Gladden had at least a little of the unconscious racial snobbery by which many Americans of Anglo-Saxon origin were marked in his time. He denounces anarchism as foreign, especially German (he was

blind to all the deeper issues involved in the Haymarket affair), and he remarks of McKinley's assassin Czolgosz that he bore a name which "no American should ever try to pronounce." He does not seem to have been quite happy about foreign influence upon American literature either. He was sympathetic toward the Negro from Civil War times on, but present-day Negro leaders would judge him benevolent from an altitude of assumed superiority. Cf. *Recollections*, Ch. XXIV; Dorn, pp. 291–302.

38 Politically Gladden was an independent, though in the early days he generally voted Republican. He admired both Theodore Roosevelt and his great rival, Woodrow Wilson. He did not support the one reform upon which most evangelicals agreed—national prohibition. It is true that in *Tools and the Man* he found the Christian state committed to the suppression of the saloon—"whatever manifestly tends to the detriment of society at large may and must be suppressed"—but he did not believe that a law which more than half the people in the country did not believe in could be enforced, and he thought that a law which cannot be enforced creates a dangerous disrespect for all law. For this reason he favored local option rather than either statewide or national prohibition. He was also convinced that neither preaching nor legislation could solve the liquor problem; if the saloon was to go, a substitute must be provided to take over its social functions. Gladden's strongest formulation of the case against liquor is in the early *Working People and their Employers*, Ch. VII.

39 *Another War with Mexico?* (Columbus: Champlin Press, 1916).

40 M, 1916. See also "Will America Yield to the Armament Madness?" *Nation*, CIII, Supplement for Aug. 3, 1916, p. 2. This begins: "I am a pacifist, if I understand that word, which is not in my dictionary." But he rejects "peace at any price."

41 *NR*, V (1915), 75–76.

42 No doubt he was influenced at last by his admiration for Wilson and his hope that his would be the guiding hand in the peace negotiations. Wilson, on his part, made no secret of his admiration for Gladden, answered his letters, acknowledged receipt of his books and sermons, and treated him with great courtesy even when Gladden disagreed with him. When Gladden died, Wilson sent a personal message to the family, in which he called the death a national loss.

43. This poem is in *Ultima Veritas*. See also Gladden, *Our Nation and Her Neighbors* (Columbus: Quinius and Ridenour, 1898); and "The Issues of the War," *O*, CLIX (1898), 673–75.

7. *Lyman Abbott: The Life of God in the Soul of Man*

Abbott's *Reminiscences* (HM, 1915) is the basic biographical document. The 1923 edition has an introduction by Ernest Hamlin Abbott. The most extensive study is Ira V. Brown, *Lyman Abbott, Christian Evolutionist: A Study in Religious Liberalism* (HUP, 1953), where see further bibliography.

The following list of Lyman Abbott's books is comprehensive but not complete: *America in the Making* (Yale University Press, 1911); *Christianity and Social Problems* (HM, 1896); *The Christian Ministry* (HM, 1905); *The Crucifiers* (Woman's Press, 1923); *The Evolution of Christianity* (HM, 1892); *The Great Companion* (M, 1904); *Henry Ward Beecher* (HM, 1903); *The Home Builder* (HM, 1908); *In Aid of Faith* (Du, 1886); *The Industrial Problem* (George W. Jacobs & Co., 1905); *Jesus of Nazareth: His Life and Teachings* (H, 1869); *Laicus; or, The Experiences of a Layman in a Country Parish* (DM, 1872); *Letters to Unknown Friends* (D, 1913); *The Life and Letters of Paul the Apostle* (HM, 1898); *The Life and Literature of the Ancient Hebrews* (HM, 1901); *The Life of Christ* (Bible Study Publishing Co., 1901); *The Life That Really Is* (Wilbur B. Ketcham, 1899); *My Four Anchors: What We Really Know in the Realm of Religion* (PP, 1911); *Old Testament Shadows of New Testament Truths* (H, 1870); *The Other Room* (M, 1903); *Problems of Life*, selections edited by Sarah Truslow Dickinson (DM, 1900); *The Rights of Man* (HM, 1901); *Seeking After God* (C, 1910); *Signs of Promise* (Fords, Howard & Hulbert, 1889); *Silhouettes of My Contemporaries* (D, 1921); *The Spirit of Democracy* (HM, 1910); *The Temple* (M, 1909); *The Theology of an Evolutionist* (HM, 1897); *The Twentieth Century Crusade* (M, 1918); *What Christianity Means To Me: A Spiritual Autobiography* (M, 1918).

Abbott's multitudinous articles in *The Outlook* and elsewhere are listed here only when cited individually in footnotes. *Outlook* articles in series began as hereinafter noted: "Christ's Secret of Happiness," Vol. LXXXIII (1906), 647–48; "The Ethical Teachings of Jesus," XCIV (1910), 532–34; "Impressions of a Careless Traveler," LXXIV (1904), 879–83; "The Last Days of Jesus Christ," CXV (1917), 317;

"The Master Builder," XCVIII (1911), 337–39. "What Is Christianity?" ran in Vols. XC–XCI (1908–9). "Summer Vesper Sermons" appeared frequently through a number of summers beginning in 1905 (Vol. LXXX). "Letters to Unknown Friends" began in Vol. XCIX, pp. 804–5 (Dec. 2, 1911), and appeared frequently under that title until 1915, but only infrequently thereafter, having been more or less displaced by "Knoll Papers," which began in CXI (1915), 654–57 and continued to appear for the rest of the author's lifetime. There was one series of six monthly articles in *LHJ*, XXX, "My Fifty Years as a Minister," beginning in the January 1913 issue.

1 Eugene Exman, *The Brothers Harper* (H, 1965), p. 319.

2 Lincoln is credited with having avowed his indebtedness to the brothers Abbott for almost all his historical knowledge.

3 The story of this catastrophe, which is too complicated to tell here, may be read in Ch. XIII of Abbott's *Reminiscences*.

4 Henry Hoyt Moore, "An Associate's Reminiscences of Lyman Abbott," *O*, CXXXII (1922), 728–29.

5 For Abbott's own spine-tingling account of how his arm had to be rebroken and reset without chloroform, see "The Good Old Times," *O*, CXXV (1920), 567–68.

6 "Impressions of a Careless Traveler," *O*, Vols. LXXVII–LXXVIII and less frequently later, show his capacity for keen observation and also testify to his having covered considerable territory. See, also, two early articles in *Harper's Magazine*: "The Eternal City," XLIV (1871–72), 1–19, and "The City of the Saints," XLV (1872), 169–86.

7 See "Using But Not Abusing," *O*, CXXIV (1920), 550, which is interesting not only for its content but for its revelation of Abbott's frank response to criticism.

8 *The Outlook* gave a reasonable amount of attention to distinguished actors, and as early as 1903 Abbott himself interestingly compared Senator Hoar's autobiography to a "cinematograph" (*O*, LXXVI, 311–18). The paper printed a statement from Ethel Barrymore on the Actors' Strike (CXXIII [1919], 11–12), and when Mary Garden became director of the Chicago Opera, she was hailed editorially: "Few who saw her as Melisande will ever escape attributing to the whole spirit of the Middle Ages something of Mary Garden's personality" (CXXVII [1921], 128–29). But many new tendencies in the drama

were met much in the spirit of William Winter. The production of *Peter Pan* in 1905 drew editorial approval "after the indecencies of *Zaza* and *Sapho*, the scarcely less veiled and more insidious indecencies of the plays presented by Mrs. Patrick Campbell, the horror of *Ghosts*, the tropical passion of *Monna Vanna*, the sinister cynicism of *Man and Superman* and of *Mrs. Warren's Profession*" (LXXXI, 645). The next week, after *Mrs. Warren* had been banned, Royal Cortissoz's severely critical article on Shaw was bolstered by an editorial on "The Yellow Dramatist."

9 In one passage he seems to give Beethoven primacy, but he found a place even for Berlioz, "with his clanging cymbals and his kettledrum" (*O*, CIV [1913], 894–95). He once published a pamphlet on the religion of *Parsifal*.

10 In *Laicus* he writes, "The most beautiful statue that Powers ever chiseled does not compare for grace and beauty with the Divine model."

11 See *O*, LVII (1899), 161–67.

12 See his "My Father," p. 409, in *O*, CXXXII (Nov. 8, 1922), which is the Lyman Abbott memorial number.

13 "I once thought that it was my business to make myself over. I took Jesus Christ as my model, imagined myself to be a man of sculptor's clay and tried to model myself according to the copy set me. It was a mistake. I discovered that either I was pleased with my work—that means self-conceit—or dissatisfied with my work—that means discouragement. . . . Long ago I gave up this copy-work, and for self-examination substituted the prayer: Search me, O God, and know me, and see if there be any evil way in me, and lead me in the way everlasting."—"The Pernicious Habit of Self-Examination," *O*, CXVI (1917), 185.

14 *LHJ*, XXX (March 1912), p. 11.

15 Abbott reviewed both the Browning and the Carlyle love letters sympathetically, refusing to be sidetracted into a discussion of whether they ought to have been published, and he was enlightened in his treatment of prostitution ("The Care of Vicious Women," *O*, LIV [1913], 101–2) and of sex education. *The Outlook* championed the film *Traffic in Souls* as a socially useful exposé of white slavery. Abortion Abbott considered murder, with mothers casting themselves into

the old roles of Herod and Pharaoh ("The Seven Ages of Man: Infancy," *O*, LIX [1898], 728–30).

16 "Righteously," *O*, LVII (1897), 519–21.

17 See especially "Why the Vote Would Be Injurious to Women," *LHJ*, XXVII (Feb. 1910), pp. 21–22. Abbott did champion woman's right "to an open door to every vocation, her right to a fair opportunity for the highest and broadest education, her right to do whatever she can do and be whatever she can become; her right to determine her own appropriate sphere, not to have it determined for her by a lord and master." See two articles in *O*, XCI (1909)—"The Assault on Womanhood" (pp. 784–88) and "The Profession of Motherhood" (pp. 836–40).

18 In later years, Abbott believed in industrial education, regretting his own lack of manual training, and even refusing to rank a literary or scholastic education on a higher plane. The perfect man should have hand and mind trained together. He does not mention the most cogent argument for industrial education, which is that the practical work of the world must be done and that there are many who are not capable of doing anything else.

19 See *O*, CI (1912), 31; CXI (1915), 65–67.

20 Oddly enough, the most detailed reference is in "Impressions of a Careless Traveler: Bermuda," *O*, XCVII (1911), 812–15.

21 *O*, CI (1912), 31.

22 "Concerning Reading," *O*, CXII (1916), 893–94.

23 "The Habit of Immortality," *O*, CI (1912), 30–34.

24 *O*, CXVII (1917), 398–99. He also reviewed *What Is Coming?* *O*, CXVI (1916), 457–60—"Mr. H. G. Wells is always interesting, often entertaining, rarely convincing."

25 "Vicarious Enjoyment," *O*, CXIX (1918), 529.

26 But see "William Jennings Bryan: A Character Study," *O*, LXXXIV (1906), 66–68. This is not unfriendly, though Abbott does express doubts about Bryan's capacity for statesmanship. See also "A Summing-Up of the Vital Issues of 1896," *Review of Reviews*, XIV (1896), 544–49.

27 See Abbott's article on the influence of Theodore Roosevelt's administration upon patriotism and the public service, *O*, XCI (1909),

430–34. When Roosevelt died, Abbott called him "the foremost statesman of his time, and because of his sterling virtues . . . at once the best beloved and the most bitterly execrated of America's public men."—*O*, CXXI (1919), 91.

28 Only, however, because he believed that public order must be preserved. In retrospect at least he felt that "morally, and in the high court of heaven, the capitalistic employers were far more responsible for the conditions in Chicago . . . than the laborers whose passions overwrought their judgment."

29 On Anarchism, see "Danger Ahead," *Ce*, N.S. IX (1885–86), 51–59 ("Repression is not remedy. We cannot suppress this growing discontent; we must remove its cause"), and "Anarchism: Its Cause and Cure, *O*, LXX (1902), 465–71.

30 One of his very few sentimental, unrealistic passages occurs in *Christianity and Social Problems* (p. 318), where he writes that the new criminology "will seek . . . not to protect society from criminals, not to inflict on criminals the vengeance of society, but *simply, solely, only*, to reform them" (italics mine). Before the end of the chapter (pp. 326–27) he has modified this.

31 P. 239.

32 See "What Shall We Do with Cyclops?" *O*, C (1912), 690–92.

33 Abbott's refusal to work for national prohibition estranged him upon this one point from many reformers within the churches. Like Theodore Roosevelt, he was not an absolute teetotaler, but both men were practically teetotalers, and this personal factor was of no importance in the views they held. There are passages in *The Rights of Man* (see pp. 148, 152, 248, 269) where Abbott tries so hard to be fair to alcohol that he leans over backwards (if he is right on p. 152, then obviously we must require independent research from schoolchildren beginning in the first grade). Actually, however, he opposed the liquor interests in many practical ways (see Brown, p. 81), and he had no objection to local prohibition where public sentiment supported its enforcement. In 1910 he wrote T. M. Gilmore, president of the National Model License League (*O*, XCIII, 623–26), of his belief "first, that distilled liquors should never be used except under the advice of a physician; and second, that beers and light wines, if taken as a beverage at all, should be taken only in connection with meals." After national prohibition was achieved, both Abbott and

Roosevelt accepted and supported it. It may be added that once at least *The Outlook* dropped tobacco advertising because of protests from readers (see *O*, CXVIII [1918], 135), but later returned to its sins like a dog unto its vomit, as the Scripture so elegantly expresses it.

34 In addition to his discussions in *The Industrial Problem* and *Christianity and Social Problems* (Ch. X), see "The Wages System" and "Industrial Democracy," *Forum*, IX (1890), 518–29, 658–69, and "Christianity versus Socialism," *NAR*, CLXVIII (1889), 447–53.

35 Yet he advised all extemporaneous preachers to do some writing habitually, "to form a habit of accuracy in expression. The more ready the speaker, the greater the necessity for this pen exercise."

36 Jacob Abbott told him: "If I were a preacher, I would make my first sermon of any convenient length. The next Sunday I would make it five minutes shorter, and I would continue to take off five minutes until the people complained that my sermons were too short. Then I would take five minutes off from that, and the result should give me my standard." The son adds: "I never followed literally my father's counsel; but I have acted in accordance with its spirit."

37 "Shall We Send Them to College?" *O*, XCIII (1909), 758–63.

38 See "Salvation by Growth" and "Salvation by Grace," in *Signs of Promise*.

39 See *Reminiscences*, pp. 373–75.

40 *Proceedings of a Council in Plymouth Church, Brooklyn, New York for the Installation of the Rev. Lyman Abbott, D.D., . . . with a Sermon . . . on The New Theology* (Brooklyn, 1890), p. 13.

41 "The Message of the World's Religions, VI—Christianity," *O*, LVI (1897), 988–93; "Hamilton Wright Mabie," *O*, CXV (1917), 49–51.

42 Of one experience Abbott wrote: "The mystic will say the message was given me by my unseen Father. The rationalist will say the message was the product of unconscious thinking suddenly made conscious by the intellectual crisis. Perhaps both are correct. Perhaps the Father gives us his message in and through our unconscious thinking." This is startlingly like Saint Joan's reply when Baudricourt tells her that her voices come not from God but from her imagination: "Of course. That is how the messages of God come to us."

43 Though Abbott admired James Russell Lowell, he never, to my knowledge, refers to "The Cathedral." It must, I should think, have made a great appeal to him, for the incompleteness of modern religious experience, based upon mystical perception, as contrasted with the old dogmatic formulations based upon authority, is the poet's essential point.

44 *O*, CVI (1914), 439.

45 Elsewhere, however, he wrote: "But when I have found what Christ teaches, that is final, that to me is truth: and when I find out what Christ commands, that is final; that is where I mean to follow, God helping me." In theory he was ready to admit the possibility of further revelations from God, but since perfect love had been revealed in Christ, he found it difficult to imagine what further revelation could achieve. In *O*, CIII (1913), see two articles: "Henri Bergson: The Philosophy of Progress" (pp. 388–91) and "Rudolf Eucken: The Philosophy of the Spiritual Life" (pp. 482–85).

46 In *Seeking After God*, Abbott says that he accepted "the Trinitarian view of tri-personality; that is, that the Trinity of manifestation apparent to us has a basis in a Trinity of Person necessarily hidden from us." But he makes this statement in a footnote and does not enlarge upon it. Though he always insisted that he was not a Unitarian, he admitted on at least one occasion that he was "by no means sure that I am a Trinitarian."—"Fragments of Knowledge," *O*, CXII (1916), 264, 273. He told the Plymouth council: "I do not use the word 'Trinity,' and I do not use the phraseology 'Three Persons in one God,' or 'essence' or 'substance,' because I do not find them helpful to other people's minds at the present time, and they are not helpful to my own." See also "The Trinity in Experience," *O*, LXIV (1900), 713–14.

47 *O*, XCVIII (1911), 776.

48 "Does God shut himself up, so that no man shall come near him except through the avenue of this or that or the other opinion? Has God no sympathy for a sceptic? Has God no love for a heretic? Has God no helpful hand to reach out to an atheist?" If so, how can He ask us to love and bless those who curse us? See also "Unconscious Following of Christ," *O*, LX (1898), 1011–16; "Whom God Elects," *O*, LXII (1899), 850–54.

49 There is an interesting eschatological passage at the end of the

chapter on "God in Nature" in *Seeking After God.* "When God's work is done, and he is everywhere,—as he is now everywhere but in the hearts of those who will not have him,—when he is in human hearts and lives, as he has been in all nature and in all history, then will come the end, and God will be all in all." This is much like Poe's *Eureka*; did Abbott know it? See "What Is the Promise of His Coming?" *O*, CXX (1918), 582–83.

50 "The New Reformation," *Ce*, N.S. XV (1888–89), 71–80, is perhaps Abbott's most useful summary of the significance of the new Biblical scholarship and its effect upon faith. Certainly it is one of his most substantial articles.

51 At least once he varied this statement to read that the two things he never doubted were God's existence and his own. See "Out of the Past," *O*, LXI (1899), 823–28. He told the Plymouth council that he inclined to believe that immortality was "not the universal attribute of humanity—that God alone hath immortality; and we have it only as here or hereafter we are made partakers of the divine nature."

52 See, among much other material, "The Ages of Man: Infancy," *O*, LIX (1898), 728–30; "The World without Christ, III: What Is Christianity?" XC (1908), 622–26; "Why I Am Not a Christian Scientist," CVII (1914), 692–94; and, for Spiritualism, reviews of some books by Sir Oliver Lodge, *O*, CXV (1917), 229–30; CXXIV (1920), 520–21. One of his few directly controversial articles is the excellent "Flaws in Ingersollism," *NAR*, CL (1890), 446–57.

53 Abbott's conception of nature as the mirror of God seems all the more inexplicable in view of a rather amazing late article, "The School of Life," *O*, CXI (1915), 654–57, in which he tells us that he went to nature not for instruction but for enjoyment, delighting most "in her wildest mood." He once spent the better part of a day as the only passenger on shipboard during a cyclone, feeling "an awful joy in the splendor of the tempest." He also felt "a strange emotion of joy and pain in the experience of human helplessness" as he watched a tornado cut a swath through a Western city. See his review of John Burroughs's *Under the Apple Trees*, *O*, CXIII (1916), 625–27.

54 There is, however, a rather surprising passage in his *Reminiscences* in which he describes a street riot he witnessed near the Five Points in 1857. "I, expecting a riot, walked down to the scene of disorder." He watched from a balcony directly over the battle and escaped a bullet only by good luck, certainly not by good judgment.

55 Abbott might have done well at this juncture to reread his 1888 sermon on "The Power of the Keys" (*Signs of Promise*): "There are not wanting Americans who would take the keys from the people and give them to the Anglo-Saxons. Ask the Chinaman, the Indian, and the Negro how this violation of the divine law works."

56 *O*, LXXVI (1903), 311–18.

57 "A Vision of Peace," *O*, LXXXIII (1906), 507–11.

58 It was in connection with the Indian problem (besides *Christianity and Social Problems*, see "Our Indian Problem," *NAR*, CLXVII [1898], 719–28), that Abbott committed himself to the view that "barbarism has no rights" against civilization. He was justifiably annoyed when the newspapers distorted this to "barbarians have no rights," but though he was forward-looking in arguing against the reservation system and advocating the assimilation of the Indian (Helen Hunt Jackson's *Ramona* was serialized in *The Christian Union*), it must be admitted that the distinction is easier to maintain in theory than in practice. "Will not some Indians die in the process? Yes; perhaps many. Will they not suffer in the process? Yes; perhaps much. But God's way of making men and women is through suffering and by struggle, and there is no other way." This comes pretty close to the social Darwinism which Abbott elsewhere deplores. Nor are his examples of superior and inferior civilizations always quite convincing; see *The Rights of Man*, pp. 219–22. As for Negroes, he demanded legal equality for blacks and whites after the Civil War, but he did not doubt the present inferiority of the blacks, always tended to overstate the progress they had been permitted to make in the South (see the first "Impressions of a Careless Traveler: Some Southern Impressions," *O*, LXXIV [1904], 879–83), and was a convinced segregationist (see *O*, C [1912], 114–16, and CII [1912], 114–16). He did, however, understand the seriousness of the Negro problem: "If we solve it aright, its solution will bring peace and prosperity in the Nation. If we fail, it will bring disaster to the Nation." He also realized (*O*, CXVII [1917], 602–4) that in many communities, segregated schools have meant only inferior schools for blacks. In *Signs of Promise* (1889) Abbott could write of the immigrants as "great hordes of half-civilized and half-heathenized population," but in *America in the Making* (1911), "the great mass of our immigrant population is made up of men and women with more energy and more initiative than their neighbors." His own insularity shows when

he remarks that it is natural for Americans to sympathize with England "because we have one blood pulsating in our veins." As a student of the Old Testament, Abbott could not but appreciate the Jewish genius for religion, and he would have been horrified by anything we know as anti-Semitism. He defended the Jews against H. S. Chamberlain's insane charges in *The Foundations of the Nineteenth Century* (*O*, XCVIII [1911], 731–34; cf. "The Debt of Modern Civilization to Judaism," pp. 774–77), and *The Outlook* did valiant service in the Leo M. Frank case, as several articles in Vol. CX remain to testify. In "Why Not?" *O*, CXXVI (1920), 56, he praised the use of a common church building for Jews and Christians in a changing neighborhood. "Nothing would induce me to undertake a mission for the conversion of the Jews. But if I were a young man I would like to apply for the pastorate of such a church and would hope for occasional interchanges of pulpit between pastor and rabbi." Yet on occasion he seems to me capable of condescension toward Jews, if not something worse: "The Jewish character has been sordid and worldly from the time of bargaining Jacob to the present day." "The man that merely obeys the Ten Commandments is at best a reputable Jew, and the man that merely obeys the prohibitions of the Sermon on the Mount is merely a half-Christianized Jew."

59 *O*, XCVIII (1911), 590.

60 *O*, CXI (1915), 165–66.

61 *O*, CXII (1916), 736.

62 "Some Commonplaces of Christianity," *O*, CXVII (1917), 92, 96.

63 Abbott himself had refuted this ridiculous interpretation in "Lenten Thoughts: Christ's Last Words—'Father, Forgive Them,' " *O*, LV (1897), 637–38: "Who knows what he is doing when he violates God's law?" Dante described the damned as those who had lost the good of the understanding.

64 Here Abbott becomes an unconscious humorist. Violent revolution is right when it succeeds, wrong only when it fails. How does this differ from Napoleon's notion that God is on the side of the heaviest battalions?

65 Abbott clearly states and realizes this in his "John Brown," *O*, XCVII (1911), 273–78, a review of Oswald Garrison Villard's biography.

Appendix: A Postscript on the Beecher-Tilton Scandal

1 Beach's conversion is denied by Paxton Hibben in the heated interchange between himself and Samuel Scoville, Jr., in *Saturday Review of Literature,* which followed the publication of Hibben's book about Beecher; see IV (1927–28), 358, 444, 510; V (1928), 563.

2 The complete record of the civil trial has been printed in *Theodore Tilton vs. Henry Ward Beecher, Action for Crim. Con.* (McDivitt, Campbell & Co., 1875). It runs to 3000 pages and is bound in three volumes. See also the other books listed in the Preface to Robert Shaplen, *Free Love and Heavenly Sinners: The Story of the Great Henry Ward Beecher Scandal* (K, 1954), which is the only modern book-length study. Shaplen does not mention J. E. P. Doyle, *Plymouth Church and its Pastor, or Henry Ward Beecher and his Accusers* (Hartford: The Park Publishing Co., 1875).

On p. 40 of my *Harriet Beecher Stowe: The Known and the Unknown,* I criticized Shaplen's book in terms which were meant to apply rather to Paxton Hibben's *Henry Ward Beecher, An American Portrait.* I did not become aware of this until I reread both books in preparation for the present study and I do not yet know how the confusion occurred. Mr. Shaplen's book is certainly not pro-Beecher, but in spite of his offensive title, he does achieve a reasonable objectivity, and he does not idealize Mrs. Woodhull and the Tiltons. My contrary statement is therefore withdrawn and apologized for.

Of Hibben's book, which more than all else has muddied Beecher's fame in our time, my opinion remains unchanged. It stands as a prime monument of the "de-bunking" biography of the twenties and ought to have been serialized in Mencken's *American Mercury.* Not many of the debunkers were as competent in their research as Hibben was, but this was all thrown away because of his obvious determination to place a degrading interpretation upon everything Beecher said or did. As Newton Arvin remarked in a not generally unfriendly review:

A thousand questions remain unanswered. . . . Hundreds of lapses from mere objectivity can be pounced upon by the dissenter. At point after point, with no real sacrifice of truth, the emphasis could be shifted from the ground where Mr. Hibben has laid it, and the whole portrait would take on, now a kindlier, now a more imposing, aspect. The central episode in the book—the story of Beecher's trial on a charge of adultery—leaves one reader not at all disposed to partisanship in behalf of a man with Beecher's religious and social views, uncertain whether the entire truth has been told. The whole affair was clearly a shady one, and not all the shadow appears to fall on the great preacher. And one may suspect that Mr. Hibben has belittled Beecher's work in England for the Union cause only somewhat less unduly than Holmes and Lyman Abbott exaggerated it. (See Arvin, *American Pantheon*, ed. Daniel Aaron and Sylvan Schendler [Delacorte Press, 1966].)

Professing objectivity ("These are judgments. They have no place in this study"), Hibben produced a book which is nothing but judgments, from start to finish, often even managing to suggest that what he has left out would be far more incriminating than what he has included. He is capable of making two statements which cancel each other out, and what has been hypothesis on one page becomes established fact on another. Perhaps the height of absurdity is reached when Hibben attributes the Chicago *Tribune*'s achievement of "first rank as an American newspaper" to its "enterprising handling" of the Beecher case. The rhetorical devices Hibben employs resemble those of a third-rate novelist; whatever the truth about Beecher may have been, Hibben's book about him is one of the most mean-minded biographies ever written.

INDEX

Note: Except at the main entry for each, the seven subjects of this book are referred to hereinafter by their initials.

Abbott, Abby Hamlin, 215, 220, 223–25
Abbott, Austin, 215, 228
Abbott, Benjamin Vaughan, 215, 228
Abbott, Edward, 122, 128, 238
Abbott, Ernest Hamlin, 215, 218, 225
Abbott, Francis Ellingwood, 134
Abbott, Jacob, 214–15, 295
Abbott, John S. C., 215
Abbott, Lawrence F., 215, 220
Abbott, Lyman. His place in the religious world of his time, 214; the facts of his life, 214–17; appearance, 218; health, 218–19; attitude toward games and sports, 219; toward the theater, 219–20; proficiency in music, 220; temperament, 220–21; strength of will, 222; attitude toward women, 222–23; family life, 223–25; learning and reading, 225–28; literary taste and judgment, 228; as fictionist, 228–29; political and economic views, 229–31; as preacher, 232–33; attitude toward war, 243–46; estimate of his achievement, 246–48
— bibliography, 290–91
— notes, 291–99
— references to in studies of others, 70, 74, 75, 78–79, 80, 90, 93, 100, 104–5, 111, 117, 119, 142, 174, 207, 249, 265, 286, 288
Adams, Henry, 274
Adams, John Quincy, 65
Addams, Jane, 209, 286
Addison, Joseph, 45
Aikin, Lucy, 41, 49, 51, 61
Alcott, A. Bronson, 50, 117
Alda, Frances, 1
Alden, Henry M., 187
Allen, Alexander V. G., 135–36, 144, 145, 174–75
Allston, Washington, 47, 51
Andrews, Horace Lee, 186
Anthony, Susan, B., 251
Aquinas, St. Thomas, 66, 135
Arnold, Edwin, 228
Arnold, Matthew, 53, 108, 200, 228, 267
Arvin, Newton, 300–301
Atkins, Gaius Glenn, 189
Atonement. LB on, 28, 31–32; WEC on, 57; DLM on, 168–69; WG on, 206; LA on, 238
Augustine, St., 238
Austen, Jane, 44

Bacon, Leonard, 1, 38–39

Baillie, Joanna, 50
Banvard, John, 219
Barnum, P. T., 220
Barrow, Isaac, 89, 103
Barrymore, Ethel, 291
Bascom, John, 187
Beach, William A., 251, 300
Beecher, Catharine, 2, 21, 22, 23–24, 35, 257
Beecher, Charles, 7, 103, 257
Beecher, David, 5, 19
Beecher, Edward, 2, 20, 21, 23, 257
Beecher, Esther Lyman, 5
Beecher, Eunice Bullard, 70, 71, 73, 75, 90, 91–94, 167–68
Beecher, Frederick, 258
Beecher, George, 1, 257
Beecher, Harriet, 19
Beecher, Harriet Porter, 4, 6, 7, 20–21, 91, 257, 258
Beecher, Henry Barton, 93
Beecher, Henry Ward. His reputation, 68–70; facts of his life, 70–73; health, 73–74; attitude toward sports and games, 75; love of nature, 75–77; intellectual gifts and limitations, 77 ff.; as reader and writer, 77–81; love of painting and other arts, 81–83; attitude toward music, 83–84; toward the theater, 84–85; in social relationships, 86–89; temperament, 89–91; family relationships, 91–94; as religious worker, 94–95; as advocate of social Christianity, 95 ff.; attitude toward Socialism, 96; toward racism, 96–99; toward war, 99–101; as preacher, 103–6; his theology, 106 ff.; attitude toward Calvinism, 107–9; Christology, 109–11; attitude toward conversion, 111–12; toward the Bible, 112; toward science, 112–13; toward future punishment, 113–14; toward the church, 114; religious toleration, 114–15; views on suffering, 115–17; various responses to his ministry, 117
— accusation of adultery brought against by Theodore Tilton, 69–70, 72–73, 249–54, 300–301
— bibliography, 264–65
— notes, 165–70
— references to in studies of others, 1, 2, 4, 10, 13, 20, 21, 23, 124, 215–16, 217, 221, 222, 232, 233, 257, 288
Beecher, Herbert, 93
Beecher, James, 1, 23, 258
Beecher, Lydia Jackson, 7, 20
Beecher, Lyman. His place in American church history, 1–2, and in this book, 2; eccentricities, 2–4; facts of his life, 5–10; appearance, 11; health, 11–13; use of sport and exercise, 12; attitude toward nature and the arts, 13–14; relations with others, 15–16; friendships, 16; family life, 16–24; attitude toward money, 16–17; as evangelist, 24–25; relationship to Calvinism, 25–30; as theologian, 30–32; attitude toward disagreement, 33–35; toward religious establishments, 33–34; interest in reform, 35–39
— bibliography, 256
— notes, 256–59
— references to in studies of others, 70–71, 73, 90, 91, 93–94, 107
Beecher, Roxana Foote, 6, 17–20, 21, 22, 24, 91, 257
Beecher, Thomas K., 2, 22–23, 187, 251, 257, 288
Beecher, William C., 93
Beecher, William Henry, 20, 22, 257
Beethoven, Ludwig van, 48, 83, 200, 292
Benton, Lot, 5
Berkeley, George, 45
Berlioz, Hector, 292
Bernhardt, Sarah, 150, 160
Bible, The. LB on, 31; WEC on, 57–58; HWB on, 112; PB on, 136–37; DLM on, 171–73; WG on, 204–5; LA on, 238–40
Blackmore, R. D., 79, 228
Blackton, J. Stuart, 245
Blaine, James G., 140

Bonner, Robert, 72, 80
Booth, Edwin, 85, 121, 125, 219, 220, 268
Borrow, George, 79
Boucicault, Dion, 85
Bowen, Henry C., 150, 252
Bowles, Samuel, 117, 187
Bradford, Gamaliel, 146–47, 158, 249, 277
Brightman, Edgar, Sheffield, 236
Brooks, Mary Ann Phillips, 119
Brooks, Phillips. His position in Boston and his reputation as a preacher, 118–19; his life, 119–21; appearance, 121; health, 122–23; attitude toward nature, 123–24; preferences in art and architecture, 124–25; interest in music, 125; in literature, 125; social relations, 125–28, 144–45; pastoral work, 128–29; attitude toward women and marriage, 129–31; preaching, 131–35; theology, 135–39; attitude toward social Christianity, 141–44; religious ideal, 145–47
— bibliography, 270–71
— notes, 271–77
— references to in studies of others, 53, 94, 105, 157, 199, 233, 265
Brooks, William, 145
Brooks, William Gray, 119
Brown, Charles R., 189, 200, 275–76
Brown, Ira D., 214
Brown, John, 97–98
Browning, Robert, 127, 144, 160, 198, 227, 229–30, 249, 292
Brownson, Orestes A., 198
Bruce, Alexander, 132
Bryan, William Jennings, 229, 293
Bryant, William Cullen, 48
Bryce, James, 134–35
Buckham, John Wright, 107
Bulwer-Lytton, Sir Edward, Lord Lytton, 80
Bunyan, John, 78, 279, 287
Burke, Edmund, 79
Burns, Robert, 226
Burton, William E., 219
Bushnell, Horace, 136, 169, 206, 232
Butler, Joseph, 5, 103, 136
Butler, Samuel, 228
Byron, George Gordon, Lord, 14, 44, 80, 226, 227

Cable, George W., 117
Calvinism. LB and, 18, 22, 25–30, 38–39; WEC and, 56; HWB and, 107–9; WG and, 183–84
Campbell, Mrs. Patrick, 292
Carlyle, Thomas, 44, 226, 292
Carroll, Lewis, 228
Cervantes, 44
Chadwick, John White, 49, 59, 67
Chamberlain, Houston S., 299
Channing, Edward T., 41
Channing, Mary, 42
Channing, Ruth Gibbs, 42
Channing, Susan, 63
Channing, Walter, 41
Channing, William Ellery. His religious toleration, 40; appearance, 40–41; health, 41, 43, 51–52; facts of his life, 41–43; as scholar and writer, 43–46; attitude toward nature, 46–47; toward the arts, 47–48; toward money, 49; toward women and children, 49–50; preaching, 53–54; attitude toward morality, 54; toward pastoral work, 54–55; emotions, 55; Unitarianism, 55–57; attitude toward the Bible, 57–58; relations with others, 59–64; attitude toward politics, 64; as reformer, 64–66
— bibliography, 259–61
— notes, 261–64
Channing, William Francis, 42
Chapman, Maria, 65
Chaucer, Geoffrey, 80
Cheverus, Jean Lefebvre de, 40
Child, Lydia M., 65
Christian Science, 115–16
Christy's Minstrels, 219
Church, The. LB on, 9, 33–34; WEC, 263; HWB, 114–15; PB, 136, 138–39, 141–44; WG, 207–8
Cibber, Colley, 47
Clark, Sir Andrew, 156

Clark, Clifford, 268
Clay, Henry, 65
Clemens, Olivia Langdon, 2, 92
Cleveland, Grover, 87, 140, 229, 252
Coffin, Henry Sloane, 214
Coleridge, Samuel Taylor, 44, 127
Conversion. LB on, 24–25; WEC on, 57; HWB on, 111; PB on, 137–38; DLM on, 170–71, 178–81; WG, 204
Cooper, James Fenimore, 48, 198
Cotton, John, 119
Cowper, William, 80
Crabbe, George, 80
Croker, Richard, 159
Cross, Barbara M., 30
Curtis, George William, 199
Cushman, Charlotte, 125

Dale, R. W., 171
Daly, Augustin, 266
Daniel, Samuel, 79
Dante, 80, 113, 206, 227, 299
Dewey, Orville, 62
Dickens, Charles, 44, 127, 159, 198, 222, 227, 267
Dix, Dorothea, 49
Donne, John, 9, 118
Drummond, Henry, 164, 174
Duffus, R. L., 162
Dumas, Alexandre, 226
Dunne, Finley Peter, 198
Duns Scotus, John, 135
Dwight, Timothy, 5, 16

Eaton, Walter Prichard, 160
Eddy, Mary Baker G., 115
Edgeworth, Maria, 44
Edwards, Jonathan, 5, 25, 27–28, 30, 35, 103, 107, 113
Eggleston, Edward, 88
Election. LB on, 30
Eliot, Charles W., 127, 131–32
Eliot, George, 127, 228
Ely, Richard T., 183
Emerson, Ralph Waldo, 43, 143
Everett, Edward, 63

Fairfax, Jenny, 130
Farrar, F. W., 89
Fénelon, 52, 263
Fichte, Johann G., 211–12
Findlay, James F. Jr., 150, 153
Finney, Charles G., 232
Fiske, John, 97, 134, 286
Fitt, A. P., 174, 278
Fitt, Emma Moody, 279
Fitzgerald, Edward, 228
Fondolaik, Constantine, 87
Ford, John, 81
Forster, John, 127
Fosdick, Harry Emerson, 279
Frank, Leo M., 299
Franklin, Benjamin, 45
Frazee, John Elmer, 25, 31, 32
Froude, James, 79
Fuller, Margaret, 63

Gannett, Ezra Stiles, 43, 60
Garden, Mary, 147, 291
Garfield, James A., 187
Garrick, David, 85
Garrison, William Lloyd, 37
Gilmore, T. M., 294–95
Gladden, Jennie O. Cohoon, 187, 188
Gladden, Washington. His fame as prophet of the Social Gospel, 183; of the New Theology, 183–85; facts of his life, 186–88; appearance and manner, 189; health, 189–90; frankness, independence, and strength of will, 190–96; love of nature, 196–97; learning, 197–98; attitude toward sports and games, 198–99; aesthetic theory, 199–200; musical proficiency, 200–201; attitude toward theater, 201–2; toward sex, 202–3; preaching, 203–4; use of Bible, 204–5; theology, 205–7; as churchman, 207–8; interest in labor problems, 209–10; in war and peace, 210–13; progressivism, 213
— bibliography, 281–82
— notes, 283–90
— references to in studies of others, 174, 230
Gladding, John, 186
Gladstone, William E., 199
Goethe, Johann Wolfgang von, 44

Gordon, George A., 133–34, 144–45
Gorky, Maxim, 228
Goss, Charles, 160
Gough, John B., 232
Gounod, Charles, 84
Graham, Billy, 279
Grant, U. S., 102
Grenfell, Wilfred T., 149
Greuze, Jean B., 83

Hamlin, Hannibal, 215
Hammond, William A., 84
Handel, G. F., 84
Handy, Robert T., 183
Hanna, Mark, 69
Harper, William Rainey, 194, 279
Hawthorne, Nathaniel, 261
Hay, John, 68, 190
Hayes, Rutherford B., 197
Hazlitt, William, 60
Hearst, W. R., 244
Hedge, Frederic, 62
Hegel, G. W. F., 242
Hemans, Felicia, 50
Hibben, Paxton, 249, 267, 300–301
Higginson, Thomas Wentworth, 92, 120
Hillis, Newell Dwight, 79
Hoar, George Frisbie, 244
Hofmann, Josef, 200
Hogarth, William, 83
Holland, J. G., 187
Holmes, Oliver Wendell, 104
Holton, Samuel, 151
Homer, 80
Hooker, Isabella Beecher, 1–2, 251, 257
Hooker, Richard, 136
Hopkins, Mark, 187
Hopkins, Samuel, 18, 25, 42, 261
Howard, H. C., 104
Howells, W. D., 186
Hugo, Victor, 80, 191
Hume, David, 45
Huxley, Thomas Henry, 196

Immortality. HWB on, 113–14; PB on, 139; LA on, 240
Infant damnation. LB on, 26, 29–30
Ingersoll, Robert G., 171
Inness, George, 83
Irving, Sir Henry, 85
Irving, Washington, 48

James, Henry, 198, 274
Jameson, Anna, 50
Jefferson, Charles E., 276–77
Jefferson, Joseph, 85, 149
Johnson, Samuel, 78
Jonson, Ben, 81

Keats, John, 227
Keene, Laura, 219
Kemble, Fanny, 47, 85, 125
Kidd, Benjamin, 206
Kipling, Rudyard, 159, 225
Kneeland, Abner, 43
Knox, John, 280
Kreisler, Fritz, 220

Lawrence, William, 118, 145
Lawson, Thomas, 230
Leonardo da Vinci, 83
Lillo, George, 47
Lincoln, Abraham, 68, 102–3, 199, 268, 291
Lind, Jenny, 84, 220
Literature. WEC and, 43–45; PB and, 125; DLM and, 159; WG and, 197–98; LA and, 226–29
Locke, John, 45
Lodge, Henry Cabot, 246
Longfellow, Henry Wadsworth, 69, 145, 198
Lovejoy, Elijah P., 66
Lovett, Robert Morss, 160, 181, 279, 280
Lowell, James Russell, 120, 199, 206, 296
Luther, Martin, 280

Mabie, Hamilton Wright, 235
Macready, William Charles, 219
Mansfield, Richard, 160
Mark Twain, 2, 91, 115, 186, 244
Martineau, Harriet, 50
Marx, Karl, 35–36
Mason, Lowell, 9, 14

Massinger, Philip, 81
Mathew, Theobald, 64
Maurice, Frederick D., 136
May, Samuel J., 65
McKinley, William, 69, 229, 244
McLoughlin, William G., 115, 116, 178, 267–68
McVickar, William, 130
Melville, Herman, 242
Mencken, H. L., 148
Michelangelo, 113, 199
Miller, William, 207
Milton, John, 14, 32, 44, 45, 48, 56, 57, 60, 79, 80, 160, 223, 227, 262
Mitchell, S. Weir, 126
Montaigne, 228
Moody, Betsy Holton, 157
Moody, D. L. As evangelist, 148; as preacher, 148–49; anecdotage of, 149; facts of his life, 149–56; attitude toward sports and games, 158; toward literature and the arts, 158–59; toward the theater, 159–60; toward music, 160–61; his social relations, 161–68; family, 163–65; theology, 168–71; belief in and use of Bible, 171–73; relations with Christian liberals, 173–74; his prayers, 174–75; attitude toward social Christianity, 176–78; as educator, 178; on conversion, 178–81; sources of his appeal, 181–82
— bibliography, 277–78
— notes, 278–81
— references to in studies of others, 17, 75, 95, 123, 137, 142
Moody, Dwight, 279
Moody, Edwin, 149
Moody, Emma C. Revell, 153, 163–64, 170, 179
Moody, Irene, 164, 279
Moody, Paul, 150, 155, 156–57, 162, 163–65, 174, 178, 179, 278, 279, 280
Moody, William R., 152, 177, 179, 279, 280
Moody Bible Institute, 155, 279–80
Moore, Tom, 80, 226
Moorehouse, Harry, 170–71
Moulton, Francis, 250, 252–53
Mount Hermon School, 154
Mozart, W. A., 84
Murillo, Bartolomé, 82
Music. LB and, 14; WEC and, 47; HWB and, 83–84; PB and, 125; DLM and, 160; WG and, 200; LA and, 220

Napoleon, 48, 60
Nature. WEC and, 46–47; HWB and, 75–77; PB and, 123–24; DLM and, 158; WG and, 196–97; LA and, 242–43, 297
Neilson, Joseph, 251–52
Newman, John Henry, Cardinal, 115, 199
New Theology, The, 183–84, 205–6
Northfield Seminary, 154
Northfield Training School, 154

Ouida, 79

Paderewski, Ignace Jan, 200, 220
Paganini, Nicolò, 14
Painting, etc. HWB and, 81–83; PB, 124–25; DLM, 159; WG and, 199–200
Palmer, Alice Freeman, 222, 224–25
Palmer, George Herbert, 224–25
Parker, Theodore, 64
Parkhurst, Charles Henry, 202
Parkman, Francis, 130
Parks, Leighton, 129
Patton, Carl S., 192
Paul, St., 81, 146, 235
Peabody, Elizabeth, 49–50, 51, 59, 61, 62, 262
Peabody, Francis G., 274
Perkins, Mary Foote Beecher, 257
Phillips, Wendell, 119, 232, 267
Phrenology. HWB and, 266
Poe, Edgar Allan, 297
Pond, J. B., 73, 74, 75, 92, 93, 97
Poussin, Nicolas, 83
Powers, Hiram, 292
Prang, Louis, 159
Price, Richard, 45
Priestley, Joseph, 45

Rauschenbusch, Walter, 183

Ravel Family, 219
Rehan, Ada, 85
Reid, Thomas, 45
Rembrandt, 125
Revell, Fleming H., 278–79
Rice, M. H., 62
Richardson, H. H., 120
Richmond, Grace S., 228
Ritchie, Anna Cora Mowatt, 47, 263
Robertson, F. W., 136, 141, 206
Robinson, John, 58
Rockefeller, John D., 187, 193–94, 210, 286
Roe, E. P., 228
Roosevelt, Edith, Carow, 92
Roosevelt, Theodore, 21, 69, 92, 126, 164–65, 217, 221, 222, 229, 231, 244, 245, 289, 293–95
Rossetti, Dante G., 285
Rubens, Peter Paul, 83
Ruskin, John, 80, 198, 199

Sabatier, Paul, 239–40
Sage, Henry W., 73
Saint-Gaudens, Augustus, 274
Salvini, Tommaso, 85
Sankey, Ira, D., 153–54, 157, 160–61, 167, 280–81
Schiller, Friedrich, 44
Schleiermacher, F. E. D., 136
Schopenhauer, Arthur, 136
Scott, Sir Walter, 14, 44, 80, 127, 159, 198, 227
Scougall, Henry, 234
Scoville, Rev. and Mrs. Samuel, 93
Scoville, Samuel Jr., 268, 269, 300
Scudder, Horace E., 187
Shaftesbury, Earl of, 158
Shakespeare, William, 44, 45, 79, 80, 81, 127, 131, 157–60, 226–27
Shaplen, Robert, 300
Shaw, Bernard, 131, 292, 295
Shelley, Percy Bysshe, 44, 227
Sheridan Richard B., 85
Sherlock, William, 103
Siddons, Sarah, 85
Slavery. LB and, 6–7, 26, 37–38; WEC and, 54, 65, 262; HWB and, 87, 97–98
Smith, Sir George Adam, 172, 174
Social Christianity. LB and, 35–38; PB and, 139–41; DLM and, 175–78; WG and, 209–13; LA and, 229–31
South, Robert, 103
Spencer, Herbert, 86, 89, 206
Stanley, Arthur Penrhyn, 136, 199
Stanton, Edwin M., 102
Stanton, Elizabeth Cady, 249, 251
Sterne, Laurence, 80
Stevenson, Robert Louis, 53–54, 145
Stewart, A. T., 176
Stiles, Ezra, 42
Story, Joseph, 48
Stowe, Calvin E., 5, 6–7, 11, 12, 15, 30, 39, 71, 106, 257
Stowe, Charles Edward, 26
Stowe, Harriet Beecher, 1, 3–4, 7, 8, 9–10, 12, 13, 14, 20, 21–22, 23–24, 31, 32, 81, 91, 100, 257, 267
Stowe, Lyman Beecher, 93
Sunday, Billy, 157, 204
Swift, Jonathan, 12, 80, 226
Swing, David, 188

Taft, William Howard, 229
Tarbell, Ida M., 230
Taylor, Graham, 284
Taylor, Nathaniel, 14, 16, 30
Taylor, W. N., 70
Temple, Minny, 274
Tennyson, Alfred, Lord, 127, 198, 227
Terry, Ellen, 85, 92
Thackeray, W. M., 80, 127
Theater, The. LB and, 14; WEC and, 47–48; HWB and, 84–85; PB and, 125; DLM and, 159–60; WG, 201; LA, 219–20
Thomson, James, 80
Thoreau, Henry David, 117
Tilton, Theodore and Elizabeth, and the accusation of adultery against HWB, 72, 88, 249–54, 300–301
Timmins, Sara Gemma, 130
Titian, 82, 125
Tolstoy, L. N., 228, 245

Tree, Ellen, 85
Trinity. LB on, 31–32; WEC on, 55–57; HWB on, 109–11; LA on, 296
Trollope, Anthony, 228
Tuckerman, Henry F., 59
Turgenev, Ivan, 228
Turner, J. M. W., 83
Tweed, W. M., 193, 194
Tyng, Stephen H., 232

Vandyke, Sir Anthony, 125

Wagner, Richard, 191, 200, 292
Walpole, Horace, 45
Walton, Izaak, 118
War. LB on, 36, 38; WEC on, 65–66; HWB on, 99–103; PB, 140–41; DLM on, 177; WG on, 210–13; LA on, 243–47
Ward, Andrew, 17
Ward, Mrs. Humphry, 228
Ware, Henry, 62–63
Webster, Daniel, 69, 81
Weisberger, Bernard, 175–76
Weld, Theodore, 37
Wells, Frances, 280
Wells, H. G., 228, 293
Wesley, John, 280
Weston, Henry, 174
Whittier, John G., 65
Wilde, Oscar, 285
Wilson, Joshua L., 7, 10, 15, 23
Wilson, Woodrow, 211, 229, 244, 289
Winter, William, 292
Woolstonecraft, Mary, 50
Woodhull, Victoria, 250–51, 300
Wordsworth, William, 44, 80, 198, 227
Wright, Conrad, 261